Pathways to His Presence

Pathways to His Presence

ENTERING MORE FULLY
INTO EIGHT DIMENSIONS
OF THE PRESENCE OF GOD

DR. PHILIP BOWLER

Carpenter's Son Publishing

Pathways to His Presence:
Entering More Fully into Eight Dimensions of the Presence of God

Published by Carpenter's Son Publishing
Christianbookservices.com

Cover and Interior Design by Suzanne Lawing

Printed in the United States of America

ISBN: (print) 978-1-956370-74-4

Dedication

To my two wonderful sons, Mathias and David.
My prayer is that through this book, they will come into a deeper knowledge and experience of the power of the Presence of God.

Contents

Part III: What Now?

Introduction

The Forgotten Birthright of Christians

As Christians, the most precious possession we have in our lives is the Presence of the Living God. This is what sets Christians apart from adherents of other religions. In Jesus Christ, the God who formed the cosmos is truly **with** us! Yet it seems that so many of us walk through our lives without fully living out of the inheritance of God's Presence in and with us granted to us through the cross. We have the most powerful Being in existence living and walking with us and yet continue to live powerless lives, little different than non-believers around us. This book is a call for us to come to a deeper realization of who we are in Christ so that the power of His Presence can be more fully expressed in and through us for His glory. As we live more fully in His Presence we become the world changers[1] the world needs.

This book is organized into three main sections: Part 1 sets the foundations for entering God's Presence by looking at why God's Presence is so crucial for us. Part 2 reveals eight "dimensions" or "pathways to" God's Presence in the world. Part 3 portrays what living in the Presence of God

1 From Romans 8:19.

brings to the world and how we can nurture His ongoing Presence in our lives so that we can truly change the world for the better.

Several assumptions influence the structure and shape of what is written here. First is the assumption that the Bible is the *true and reliable Word of God*[2] and as such brings essential insights and understandings to how we must relate to God and the world. It is the touchstone around which we orient our lives and it reveals truths about God and the world we must grapple with if we hope to live lives abundantly full of His Presence. The Bible is assumed to be authoritative and normative for our lives and practice.

Second, a key assumption is that all truth, all knowledge, must be integrated into all parts of our lives including our bodies, souls, spirits, minds, emotions, wills, and hearts. One of our modern heresies is that we have somehow embraced the lie that "knowledge" is primarily a cognitive thing. It is not. *Knowledge must be believed to be understood.* Belief precedes understanding.

A third assumption is that *application empowers transformation* and is how knowledge becomes integrated into our lives. Therefore, the main points of each chapter need to be applied to our lives by the work of the Holy Spirit in us. This explains why each chapter ends with a summary of the chapter's key points, application points which encourage you, the reader, to spend transformational time in the Presence of God, and a concluding prayer asking God to make the truths of the chapter come alive in your experience.

Our overarching goal is to develop a vital experience with God that conforms to sound theology rather than limiting our theological understanding to what we already "know" and experience. The tendency is to reduce our Biblical understanding to our current level of experience when we are meant to press into the truth of the Word and invite His Presence until our experience with God reflects truth.

---

2 Timothy 3:16.

This process is empowered by two more truths: A fourth assumption is that God is *already active* in our lives calling us deeper into His Presence.[3] The living God of the Bible is One who acts in history to call us into intimacy with Himself. The application points and prayer that end each chapter are intended to encourage the engagement of our whole being, body, soul, and spirit in this process.

A fifth truth is that *we all,* regardless of age, education, or maturity, *need transformation.* The goal of the discipleship process is, according to Romans 8:29, to be formed and shaped into the image of Christ. Since none of us are yet like Christ, we all need to humble ourselves and submit to this process of change. The concluding prayer of each chapter gives you a chance to respond to God and to ask for His intervention in your life so you can grow and mature His way. Without His involvement, we will not get to the right destination, yet He waits for our invitation to do so.

Learning to live in God's Presence is one of the developmental tasks we have as Christians. We can only learn this while living on earth. It is God's Presence alone that releases us into **life**. Heaven is coming fully into the Presence of God that we began to embrace and taste on earth. The tragedy of sin is that it cuts us off from God's Presence. The coming judgement on this sin is simply a release into the fullness of one's rejection of God and His Presence. In the end, we get what we truly wanted with respect to Him. God loves us and this is why so many people have access to so many good things despite their rejection of God. Yet that time of grace will come to an end. Our sin and righteousness choices **now** have powerful and eternal implications for our ability to live fully in the Presence of God both now and later. Now is all the time we have to pursue God and the wonder of His Presence.

---

3 Deuteronomy 31:8.

This book is intended for those who hunger and thirst for more of God[4] and want to divest themselves of all that prevents God from having more of us so that we can have more of Him.

Let's take the closing prayer in each chapter seriously and engage with the Holy Spirit. Together, let's press into God and ask for His deeper Presence in our lives so that we can be transformed into world changers for the greater glory of God. May each one of you live more fully in the power of the Presence of the Lord through this book.

THE RIVER OF LIFE THAT FLOWS FROM THE PRESENCE OF GOD.

When the Lord is established in His temple (Ezek. 47:1-12) and on His throne (Rev. 22:1-4), there is a river of life flowing from His Presence. It goes to the barren places, the dead places and everywhere it goes it brings life. Ezekiel 47 describes how its flow deepens and becomes more powerful as you walk along its length. It starts off small, barely a trickle. After 500 m., the water is now a creek, but only ankle deep. Five hundred meters later, it has deepened to a river and is knee deep. Then another 500 m., it is waist deep. A further 500 m., it is a mighty river, so deep you cannot ford it. Life births everywhere the river goes. Salt water becomes fresh. All kinds of fish teem in its depths. There are trees along the sides of the river that sink their roots deep into its life-giving flow. Life births so powerfully that these trees bear fruit all year long and even the leaves of these trees can be used for the healing of the nations.

This is a metaphor for how life flows from the Presence of God. It flows from the altar in the temple, a place of consecration (Ezek. 47) or from His throne (Rev. 22), a place of His Lordship. We must do some work to get to the point where we can swim in this water (walking at least 2 km.). Yet how much of His Presence do we want? How much work are we willing to put in? Are we happy to just dabble in His Presence, just get our

4 Matthew 5:6.

feet wet? Or do we want more? This book is about seeking the Presence of God and daring to, as much as we can, immerse ourselves in it.

Swim in Him. Find more of Him. He is the source of life. He wants to bring life to your dead and barren places. He wants to release healing to you. Sink your roots deep into the living water that flows from His Presence. I encourage you, invite God's Presence and float in His river of life.

Part I:

Setting the Foundations for Entering Into His Presence

In this section, before we talk about the eight "dimensions" of God's Presence[5], we lay the foundations for understanding why God's Presence is so good for us and how God's loving Presence with and in us can transform and impel us into our destiny.

When Augustine said, "You have made us for Yourself, and our hearts are restless, until they can find rest in You,"[6] he was expressing the reality that our lives miss a significant part of who we are when we do not embrace the Presence of the Lord. This hunger, this ache for the Lord, yearns to be satisfied, but why do we have this yearning and why do so many people around us seem oblivious to it? One of the problems is that we have related to truth incorrectly and so this section explores how we relate to truth so that it can more effectively transform us.

In addition, the Western view of the world is fundamentally flawed. We, with our emphasis on science and technology, view the world as primarily physical in nature even while we may at times allow for the occasional penetration of the "spiritual world" into our lives. Yet the truth

5 In this book I will capitalize "presence" when it refers to the presence of God Himself.

6 In Augustine. *Confessions*, translated by Rex Warner. New York: Mentor, 1963.

is different. The reality is that our world is primarily spiritual rather than physical in nature. God spoke and the entire universe was created. This demonstrates that the source and foundation of all things arises from the spiritual world. So when we do not relate rightly to the spiritual world, we will never understand or relate rightly to the physical world that has its source in God. My parents were missionaries in Africa for 49 years and I grew up there. Currently I am also a missionary in Africa. People often ask me why miracles and healings are more common in Africa and the answer is precisely the point mentioned above: for the African, the world is primarily spiritual in nature and so their understanding at a fundamental level is that the answers to their problems will or can come from the spiritual world. They may disagree whether their answers will come from Islam, Christianity, or animism, but they seek to access spiritual realities to deal with their problems. Their recognition of the prominence of the spiritual world naturally produces more faith for miracles. Yet the Western world tends to turn to science and technology for those same answers although it is changing due to the rise of New Age philosophies. Until we recognize and embrace that God is the source of all reality, we will not be able to fully enter the power of His Presence to both transform us and the world around us.

God is calling each one of us to come to Him. This section and book seek to identify some of the barriers present in our lives that prevent us from living in His Presence and hearing Him calling to us.

1

The Presence of The Lord Calls Us Into Our True Identity.

'Then God said, "Let us make mankind in our image, in our likeness, . . . " So God created mankind in his own image, in the image of God he created them; male and female he created them. (vs. 28) Then God blessed them, . . . ' (Gen. 1:26-28, NIV)

'Then the Lord God formed a man from the dust of the Earth and breathed into his nostrils the breath of life, and the man became a living being. . . . But for Adam no suitable helper was found. So the Lord caused the man to fall into a deep sleep; while he was sleeping, he took one of the man's ribs he had taken out of the man and then closed up the place with flesh. Then the Lord God made a woman from the rib he had taken out of the man, . . . "(Gen. 2:7, 20-22)

FOUNDATIONS

Most people have questions about who they are. Why am I alive? What makes me unique? What can I do with my life? Living in the Presence of the Lord reveals answers to these kinds of questions. In Him, we discover who we are and are released into our true identity through God's active

Presence in our lives. The foundation of what it means to really endeavour to live in God's Presence continually is found in Genesis chapters 1 though 3.

The culmination of the creation account is the creation of mankind. God speaks and, little by little, the cosmos and the world are formed by the power of His spoken word. Then there is a transition. Previous to Genesis 1:26, God declared, and it was so. Now in verse 26, the fullness of God's nature becomes involved in the creation process. Rather than just calling humans into being, God's creation of mankind arises from relationship and the model for what God is about to create becomes God himself. God gets down and dirty; He reaches into the dust of the Earth to craft humans. The glory of the created world ramps up. Until this moment, all of creation was "good;" now it becomes "very good."[7]

Previously, creation reflected the goodness of its Creator; now it fully displays the intrinsic good nature of its Creator.

WE ARE MADE FOR RELATIONSHIP WITH GOD

The words *"Let us"* of Genesis 1:26 are a crucial part of the story. It demonstrates that God as three-in-one is primarily relational in His inner nature (Father-Son-Holy Spirit) and all three persons of the Godhead are agreed in the decision to create humans in their own image. This means that humans, as created in the image of God, are also relational in nature. This means *we were created for relationship* and that, as male and female, the model of how we are to relate to each other arises from God Himself.

Part of being relational, created "in the image of God," implies the need for relationships with others. No person is an island in themselves. We need one another. The "image of God" can be displayed through people as we relate to others. Later I will say that we cannot know ourselves unless we first know God. A parallel truth is that not only God's Presence, but also relationships with others can confer true identity, particularly when those relationships reflect the character of God. Part of God's gift

7 Genesis 1:31: creation is now "very good".

to us is the relationships around us and the family of God He calls us into, or at least they are meant to be. Unfortunately, in a fallen world, at times what is meant to be a gift is turned into a source of hurt and pain. Yet as we find ourselves in the Lord, He changes us and empowers our relationships to reflect Him so that love blossoms and we settle into our destiny through safe relationships that call us into God's life. One implication of this is that when we do not have relationships that are safe, particularly when we are young, our self-concept gets distorted and we will struggle to develop a self-identity that lines up with who God has created us to be. Yet God has created us. He knows us best. He loves us. His intention is that relationship to Himself and others will provide the relational context in which we will thrive. *We were made for relationship with God and we need this in order to know ourselves.*

GOD IS THE SOURCE OF OUR LIFE

Normally the account of Genesis 2 is taken as a more detailed description of the events of day six and of the creation of mankind found in Genesis 1. The second aspect of the creation of humans to emphasize is from Genesis 2:7. God took the creature formed from the dust of the Earth, breathed into his nostrils and he became a living being. In other words, the source of life for this newly created human was God Himself. This has never changed. The Presence of the Lord breathed into us continues to be what truly gives us life. We cannot be fully happy or fulfilled, without receiving His life. His "breath" in us is what makes us fully "alive." *Life flows from the Presence of God.* In the creation of the first human being, God freely gave of His Essence to birth life in Adam. God's willingness to birth life in humans through breathing His Spirit into them continues to characterize who He is. God is, always has been, and always will be a "Life-Giver." In addition, we discover that we are much more than just physical beings; we have something of His spirit within us that empowers us to communicate with and relate to the spiritual world. God's Spirit makes our spirits alive. This is part of what Jesus was talking about in John 3. We must be "born again" by the Spirit of God in order to understand the things of God. Sin kills our spirits,[8] whereas God's Spirit and holiness working in us brings us life.

GOD'S PRESENCE CONFERS IDENTITY

Thirdly, since mankind is created in the image of God, the definition of what it means to be truly human originates in God Himself. *We find out who we are through knowing God.* When we discover what God is like, we discover who we are meant to be. One of the fruits of pushing into the Presence of the Lord and pursuing a more intimate relationship with Him is that we come to know who we are, and what we are called to do in this life. We discover our humanity in communion with Him. It is being with Him, being in His Presence that releases us and calls us into our destiny. Our part is to press into the Lord and allow His Presence, His love to remove the barriers that prevent us from hearing His voice and from accepting who we truly are. Part of this includes saturating ourselves with His Presence so that we are conformed to the image of Christ.[9] Holiness empowers our ability to enter our destiny.

Do you want to know who you really are and why you are on the earth? The language of destiny is really very simple. It involves living in two words: "Yes, Lord." When convicted of sin, agree with God about it and submit to his way, saying "Yes, Lord." When challenges come your way, embrace and enter into God's love for you and His will for you. Jesus entered His destiny in the Garden of Gethsemane when He said to God, *"Not My will but Yours be done."*[10] The world became forever changed through His sacrificial obedience. You truly do find out who you are through living in intimacy with the living God and are empowered to enter into your destiny through submission to His love for you.

An implication from this is that those who do not know the Lord cannot fully know who they are and what they are called to be. Although,

8 Romans 6:23.

9 Romans 8:29.

10 Matthew 26:39, 42, 44.

since God's Presence is available for those who seek it,[11] non-believers can get glimpses of their own calling. Our problem is that too many believers follow the world's pattern of seeking their significance and value from sources other than God and so do not know who they are. In addition, wounds and hurts prevent people from fully stepping into the Father's love for them. Yet the Presence of the Lord is the *environment in which we were designed to thrive* and truly find identity. Mankind was created in the "image of God" not in the "image of society." If we do not seek and pursue relationship with the Lord, we will live unfulfilled lives weighed down by false identities that do not satisfy, and we will never become the people we need to be to truly bless those around us. Every child, every person, is created for a destiny they will only fully discover through living in the Presence of God.

As I connect to God, I realize that I have dignity, value and significance. This causes me to value others and their uniqueness. Societies that do not understand the creation of mankind in the image of God end up defining people by things like their power, position or wealth. This opens up the possibility of abuse towards others with less power, wealth or authority. When we connect to God and find our value in Him, we are able to embrace differences. Equality of value does not necessarily mean equality of role or sameness.

When we understand that God's Presence confers identity and link this with verses such as Psalm 139:13-14: *"For you created my inmost being; you knit me together in my mother's womb. I praise you because I am fearfully and wonderfully made; your works are wonderful, I know that full well,"* we see that God was actively present in our own creation even prenatally in our mother's womb. The dignity, value and significance of each person starts prenatally at conception, when we become a genetically complete individual. He formed us and shaped us to be who we are. Yes, the environment of our upbringing can sometimes distort and wound us as we are becoming adults, yet as we press into God and make Him the

11 Jeremiah 29:13; 2 Chronicles 15:2.

environment of our lives, His affirming Presence frees us to become who He always intended us to be.

One implication of this is that no person, no matter the circumstances of their conception, is a mistake. The goodness of God is seen in the fact that He takes what at times can be a very difficult situation and uses it to form and shape a masterpiece. There is so much beauty in every person.

The world around us needs us to know who we are through knowing God so that we can bring others into what they are called to be in God. We are a blessing and the source of that blessing flows from being carriers of the Presence of the Lord.

We need to press into God to find ourselves. The world is trying to be "human" through eliminating low self-esteem, removing limits, eliminating discipline, etc. They will never find it that way. The fullness of what it means to be truly "human" is only found in the Presence of the Lord.

FRUITFULNESS FLOWS FROM THE PRESENCE OF GOD

A fourth point is that fruitfulness flows from the Presence of God. In Genesis 1:26, God created mankind in His image and then, out of the context of that creation environment, blesses them to be *"fruitful and increase in number"* (Gen 1:28). This is a theme in Scripture. Blessing or fruitfulness comes through obedience to the Lord and staying connected to Him.

In Genesis 3 we see that sin broke the intimacy that existed between God and Adam and Eve and cut them off from the Presence of the Lord (see Gen 3:8-10). Instead of running to embrace the Lord, mankind hid from His Presence (vs.10). Later, after Cain kills his brother Abel, he says to God, "*My punishment is more than I can bear . . . I will be hidden from your presence.*"[12] Then Cain goes out "from the LORD's Presence"[13] into the world. One of the consequences of sin is that the Presence of the LORD becomes hidden from us and becomes something we are afraid of even while we long for it. In addition, as soon as mankind is cut off from the Presence of the Lord through their sin, their relationship with each other becomes characterized by blame and discord (compare Gen. 2:23 and Gen. 3:12):[14] mankind starts to die, they lose a sense of who they are and fruitfulness becomes harder. After Adam and Eve's sin, the ground becomes cursed and hard to work.[15] After Cain's sin, the ground becomes unfruitful.[16] The good news is that since we were designed by God to function best with access to His Presence, immediately after mankind was cut off from His Presence, God instituted a redemption plan to bring us back into His Presence through Jesus Christ. It is no surprise that in John 15: 4, 5, Jesus promises fruitfulness for those who remain and "abide" in Him.[17]

Sin disrupts our connection to God and breaks our intimacy with Him. It separates us from an awareness of what it means to be human. Our connection to God, restored through Jesus Christ, empowers us to know and accept what gives us life, and how we were designed to thrive in a context of holiness. Human identity comes out of holiness, out of separating ourselves from sin and coming into the Presence of God. Staying connected to the God who formed us and shaped us according to His "image" is the key to being truly "human".

---

12 Genesis 4:13-14.

13 Genesis 4:16.

14 We also see the loss of identity that comes through sin. In Gen. 2:23, Adam knows who Eve is, by Gen. 3:12 sin has caused him to be blinded to who she is and he no longer treats her as "bone of his bone and flesh of his flesh." Sin has brought disintegration to the relationship between them and to their sense of self.

15 Genesis 3:17-18.

16 Genesis 4:12.

17 John 15:4-8.

PEOPLE LIVING IN GOD'S PRESENCE DISPLAY THE IMAGE OF GOD TO THE WORLD

The next point has implications for marriage.[18] In Genesis 2:7 Adam is created. He names all the creatures God has created, but, despite the variety of God's creation, *"for Adam no suitable/similar helper was found"* (vs. 20). So God caused Adam to fall asleep and then created Eve out of Adam's rib (vs. 22). Eve is then given to Adam and now creation is complete and is "very good."

The Adam of Genesis 2:7 is not the same as the Adam of Genesis 2:22. The first Adam is created in the image of God as one unit. The second Adam has part of his nature changed and the image of God becomes separated into two parts, one masculine and one feminine. Both men and women are created in the "image of God" and both display this in their ability to love, communicate, relate to others, create, steward, and reflect other characteristics that are seen in God. Yet it is interesting that the final, complete, image of God is neither male nor female by themselves, but only the two of them together (I will briefly discuss singleness below). Another way to say this is that when male and female come together in a unity, they represent a completion of the image of God in a way that neither of them does separately. Neither one is more completely the "image of God" than the other. Both need the other to reflect the fullness of the image of God to the world. This is one reason that the *Biblical* idea of marriage is when one man and one woman come together in a union that represents the completeness of the image of God as seen in Genesis 2. No other type of union does this. Of course, to get the full idea of what the image of God is meant to be, the marriage must be submitted to the Lordship of God and lived in the Presence of the Lord. It is not automatic that any marriage will display what God is like to the world. It is God's love and Presence that empowers the two to function as one and display the image of God.

---

18 I will only give a thumb-nail sketch of this here. It needs to be developed further in another place.

Marriage as well as community lived in the Presence of the Lord is evangelistic, displaying to the world the true nature of what it means to live out our identities as those created in the image of God. As men and women function together while mutually honouring one another and God, the image of God becomes visible in the world and calls people towards God. Godly marriages and communities display all of the things already mentioned: the relational nature of God; the life-giving nature of living in God's Presence; the fact that identity comes from our relationship with God and not from what we do; and the fruitfulness of living in God's Presence. A marriage and community that is God centered, God honouring, and cleansed by the cross displays to the world the nature of God just like Jesus does. Both are the image of God, although Jesus would more exactly model this due to His sinlessness.[19] In contrast to this, a flawed marriage and flawed community displays a flawed image of God to others. Godly marriages and communities are like a river of life, calling people around them to experience the life-giving Presence of the Lord. One person in the community or marriage calls and releases the other into their destiny in the Lord just as God, through His Presence with us, does the same.

An implication of this is that when God pours out His Spirit as He does in Acts 1 and 2 and as is prophesied in Joel 2:28, He does not pour out His Spirit on only part of His image – He pours out His Spirit on *both* men and women. Both are recipients of His empowering Spirit and the clear expectation is that both will be able to express their spiritual anointing in the Church in the Presence of the Lord.

When Eve is brought to Adam, he calls out in joy that she is *"bone of my bone and flesh of my flesh."* Adam and Eve are one. In Genesis 3, Satan comes along and his strategy is to separate bone from bone and flesh from flesh so that the two, joined in unity under the Lord, start to function as two separate units at war with one another outside of the Presence of the Lord. When God comes to Adam and asks what happened, Adam blames

19 Men and women are sinners, yet Jesus is not, so He more exactly reflects without distortion the image of God (see also Colossians 1:15).

Eve, the *"one You gave me"* and the image of God no longer functions as a unit. Satan's strategy has not changed. If he can get men and women to believe that the problem is the other, discord sets in, and the war is on, and the image of God is marred from presenting to the world a display of what God is like. This is one reason marriages are under attack today. Marriages lived in submission to God that are rich in His Presence powerfully display the truth about God and are powerfully used to bring His kingdom to the earth. The center of our marriages as well as our other relationships needs to be the Presence of the Lord so that we can display Him to the world.

SINGLENESS AND THE IMAGE OF GOD

My wife and I married later in life and lived and ministered for years as singles before we married so I understand the perspective and challenges of being single in the Church. I was at a leadership retreat with our church at one point and one of the activities the leadership had decided to do was to have the husbands wash the feet of their spouses. I was the only single among the leadership group and was asked to absent myself for that session. It was a difficult moment for me and I want to be sensitive to the perspective of those who read this who may find themselves single at this time.

As beings created in the image of God we were created for relationship. Each of us, no matter whether we are married or single have been created in the image of God and as we live in relationship with God have the potential to powerfully display the "image of God" to the world. Yet everyone needs loving relationships with others to thrive. Singles need to be embedded in nurturing and caring relationships that affirm and accept who they are and work to release them into their unique calling in the Lord. Part of God's gift to each of us is His body, the Church. Families in the Church need to enlarge their sense of family to include those in their church (and wider) community who are single. In fact, people in the Church who love Jesus become our true family. As a married person, I can find my completeness in my spouse (in the Lord) and as a single I can find my completeness in the community formed within the Body of

Christ (also in the Lord). There is also a sense that as a married person I will never truly find my completeness in my spouse unless I find it *first* in God. Even as a married person, I need godly relationships with a wider community to help me thrive. The challenge for everyone, whether married or single, is to find their completeness in the Lord *first* before they seek to find it in relationships with others. For both married and singles, the ability to fully express who I am as one created in the image of God comes through God-saturated relationships with others. Together we express more of the image of God than we do separately. Because of who we are created to be, we find out our true identity as individuals and as male and female through encountering the Presence of the Lord. Also because of who we are and were created to be, we find out our true identity through the Presence of God-saturated community.

THE PRESENCE OF THE LORD CONFERS DIGNITY AND HONOUR

Another aspect of the story of the creation of humans is that the Presence of the Lord confers dignity and honour upon them. The creation of mankind shows that the Lord of the Universe places great value on us and His great desire to be present with us emphasizes that we are incredibly special. Just think of how we would feel if the president of our country or someone we respect highly went out of his/her way to clear their schedule to spend time with us, then magnify that about a million times and we have a glimpse of how God's intense desire to be with us confers honour upon us. God's Presence with us emphasizes how precious we are. Because of this, when we are in God's Presence our love for Him is stirred up, our worship of Him is released, and we are changed by our encounter with His Presence.

WE WERE MADE FOR MORE THAN THIS WORLD HAS TO OFFER

Lastly, the passage from Genesis 1 and 2 shows us that we were made for more than this world has to offer. We were created with eternity in our souls and a hunger and a thirst for something greater than what this physical world around us has to offer. The creation account shows us that the entire Universe has its source in God Himself. As mentioned earlier, contrary to the Western mindset, the world is primarily spiritual rather than physical in nature and as long as we ignore this, we will always be restless and never fulfilled. If we were made to find our identity through our relationship with God this means that relating rightly to the spiritual world is the foundation of a proper self-image. Since God is the source of all creation, all of creation displays aspects of who He is and of His love for His creation. We will never be completely happy, we will never be completely fulfilled, without being in a loving relationship with our Lord. Being spiritual in nature, even at the subconscious level, we recognize the spiritual nature of life and ache and long to be connected rightly to it. This world alone leaves us busy but empty. We were designed for a greater destiny that can only be found in God.

Summary

In this chapter, the creation account was used to show several ways in which our very nature as humans finds fulfillment through relationship with God and living in His Presence.

These include:

1. God has made us relational in nature and we function best when we are rooted in relationship to God's Presence and allow that Presence to flow into and through us in our relationships with others.
2. God's Presence gives us life and He is always willing to breathe His Spirit into us again.
3. We find out who we are through living in God's Presence. His Presence confers identity. He needs to be the context in which we live so that we can become who He has designed us to be.
4. Fruitfulness comes out of living in the Presence of the Lord.

5. Marriages lived in the Presence of the Lord are a coming together of the image of God into a unity that displays the beauty of the Lord and calls others towards Him.
6. The above point is true for other relationships. Communities that are characterized by the Presence of the Lord display the image of God to the world and call us into and affirm our true identity in the Lord.
7. We discover our incredible value and worth when we come into the loving Presence of God.
8. The world we live in, by itself, does not offer us what we need to find fulfillment. We were designed for more than this world can offer us.

Entering Into His Presence

Spend some time worshipping the Lord and then just rest in His Presence. Ask the Lord to show you any false identities that you may have believed. If He shows you anything, repent and ask the Lord for forgiveness and then ask Him to show you something about you that He loves, the truth that is the "real" you. For some people this may be hard especially if there was not a lot of affirmation in your own family.

Ask the Lord to pour out His life on your soul and drink it in like water on dry soil. Let God come to you with His life-giving Spirit. If you are married, turn your thoughts to your marriage and ask for the Lord's blessing on it so that you and your wife or husband can be the reflection of God to those around you. If you are single, turn your thoughts to the Lord and give Him your relationships. Receive His love for you. Give to Him any difficulties you may be having (whether married or single) and ask Him for His strength and light. Let the love of the Lord pour down upon you.

Forgive where you may have been wronged and accept the affirmation of the Lord. Accept that He loves you and loves being with you.

Prayer

Lord, I am taking this moment to repent of any ways that I have tried to take my significance and importance from other sources. I want to acknowledge and declare right now that You are my one desire. In the name of Jesus, I receive Your life in my heart, mind, soul, spirit and body.

Help me, Lord, to find my identity in You. I repent of any false identities that may have come into my life through my work or my insecurities (if God shows you specific things, lay each of them down and repent specifically). I lay them all down. Show me, Lord, who You have made me to be. I choose right now to accept who I truly am and ask You to help me to love myself as much as You love me. Help me to so value Your Presence that I seek it at all times.

I give You my work. Help me to be able to bring Your Presence into my workplace so that I can be fruitful in the right way. Help me not to take my identity from what I do.

I give You my marriage. Make my marriage so full of Your Presence that I am able to affirm my wife/husband so that our marriage will sparkle with Your love and Presence. Help me to forgive fully from my heart for those times I have been hurt. Help us to show Your beauty to those around us. (If you are single you can replace "marriage" with "friendships" and "wife/husband" with "friends")

I give You all my relationships. May You be the center of them all. Help me to not get my identity from people but instead from You. Lord I pray that You would release to me those relationships I need to mature and grow. Fill me so full of Your Presence that You overflow from me to touch all of those who need Your love.

I declare right now that You are my God and ask You to unite my heart to fear You only. Help me to rest in Your love and more fully live in Your Presence.

In the precious name of Jesus I pray,

Amen.

2

The Living God of The Bible Is Different From Any Other "God"

*'The Lord said, "**I have indeed seen** the misery of my people in Egypt, **I have heard them** crying out because of their slave drivers, . . . **So I have come down** to rescue them from the hands of the Egyptians . . . **So now go. I am sending you** to Pharaoh to bring my people the Israelites out of Egypt. . . . And God said, "**I will be with you. . . .**"'* *(Exodus 3:7, 8, 10, 12,* emphasis added*)*

"Moses said to God, 'Suppose I go to the Israelites and say to them, "The God of your fathers has sent me to you," and they ask me, "What is his name?" Then what shall I tell them?' God said to Moses, 'I AM WHO I AM. This is what you are to say to the Israelites: "I AM has sent me to you."'" (Exodus 3:13-14)

THE IMPORTANCE AND SETTING OF EXODUS 3

There is a pivotal revelation of God in Exodus 3 giving us key information about the living God that will empower our ability to draw life from His Presence. The Presence of God is so powerfully healing for us because of who He is.

Exodus 3 is the familiar story of Moses' encounter with God at the burning bush. At that time the Israelites were suffering terribly as slaves of the Egyptians. The Moses we see in chapter 3 is a different man from what we saw in the previous chapter. In chapter 2, he was raised in the court of Pharaoh, was highly educated, and filled with a sense of his own power and authority. He wanted to do something about the slavery of his people. Perhaps he had a sense of his own calling from God: that he would one day be the one who would bring deliverance to his people. Yet when he stretched forth his hand to bring this about in his own flesh, he failed miserably and had to flee for his life.[20] It is deeply ironic that in Exodus 2:14 a Hebrew man says to Moses, "Who made you ruler and judge over us?" At that moment Moses was trying to act in this role through his own power and authority. From chapter 3 on, it is clearly God who places Moses into this position of leadership. Just because one has a correct sense of one's own calling does not mean that it should be forced into existence. There is always a mystery to God's timing. Trying to force the fulfillment of what we feel we are called to do by God on our terms will always cause us problems and may even cause our destiny to remain unfulfilled.

Moses almost loses his destiny through two opposite mistakes. First, he tries to fulfill his calling through his own strength and power,[21] and later, he resists his calling and almost loses it through lack of obedience to God.[22] Here is where the Presence of the Lord makes all the difference. Moses starts to enter into his calling when he dialogues with God and spends time in His Presence. There is no evidence of Moses dialoguing with God in chapter 2.

Chapter 3 finds Moses in the desert shepherding his father-in-law's sheep. He is poor and in the middle of the desert where he has been a shepherd for 40 years. He is not the proud man he used to be. His self-im-

---

20 Exodus 2:11-15.

21 Exodus 2:12-14.

22 Exodus 4:10, 13.

age is shattered[23] and he does not have a lot of self-confidence when God starts to speak to him about His plans for him and for the Israelites.[24] While in the desert, he became meek and humble enough that God could trust him to lead a nation. We see here that pride[25] often *blocks* us from entering our calling while humility *opens the door* for us to walk into it. Humility empowers us to see God more clearly and enables us to encounter God in a more meaningful way.

While Moses was in the desert shepherding sheep, God caused a bush to burst into flame without being consumed by those flames. Curious, Moses drew near to the burning bush. God called to Moses by name and we see the start of a dialogue between Moses and God that changed Moses' life and impacted all of history. In this significant event, it is Moses' encounter with the Presence of God that shifts the future trajectory of his life.

In the preliminary verses of this chapter, we see that God knew exactly where Moses was, what he was doing, and He also knew his name. God used what He knew about Moses and his curiosity to draw him into a place where He could speak to him. God does the same with us. He knows who we are, where we are, and will use what He knows about us to draw us into His Presence so He can speak to us and we can hear His voice.

In the subsequent verses in Exodus 3 we see three key self-revelations of God that enable us to understand who God is and how He is so different than any other "god." The first is from verses 5-6, the second from verses 7-12, and the third from verses 13-15.

---

23 Compare his vigorous actions in chapter 2 to his halting rebuttal to God in Exodus 4:10.

24 Exodus 4:10: "... I am slow of speech and tongue." See also 4:13: 'But Moses said, "Pardon your servant. Please send someone else."

25 Pride often comes when we try to define ourselves in comparison to others outside the Presence of God.

THE LORD COMBINES HOLINESS WITH A PASSION FOR RELATIONSHIP

In verses 5-6, after calling to Moses so that he would come closer, God somewhat contradictorily says (vs. 5): *"Do not come any closer. Take off your sandals for the place where you are standing is holy ground."* God in His holiness is completely "other" than us. We cannot come into His Presence without coming to terms with that holiness. Just as Moses had to take off his sandals in God's Presence, we also must put off something of ourselves to come closer to the living God and enter His Presence. What do we need to "put off" in order to draw closer to God? Is it fear? Pride? Self-sufficiency? At different points in time, I have had to "put off" all of these. If we are not willing to change, coming face to face with God's holiness can be shattering. It is instructive that a common introductory phrase on the lips of angels in the Bible is: "Do not be afraid."[26] Holiness clings to them because they spend time in the Presence of God and real holiness can be terrifyingly confrontive to all that we are. In Isaiah 6 we see a good example of this.[27] Isaiah is worshipping in the temple and suddenly sees the glory of the Lord. The foundations of the temple are shaken as angels cry out, the holiness of the Lord is revealed and Isaiah is convinced he is going to die. There is a truth here that through embracing the holiness of the Lord we die, and through dying we enter our calling from God.[28] If we are not willing to let go or to "put off" those things that keep us from God's holy Presence, we will never find our destiny.

In Exodus 3:5, God very powerfully introduces Moses to His holiness, but then He quickly goes on to something else (vs. 6): *"Then He said, 'I am the God of your father, the God of Abraham, the God of Isaac and the God of Jacob.'"* After calling Moses into His Presence and confronting him with His holiness, God now identifies Himself as the God who is intertwined with Moses' own personal history, connecting the God who

26 See Daniel 10:12, 19; Matthew 28:5; Luke 1:13, 30; 2:10.

27 Discussed in more detail in chapter 5.

28 See John 12:24-25.

is speaking to Moses to all that he knows about the God who previously encountered his ancestors, Abraham, Isaac, and Jacob. The God who is speaking to Moses is THAT God, the one he has heard about who called and set apart his forefathers. Three times in this chapter (vs. 6, 15, 16) God calls himself the God of Abraham, Isaac and Jacob and thus connects for Moses and for the Israelites the fact that the God currently acting is the same God who acted in the past in the lives of these people. Part of what is happening here is that God is such a personal God that He defines himself by His relationships. When I go onto the campus of my sons' school the other children do not necessarily know who I am. They know my children but not me. A child once asked me, "Are you the father of Mathias?" When I said "Yes," he knew who I was and could place me. It is the same with God. He is defining Himself relationally so that Moses would know who He was. Think of this: God is such a God of "Presence" that He defines Himself by both His current and past relationships. One of the ways in which God is known to others is through the lives of those who know and reflect Him faithfully.

It is interesting that Moses does not truly seem to understand who is speaking to him until these two things are joined together – holiness and relationship. And when this happens Moses hid his face. He is afraid. He "gets" who he is talking to and is overwhelmed. It is a conundrum: a God who is holy, yet supremely relational, yet that conundrum is resolved in Christ. This tension defines a key aspect of who God is.

GOD SEES US, HEARS US AND COMES DOWN TO RESCUE US

A seminary professor once told me that if you want to know the key distinction between the Biblical God and the gods of Hinduism, Islam, Buddhism or any other religion, it is found in Exodus 3:7-8. Here is the key truth: The living God is a God who sees (vs. 7), hears (vs. 7), becomes concerned by what He sees and hears (vs.7) and so comes down to rescue us (vs. 8).[29] It is really that simple. The God of the Bible saw what the Israelites were going through just as He knows what you are going through. He heard the prayers of the Israelites just as He hears your prayers and the groanings of your spirit. And the living God does not hold Himself aloof from what He sees and hears but responds in love to rescue and deliver. I work among Muslims and this is definitely NOT the god of Islam. The god of Islam is normally seen as aloof and far off. He may "see" and "hear" but he cannot be counted on to rescue or deliver. There is a fair bit of hopelessness and a type of fatalism within Islam. I have found also that one key strategy of the enemy is to try to convince us that God does not see us, that He does not hear us and that our failings are such that He will not come down to rescue us. But God *does* see you, He *does* hear you and He *is* coming down. Let me relate a story that illustrates the power of this passage.

I was in Togo teaching a class, and my wife called me from Senegal and said that she had just had the best day of her life. She and a national pastor's wife went out to a village teaching the ladies how to tie-dye cloth. As a part of this, they normally tell a Bible story and then pray for the sick. My wife told the story of Jesus and the healing of the woman with the issue of blood.[30] On hearing this, one woman jumped up and said, "That's me! I have gone everywhere to try to get well. I have been to the doctors, to the marabouts[31] and to witch doctors and no-one has been able to help me. Do you think Jesus can heal me?" My wife said, "Jesus can heal you just like He did the woman in the story." Then another woman said, "I have a problem with my eyes." My wife said, "Jesus can heal you too." Due to time constraints, they went into the tie-dye training and did not get to the prayer time. A little later, the first woman jumped to her feet and started to dance. The whole room erupted and several ladies jumped to their feet and joined in. As they danced,

29 See also Deuteronomy 26:7-8 where God is described in a similar fashion.

30 Matthew 9:20-22; Mark 5:25-34; Luke 8:43-48.

31 Islamic religious leaders, leaders of the local mosques. They often practice a type of Islamic sorcery.

they started to chant a phrase in their language. Asking for a translation, my wife discovered they were chanting, "Jesus healed me!" Once things calmed down they found out that both of the above-mentioned women were healed! Half the women there were Muslim yet both Muslims and Christians were dancing and shouting out: "Jesus healed me"! I told my wife it was not fair that I was teaching a Seminary class and she was having all the fun!

A couple of months later we were able to go back to the village where all this happened. I started by asking if the two healed women were there. When they were, I had them share their testimonies. I taught from Exodus 3 that the God of the Bible is a God who sees, hears, and comes down. I told them that they already knew this to be true because of the miracles they saw when my wife was there before and the stories the ladies had told earlier. They nodded their heads. Then I invited them to come forward for prayer. Of the 45 or so people present, over 20 pushed to the front of the small room. Headaches were healed. Frozen shoulders were healed. Painful knees became pain free. It was amazing! Then we had them share testimonies and I finished with – "See! God sees, hears and comes down!" I told them that they now knew that what I had been teaching was true! Then we sang the Sunday school song: "God is good!" All of us were blown away by what we had seen and experienced. Our God is truly a God who sees, hears and comes down to rescue us!

The above story shows a truth that applies to each one of us. Our God is a personal God who sees the circumstances of our lives, He hears our prayers and He comes down to rescue us. This is our God! Nothing is so overwhelming that the answer is not found in the heart of our God who exerts Himself to save us.

We see this supremely in Jesus Christ, who is God's response to what He has seen and heard: God's response to the pain in the world, sent down to Earth by our Heavenly Father to rescue us from our sins.

GOD'S PRESENCE WITH HIS PEOPLE EMPOWERS THEIR OBEDIENCE TO ACCOMPLISH HIS WILL

I want to make one more point from verses 7-12. God says to Moses, *"I have seen, heard and I have come down ... now you go (vs. 10) . . . and I will be with you (vs. 12)."* God came down to rescue the Israelites but then sent Moses to do it. God's will is expressed when God's people are obedient. The implication is that we can thwart God's will through our disobedience. If Moses had refused to go, the Israelites would have remained slaves. God comes down in response to the need He sees and hears and then calls Moses to do what is absolutely impossible for one man to do – free an entire nation from slavery. It only becomes possible because God promises that He would be *with* Moses. The man who is sent by God to do the impossible task can do it because the LORD is with him. We are the hands and feet of God in the world today, accomplishing His will. As we go in obedience, carrying His Presence, the impossible becomes possible. Our obedience or disobedience impacts the world around us and determines whether the fullness of God's will is accomplished. Another way to say it is that because of who God is, all things are possible. Because of who God is, He empowers what He commands. The kingdom of God is released through obedience. Even baby steps of obedience are much more powerful than no steps of obedience at all.

The second key revelation of God in this passage, then, is that the living God of the Bible is one who sees, hears and comes down and that He will accomplish His will to bring deliverance to others as we go in obedience with His Empowering Presence.

THE FOUNDATION OF ALL REALITY IS A GOD OF PRESENCE

In verses 13-14 we see the famous "I AM" passage. It brings into focus a key aspect of who God is and why we must relate to the Presence of God in order to come into a proper understanding of reality. Knowing God centers us and balances us and enables us to relate rightly to the world around us. God's Presence is so powerful simply because of who He is.

When Moses asked what the name[32] of God was, God said, *"I AM WHO I AM. This is what you are to say to the Israelites: 'I AM has sent me to you.'"* From this point on, the main name for God is "Jehovah" or "Yahweh[33]" which is a derivative of the "I am" verb in Hebrew. It is used over 6500 times in the Old Testament. Moses is being very daring[34] in asking for a fuller, deeper revelation of the essential nature of God by asking for the name of God, yet God responds. His response seems ambiguous to us but is packed with power.

There are at least three things God is saying here. First, He is making it clear that He is the basis and source of all reality. He is the ground from which reality emerges. Nothing else makes God who He is. He is who He is. We cannot shape God into what He is not. We must simply take Him as He is and relate to Him on His terms not ours. We must accept who He is and not seek to make Him what our understanding thinks He should be like. He is more solid than the mountains, more eternal than the stars. He is the God who simply spoke and all of these, seemingly durable things, came into being. The truth is that the foundation of all that we see is the spiritual world (as mentioned earlier). The physical world is just the shadow of a deeper reality.[35] In Genesis we see that from the spiritual world, came, by the exertion of God's spoken Word, all that we see around us. God is the one who "is" and from Him flows all things, from Him flows all power. There are no other gods like this God. God makes no apologies for who He is. He is simply who He is and Moses and the elders of Israel must take Him as He is. We must do the same. This means

32 In Hebraic culture, the name of someone described his inner essence. This is why it was startling that God knew the name of Moses (which means 'one drawn from the water' see Exodus 2:10). Moses is asking God to reveal who He really is to him.

33 "Normally "Yahweh" is translated as "LORD" in the NIV. If you see "LORD" in the text of this book, I am referring to this name for God which is explained in this chapter.

34 Often once you come into deeper relationship with God, you do get very "bold" with what you ask of him!

35 Hebrews 8:5; Colossians 2:17.

that we cannot come into a true understanding of reality if we do not relate rightly to the God who is the source of all reality. It also means that the only solid foundation for a correct perspective on the world around us is God Himself.

Tension arises here because in the Western world, people generally do not believe this. Many Westerners do not even believe that the spiritual world exists, or if they do believe it exists, see it as largely irrelevant to their lives. Even among Christians we see many functional atheists.[36] However, in Africa from cradle to grave, people see themselves as embedded in a spiritual world that is the source of what they see around them. And the answers we need when faced with physical challenges can come from the spiritual world (whether for money, health, or food). This is closer to the Biblical perspective. As a missionary in Africa, I have seen many people healed of various diseases and Westerners will comment that healing and deliverance seem to occur much easier and faster in non-Western contexts. They also often comment that this must be because there is less access to medical and other resources and so people are more open to non-medical healing modalities.[37] While this may be true it is only part of the reason. A large part of it is that Africans fundamentally believe that the spiritual world is the foundation of the world they see around them and that it holds the answers they need. They are very open to your prayers and the expectation for God to act is high. In large part in the Western world we are so divorced from this Biblical viewpoint that we will seek naturalistic explanations for why faith seems to be more evident in non-Western settings. Yet God spoke and the world was formed. From God Himself came all we see. Since this God is the ultimate source of reality, all answers flow from Him, even if it involves setting an entire nation free from their slavery (as was the case with Moses) or healing

---

36 A "functional atheist" is someone who says they believe in God but functionally, in their day to day lives, they live as if God does not exist.

37 For example see Randy Clark and Craig Miller. *Finding Victory when Healing doesn't Happen: Breaking through with Healing Prayer.* Global Awakening. Mechanicsburg, PA. 2015 page 103 where this very point is made.

sickness. Once we truly believe that our God is the source of all reality, we are closer to discovering the answer to our need in Him. This may require us to make a conscious shift in our worldview so that we truly see the Lord as the source of all we need. Faith will come easier when we perceive God and His world in the right way.

GOD MAKES HIMSELF PRESENT TO US

A second aspect of what God is saying in Exodus 3:13-14 comes out of the Hebrew culture. You see a bit of a glimpse of this when Moses responds to God's call with "Here I am." (vs. 4). In the country I served in Africa, after the initial greeting, you say: Na nga def? (How is it going?), and the response is: Maa ngi fii (I am here). If you were to ask how the man's wife was, he would say, "She is here." How are your children? "They are here."[38] When I was first learning the language, this seemed crazy. Of course they were here: I was talking to them! However, what they were saying is when I am present to you and you are present to me, that is enough. Presence! All we need is to be present one with the other.

The "I am" verb in the Hebrew culture is an indicator of "presence." This is why Moses himself responded to God with "Here I am." – I am present.[39] Moses is saying he is present to the one who is calling to him. In our Western culture we have lost this sense of the value of being "present" with one another. God is saying in this verse: "I am the one who makes myself present (with you), tell them that the God who makes Himself present to His people (their forefathers) is the one who has sent you." But it is more than just being "nearby", it involves an attentive or focused presence. It is about relationship. In this chapter, three times God indi-

38 And you CANNOT skip the greetings and get to the task at hand!

39 You also see this same thing in John 6:21 when Jesus is walking on the water. When the disciples are afraid and cry out, Jesus responds with "I am (here). Do not be afraid." He is saying, "It is me! I am here. I am present." When the disciples hear this, they recognize Jesus and are no longer afraid. When Jesus is with them, they can deal with anything. Jesus here is both using the Hebrew phrase indicating "presence" as well as using the recognized name for God from Exodus 3:13-14. There are multiple strands of meaning in this passage.

cates his relational ties to the Israelites (vs. 6, 15, 16), one time emphasizes that He will be with Moses as he goes (vs. 12), and twice that He is the God who sees and knows what is happening in Egypt (vs. 7-8, 16-17). God's attentive, relational Presence with the people of Israel is a clear distinctive of His nature: our God is a God who makes Himself present to His people.

This is why it was so tragic when God became angry with the Israelites after they had made a golden calf (Exodus 33:3) and said He would not go with them into the Promised Land. Moses pleads with God to go with them. Finally, God says in Exodus 33:14: *"My Presence will go with you and I will give you rest" (vs. 15). Then Moses says, "If your Presence does not go with us, do not send us up from here. . . . What else will distinguish me and your people from all the other people on the face of the earth?"*

Oh! That we would have the same passion for the Presence of the LORD that Moses had. If He is not with us, we are nothing. The God of the Bible is distinguished by the fact that He is the only God who makes Himself fully present to His people.[40] This is what sets both God and His people apart from every other nation.[41] This is what brings us hope and joy.

God longs to be present with His people. Sadly, sin and rebellion break down access to His Presence. At the fall of mankind in the Garden, sin destroyed the intimacy that God had with Adam and Eve but God had a plan. Matthew indicates the birth of Jesus is a fulfillment of Isaiah 7:14

---

40 This point is so important that you can almost say that the sign of a false "god" is that he does not make himself present to his people. The God of the Bible makes himself accessible to us. Yes, there are barriers, but He has gone through all the hard work of eliminating them. It is not up to us to tear them down. We just step into what He has done and receive what God has already done to make relationship with Him possible. This point also assumes personhood. God is not a force but a person who makes relationship possible. In addition, one of the strategies of Satan is to convince us that barriers exist between us and God that the cross cannot deal with.

41 There is a repeated refrain in Scripture where God says he will be the God of Israel and they will be his people. See Exodus 6:7; Jeremiah 7:23, 11:4; 30:22; Deuteronomy 26:18-19; 29:13 Ezekiel 36:28; Joel 2:27 as examples. See especially Leviticus 26:11-12: *"I will put my dwelling place among you and not abhor you. I will walk among you and be your God and you will be my people."*

which says that the Messiah would be called 'Emmanuel' meaning 'God with us' (Matt. 1:22-23). In and through Jesus Christ, God can be once more fully present with His people, with us. This truth about God's passion to be present with His people is so characteristic of Him that the Son of God sent by the Father to destroy all the barriers that existed between man and God was called "Emmanuel." The passion of Jesus involved His willingness to embrace the cross so that we could once again be present to the God who loves to be present to us.

The power of what Moses told the Elders of Israel is that this God who has sent Moses is the one, who in His very essence, is the God who makes Himself present to those He loves. There is no other God anywhere who makes Himself present to us like this God. We are never far from His love. In His very nature, He is a God of Presence. This brings us hope no matter how dark things get. We have the possibility of change no matter the situation. All we need to do is turn towards this God, call upon His name[42] and trust in who He is to deliver us. This was the message for the Israelites in their slavery and this is the message for us today.

GOD CAN CAUSE ANYTHING TO COME INTO BEING

The third aspect of God's nature that comes out of the "I am" saying of verse 14 comes from the fact that the Hebrew worldview is much more dynamic than ours.[43] It is likely that the "I am"[44] name for God has a

42 Jeremiah 29:13: "You will seek me and find me when you seek for me with all of your heart."

43 Which stems from the more static Greek view of the world. The Hebrew worldview is more holistic. In addition, the Hebrew verb "hayah" (I am) can mean "to be", "to become" "to exist" or even "to create". (from Robert E. Stone. "I Am Who I Am". Eerdmans Dictionary of the Bible. David Noel Freedman & Allen C. Myers (eds.). Eerdmans. Grand Rapids, MI. 2000. P. 624).

44 Translators differ on whether Exodus 3:14 should be translated "I am who I am" (present tense) or "I will be who I will be" (future tense). The latter indicates that God will be whoever He needs to be for whatever problems are encountered in the future. He is big enough and powerful enough to handle anything and will be the answer that is needed when we need it.

causative implication. Since God is the basis of all reality and the source of creation, He is the one who can cause anything "to be." His Presence in the world is dynamic and vibrant with activity. He is not limited by anything. So, when God sends Moses to do the impossible, to go to one of the most powerful leaders in the ancient world to deliver an entire nation from their slavery, it is possible because the God sending him can cause even this impossible thing to come to pass.

In summary, the great "I AM" is the source of all reality and the foundation of all things. He is characterized by "Presence" and He is the God who can bring anything into existence. To put it another way, because God is the ultimate source and cause of all things, when He is present, anything becomes possible. We have hope because this God is not a God who stays aloof from His creation but instead is passionately in love with it and is characterized by His desire to be present to it. His heart stance is to relate to His people in love; sustaining, nurturing and calling them into deeper intimacy.

HEALING IS NOT SOMETHING GOD DOES, IT IS SOMETHING HE IS

I have found that the above understanding of the essential nature of God empowers prayer for the sick. God is a unity. When His Presence comes, all of Him comes. He is the creator God who is the source of all things, and He can cause anything to come into existence. He loves to be present with us and knows exactly how our body works and what needs to be done to release healing. I believe healing should not be seen as something that God does separate from who He is. It *is* who He is. He is the source of life. Because of who God is, healing erupts where His Presence is. This is part of the message of Isaiah 35 which we will discuss in another chapter. When God is present, healing bursts forth. This is also why a key sign of the anointing of the Lord on the Messiah (i.e. the sign of God's Presence with him, see Luke 7:21-22) are the miracles that would burst forth in his ministry because of the Presence of the Lord.

Just to emphasize this point, when we have compound names for God like Jehovah-Raphah (Exodus 15:26), often translated "the Lord who heals you", but more correctly "the Lord, the healer" or "the healing Lord," what this expression is saying is that healing comes out of who God is. Because he is "Yahweh" or "I am," He heals. So, healing comes out of the active presence of Yahweh with us. In the same way, when it says God is "Jehovah-Jireh" (God the provider or the Lord will provide, Gen 22:14), provision comes out of who God is and becomes possible when God is powerfully present. So Jesus, knowing God was with him, broke a few loaves and fishes and fed 5000 people.[45] Life births where the living God is present. Another example is "Jehovah-Shalom" (The LORD our peace, Judges 6:24). Peace is not something separate from God but a part of who He is in His inner nature so when He is powerfully present, there is peace.

Summary

The Presence of God is good for us because of who He is. There is no God like the God the Bible describes who loves His creation and whose heart is always inclined to hear, see and help those who love Him and call on His name. He is a God who loves to make Himself present to those who seek and honor Him.

In summary:

1. The God of the Bible is a God who sees every detail of our lives and calls us to draw closer to Him.
2. He is a God who uniquely brings together holiness and relationship. He is the holy God whose passion is to relate with intimacy to His creation. Since He is so strongly relational, He is committed to doing whatever is necessary to break down that which prevents us from walking in His holy Presence. He calls to us to "put off" in order to "come in closer."

45 John 6:1-15.

3. The Living God is a God who sees us, hears our prayers and comes down from heaven to rescue us. This is supremely seen in Jesus Christ.
4. God accomplishes His will through the obedience of His people. While He can call us to do impossible things, He always goes with us into what He has called us to do. He calls us and equips us by His Presence for the task He gives us.
5. The living God is the eternal source and cause of all reality who is characterized by His desire to be present to His creation. Where God is present anything becomes possible.
6. Many things flow from God's Presence. One of these is healing. Healing is not something God does, it is something that He is. Where God is present, healing erupts. Where God is present, provision and peace also erupt.

Entering Into His Presence

Spend some time worshipping the Lord. Confess to the Lord those times when you have felt ignored or unseen by Him. Receive the assurance that God does see you and does care for all you are going through. Talk to Him if you have any feelings of unworthiness and give them to the Lord.

Is He asking you to "put something off" in order to come more fully into His Presence? What does the Lord need to do to "rescue" you? Receive from the Lord the hope that He is already acting on your behalf. He has not forgotten you. Rest for some time in the assurance that God is Lord of all and He is the one who is able to do all you need for Him to do.

Receive His love. Give any confusion to Him and just receive His love for you. As you receive the Presence of the Lord, also receive His healing for your body, soul and spirit. Just spend some time drinking Him in.

Listen to the LORD calling your name. Say, "Yes, Lord" and receive His love.

Prayer

Lord, I ask Your forgiveness for believing the lie that You do not see me or know me or know about the details of my life. I receive Your love and acceptance of me. I choose to believe You are, even now, working in my life to bring about the deliverance and rescue that I need. Forgive me for believing You are not doing this. I choose right now to trust You.

Lord, right now I choose to believe that You are hearing me even when I pray quietly in my heart. I choose to believe that You are acting to save, heal and deliver; that right now You are acting on my behalf.

Lord, I cry out to You, "Show me Your Presence! Don't let me go from here unless I know Your Presence!" I want You to be my God, my only God. I want to be part of the people You are forming for Yourself on the earth.

I repent of the ways I have embraced the world and run from holiness. I accept the forgiveness Jesus won for me on the cross. I receive the forgiveness of Jesus for my sin and accept the gift from Jesus of His righteousness. I place my sins right now onto Jesus and His cross and clothe myself with the righteousness of Christ.

Thank You, Lord, that You long to be present with me. Show me where there are barriers to Your Presence so that I can cast them down and open up my heart more fully to you. I hunger and thirst for more of You. I need You to be my source and my foundation. As I receive Your presence, I receive also the healing that I desperately need. I bless You for all that You are doing and have done in my life.

In the precious name of Jesus I pray,

Amen.

3

The Presence of The Lord Can Transform Everything!

The desert and the parched land will be glad; the wilderness will rejoice and blossom. Like the crocus, it will burst into bloom; it will rejoice greatly and shout for joy. The glory of Lebanon will be given to it, the splendour of Carmel and Sharon; they will see the glory of the LORD, the splendour of our God.

Strengthen the feeble hands, steady the knees that give way; say to those with fearful hearts, "Be strong, do not fear; your God will come, he will come with vengeance; with divine retribution he will come to save you."

Then will the eyes of the blind be opened and the ears of the deaf unstopped. Then will the lame leap like a deer, and the mute tongue shout for joy. Water will gush forth in the wilderness and streams in the desert. The burning sand will become a pool, the thirsty ground bubbling springs. In the haunts where jackals once lay, grass and reeds and papyrus will grow.

And a highway will be there; it will be called the Way of Holiness; it will be for those who walk on that Way. The unclean will not journey on it; wicked fools will not go about on it. No lion will be there,

> *nor any ravenous beast; they will not be found there. But only the redeemed will walk there, and those the LORD has rescued will return. They will enter Zion with singing; everlasting joy will crown their heads. Gladness and joy will overtake them, and sorrow and sighing will flee away. (Isaiah 35:1-10)*

Isaiah 35 is all about how the Presence of the Lord can powerfully transform the devastated parts of our life into something beautiful. It is a powerful passage that changed the way I saw God and drew me more deeply into His Presence. This passage is rich with key characteristics of God we need to know and embrace in order to receive our transformation.

We all have "wilderness" experiences. They are a part of life. None of us grew up in perfect homes or among perfect people. All of us carry hurt and devastation. This passage shows us that in the midst of these times, these places, we can find His Presence. No wilderness is beyond God's ability to transform.

THE ARABAH

There are a number of exegetical points that make this passage come alive. The first is to realize the historical context of this passage. Isaiah 6:1 mentions that Isaiah received his "call" the year King Uzziah died. King Uzziah was a brilliant general as well as leader, and the nation of Judah under him had the largest boundaries and the strongest armies since the time of King Solomon.[46] Under his son, Jotham, when Isaiah became a prophet, the size and strength of the nation started to shrink. Then, Jotham's son, Ahaz, became king. He was an ungodly, idolatrous man and one of the most foolish kings Judah ever had. Increasingly, the Aramites, the Israelites, the Edomites, and the Philistines all invaded the nation of Judah during his reign. Gradually the boundaries of the nation became smaller and smaller. The people were left unprotected and helpless before the attacks of all of these surrounding peoples. The worst hit

46 We will look at Uzziah in more detail in chapter 5.

area was the Arabah, the region farthest from the capital of Jerusalem (II Chron. 28:15-27), an area south of Jerusalem bordering on Moab, Edom and Philistia. In Isaiah 35, the word translated "wilderness" in verse 1 and "desert" in verse 6 is actually "Arabah". At the time Isaiah 35 was written, the Arabah was a sin-scorched landscape, a wilderness devastated by Moabite, Edomite and Philistine bandits, inhabited by the remnants of a once great people who were without hope in a desperate situation. It is precisely this Arabah, this wilderness, which God comes to visit and transform.

Look at the areas of your life that are represented by this sin-devastated landscape. All of us have been sinned against. Yet, we are never without hope, because our God is one who comes first to those desperate places to bring His love. Our God is a God who sees, hears and comes down to rescue us.

One caveat is that this shows us the influence of leaders who are passionate followers of God. Sin, in the lives of leaders, makes everyone under their leadership vulnerable to the ravages of sinful people. This applies to families all the way up to nations. When I sin, my family becomes vulnerable. When leaders of organizations sin, their organizations become vulnerable. Holiness protects those who conform their lives to it as well as those they lead. Holiness is extremely powerful and reaps a harvest mostly unseen by those who embrace it.

MOUNT ZION AND THE PILGRIMAGE THERE

If the beginning of this passage is the sin-scorched wilderness of Judea, the destination, the ending point, is Mount Zion. Mount Zion is the hill that Solomon's Temple was built on, and this term had come to symbolize the Temple itself. This was the place where God's Presence was real and powerful. God had promised[47] He would always answer the prayers prayed in this Temple and it became a place of hope. Every year thousands of Jews would make a pilgrimage to pray and seek the Lord

47 2 Chronicles 7:15-16.

on Mount Zion. The thought was that if they could just get to Jerusalem, to the Presence of God in this wonderful Temple, He would hear their prayers and help them in their need.

Every year as people traveled to Jerusalem for the great Jewish feasts, those making the journey would sing and chant certain Psalms[48] as they journeyed. Isaiah 35 became a song pilgrims sang that Isaiah wrote to encourage those who had been devastated: to build hope that God would see their plight and meet them on the way. As the pilgrims journeyed towards Jerusalem, towards the Temple, towards the living Presence of the Lord, the pilgrims would sing Isaiah 35 and rejoice in God their saviour.

The images are clear – you start the journey a long way from the Presence of God, in a sin-devastated wilderness, and step-by-step you journey towards the great Temple of Jerusalem characterized by the Presence of the Lord. The journey is one of hope and excitement.

THE GLORY OF LEBANON

The transformation of the Arabah is stunning! It begins as a desert that is barren and dry. Then flowers bloom, water gushes forth; grass, reeds and papyrus grow in what used to be desert places. And this devastated place now is characterized by the glory of Lebanon, Carmel and Sharon. Lebanon at this time had many huge forests and was the source of the magnificent lumber used for building the Temple in Jerusalem. Carmel and Sharon were characterized by beauty. Beauty and glory had come to the Arabah because God had come to it. This is why verse 2 says, *"they will see the glory of the LORD, the splendour of our God."* They will "see" God's glory and splendour because the beauty that overtakes the desert reveals God's transforming Presence in it. The living God is the one who transforms our desolated places. When He comes, the desert and sin-blasted landscapes of our lives burst into joyful celebration. He changes everything! This also shows that no matter what hurt, devasta-

48 Such as Psalms 120-134.

tion, and pain you have experienced, God is able to transform your life into something of incredible beauty.

THE IMPACT OF GOD'S COMING ON THE HURTING

In this passage, the hands are feeble, the knees are shaking, and the hearts are fearful: they have suffered so much at the hands of those raiding bands of Edomites and Philistines. The people who live in the Arabah are vulnerable and afraid. Isaiah boldly reassures them (verse 4): *"Be strong, do not fear, your God will come, he will come with vengeance; with divine retribution he will come, he will come to save you."* God will come with justice for the oppressors and salvation for the hurting. Not only does He help the fearful and hurting, He comes with healing. The blind will see, the deaf will hear, the lame will leap like the deer and the mute will shout out the praises of God. The burning landscapes that hurt you will now become a place of cool pools and refuge.

It is important to note here that these miracles mentioned in verses 4-6 are so characteristic of God that they became landmarks identifying the Presence of the anointing of God on the Messiah. This is why in Luke 7:18-23 when John the Baptist sent his disciples to ask Jesus if He was the Messiah, Jesus pointed to the miracles happening in His ministry and paraphrased parts of Isaiah 35. The miracles the disciples of John saw were proof that the Lord was powerfully present in the ministry of Jesus, thus proving that He was indeed the promised Messiah. The works Jesus did evidenced who He was where only words would not have been convincing. In Jesus we have the powerful Presence of the living God at work birthing life as only He can.

THE HIGHWAY OF HOLINESS

Verse 8 emphasizes that there is a level of protection present for those who walk on the Way of Holiness. God provides in the wilderness a highway for the redeemed to walk on. In this passage, no lion or ravenous beast will be found on the Way of Holiness. In addition, no unclean or "wicked fool" will walk on that highway. We are not only protected from "beasts" that would attack us, but also from unclean or wicked fools that would lead us astray. Holiness is not something that inconveniences us, it is something that protects us and gives us a measure of covering from the "beasts of this world." Of course, Satan is a "lion" who prowls around seeking someone to devour.[49] Holiness protects us from Satan's attacks. This is one strategy Satan even used with Jesus – if he could get Jesus off the Way of Holiness in His temptation experience, he could win the battle.[50] Yet before His death, Jesus could say that Satan had no hold on Him at all.[51] Sin opens the door to Satan. Holiness closes the door to him.

Even in the natural, there is protection that comes from living in holiness. If you remain faithful to your wife or husband and do not engage in pre-marital or extra-marital sex, for example, it would be difficult for you to get AIDS, Syphilis or other STD's. In Malawi, I heard a story of a pastor who had a daughter who was very sick. He brought her to the Church and they prayed for her and she was not healed. Then he decided to take her to a witchdoctor. In Malawi, AIDS is often spread by witchcraft as they cut the skin to let the bad spirit out of the body that is causing the sickness (in their view) and then use the same unwashed utensil on the next person. The daughter became infected with AIDS and died soon after. Sin opens the door to problems that Holiness closes the door to. Embrace and walk on the way of Holiness!

THE JOY OF THE REDEEMED

This passage ends with a note of tremendous joy. Now in place of scattered remnants of a devastated people, we have a band of singing, joyful people who have experienced the Lord's salvation and the transformation that only His Presence brings. Now joy and gladness have overtaken

49 1 Peter 5:8.

50 Matthew 4:1-11: the temptation narrative.

51 John 14:30.

them on their journey towards the Lord's Presence. The goodness of the Lord has overcome their sorrow and pain.

For us also, there will be a day when "sorrow and sighing" will finally flee away.[52] One day we will feel the full impact of being completely in the Presence of the Lord. Now we can taste it – but one day – glorious day - we finally come into God's Presence freed of all the heaviness of this life!

Sometimes we can get discouraged because we still encounter "wilderness times" in our lives. However, the end of our story has not yet been written. One day there will be no more "wildernesses".

This passage tells us that there is a destination for the redeemed – a place where there is no longer sorrow and sighing and that place is the Presence of the Lord!

LET US STEP INTO THE PASSAGE

Just for a moment let yourself imagine that you are one of the people in the Arabah, that you are one of those who have been so devastated by the raiding bandits. I knew people in Malawi who lived along the border with Mozambique during the civil war there. Often bandits would raid over the border and rape and pillage the villagers. Husbands would be shot, girls taken, boys beaten. The people were vulnerable and terrified. This is what it was like for the people living in the Arabah during the time of Ahaz. There was no one to protect them from the raiding bands of Edomites and Philistines.

Now, imagine that you were one of the ones in the Arabah. Then, you started to remember Jerusalem. Maybe someone reminded you that there was a Temple in Jerusalem where God had promised He would hear every prayer uttered in that place. You thought, "If only I could get there, everything would be OK!" Surely, then, God would hear you and would act! So, you dared to hope and together with others started towards Jerusalem and the Temple. You could not go on the roads, they

52 See Revelation 7:17 and 21:4.

were too accessible to the bandits, so you walked through the countryside, through the wilderness.

Gradually you noticed others on the same journey. One so devastated by the trauma she had experienced that she could not talk at all. Another was crippled by the bandits. Here was a man leading another who had been beaten on the head so badly that he went blind. You were a motley crew, but you all had the same hope: "If only we can get to where God is, then He will hear us, and He will come down to help us in our need."

Suddenly something changed: as you turned a corner, there were birds singing. You could hear the sound of water rushing by. How was this possible? There was no water in this desert! Then, the blind man stopped – he could see the flowers blooming. The lame man started to jump and shout. Joy filled the air! What was happening?

You realized that you were hoping to get to the Temple to meet God, yet He had come to meet you on the journey. The living God was present! Everyone is running around and rejoicing. Kids are swimming in pools of water. Everything has changed. God has come!

You start to celebrate and sing with the others and you notice that God has placed in the desert a roadway ahead. It is a protected place, not like the other roads where the bandits are. You knew instinctively that no one could touch you on this road! God would protect you. No beasts, no wicked bandits dared to come to a place so rich with God's love and holiness. In fact, bandits are terrified of God's holiness. You were safe! God had come and you are safe in the shelter of God's Presence.

All of life is a pilgrimage, a journey towards God. We all have our areas of pain and challenge as we live in an imperfect world. Yet we can start the journey towards Him, embrace hope, and know that God has the answer for our need. As we step towards Him, He meets us on the way. Our God can transform anything!

His Presence births life like nothing else can. Our God is the true transformer!

GOD IS THE LIFE GIVER

The God of the Bible, Yahweh, is **THE** giver and source of life. From the creation story in Genesis 1 to the end of Revelation with the formation of a "new" heaven and earth, God is so vibrant with life that He releases it by His words and actions and by His Presence. He spoke and His words birthed life: the trees, animals and all of the created world came into existence at His command. When He created mankind, He stooped down and breathed the "breath of life" into Adam's nostrils, imparting some of that life-essence into Adam and he became a living being.[53] God **IS** the source of life in His creation. He designed it to function that way. It is incongruous that many in the world today want a greater "quality" of life yet they reject and even despise the One who alone can give it! True life is only available through intimacy with the Living God. True life thrives when lived according to the pattern of holiness.

The ultimate example of God bringing life to the world is found in Jesus. The New Testament teaches that Jesus is the exact image of the invisible God.[54] What this means is that Jesus expounds for us the hidden, invisible nature of God. If God IS the embodiment of life, then Jesus Himself is also "life". It is no surprise that Jesus says such things as:

- *"I am the resurrection and the life"* (John 11:25) as He stands before the tomb of His friend Lazarus who has been buried for four days. He knows He alone can release life to Lazarus' corpse. Then He goes about proving it by calling Lazarus back to life.
- *"If you knew the gift of God and who it is that asks you for a drink, you would have asked Him and He would have given you living water."* (John 4:10) with the Samaritan woman. He also adds: ". . . *Indeed, the water I give them will become in them a spring of water welling up to eternal life."* (John 4:14). Jesus is the source of life symbolized by

53 Genesis 2:7.

54 Colossians 1:15; Hebrews 1:3.

the water He is talking about. In this passage, Jesus brings honour and dignity, "life", to the wilderness of a broken woman's life.

- *"Let anyone who is thirsty come to me and drink. Whoever believes in me, as the Scripture has said, rivers of living water will flow from within them"* (John 7:37-38). This occurs during the last and greatest day of the Festival of Tabernacles which commemorates the moment when Moses struck the rock in the desert and life-giving water gushed out to nourish the Israelites. Jesus is saying that, like that rock in the desert, He is the source of life for the nation if they would only believe.
- *". . . I have come that they may have life, and have it to the full (or more abundantly)"* (John 10:10). The purpose of Jesus' life was to make it possible for us to have life – fully, completely, abundantly.
- *"For God so loved the world that he gave his one and only Son, that whoever believes in him shall not perish but have eternal life"* (John 3:16). Jesus was sent into the world by His father to give life to whoever believes in Him.
- *"I am the Living One; . . . who holds the keys of death . . . "* (Rev. 1:18). Jesus in His exalted state in Heaven is the one who "embodies" life and because of this has power over death itself.

Jesus is the mediator of the life of God to us. How? On the cross Jesus died our death so that we would be able to live His life. Since we are now cleansed from all unrighteousness through applying the cross to our lives, we are clean and holy and can be in the Presence of the Living God without being destroyed by His holiness. Through Jesus the life of God becomes available *now* for all who humble themselves and seek it.[55] The eternal life we have through believing on Jesus is not just about "not perishing" and having a life that endures eternally.[56] It involves a quality of life, the life of the kingdom of heaven, that starts now when we receive

55 Jeremiah 29:13; Isaiah 51:1.

56 John 3:16 quoted above.

Jesus into our lives, and then continues into eternity. The reason it starts now is that when we receive Jesus into our lives, His Presence comes in[57] and His Presence births life everywhere it is. This is why God's life can come to a desert wilderness and transform it into a paradise. Yet, do we know our need for God? Do we know our need for the life that only He can bring us? Hunger for God is the precursor for finding and experiencing His life.

"Blessed are those who hunger and thirst for righteousness, for they will be satisfied." (Matt. 5:6). I challenge each reader to hunger and thirst for those things that prepare the way for the Holy One of Israel to come into your life and birth true, abundant life within you! This is the only way you will be satisfied.

Summary

We can have hope because of the life that flows from God's Presence. He is the life-giving God who can transform any hurt by His love and His Presence. He specializes in blessing the barren wildernesses in our lives with His restoring, renewing life. He replaces sorrow with joy, barrenness with fruitfulness, woundednes with healing. As we turn towards Him, He meets us on the pathway into His Presence.

In summary:

1. The living God of the Bible is one who is characterized by visiting the sin-devastated landscapes of our lives to bring healing, wholeness and life. He transforms all He touches by the power of His life. No devastation is beyond His ability to transform.

2. The glory and splendour of our God is seen by how He transforms all He touches. Only He can do what He does.

3. Life giving miracles characterize the Presence of the Lord. Life erupts where the Presence of the Lord IS.

---

57 Which is made possible through the cleansing, sanctification and justification of the cross. His life-giving Presence with us is mediated to us through the Holy Spirit.

4. Embracing the Way of Holiness releases protection over our lives. Part of God's provision for us is the holiness that keeps us in His Presence and covering.
5. Those who experience the love of God will come into His Presence with joy and celebration. Sorrow and sighing disappear in His Presence. God brings His Redeemed joy *now* as they walk on the Way of Holiness. God's Presence changes fear and sickness into joy and health.
6. The God of the Bible is the only true source of Life. This is seen particularly through Jesus who was sent by God to die for us, taking our place so that we could live the abundant life of the kingdom of God now through having access to God's life-giving Presence.

Entering Into His Presence

Spend some time worshipping God and just basking in His Presence as the God who sees you, hears you and comes down to be with you. Let God bring you His life and love.

If you have areas of your life that feel "blasted" by the actions of others, acknowledge them to God and give them to him. Invite Him into these wounded places. Ask God to change your heartache into joy. Receive His forgiveness and release forgiveness to those who have hurt you. Let the Presence of God bless you with His life.

Thank God for His gift of holiness and ask God to help you to walk on His Way of Holiness. Repent of any sin that plagues your life and give it over to the Lord. Ask God to show you where you have run after false sources of life and repent where necessary. Make a choice now to seek God and open up your life to His life-giving Presence. Let God bring His healing to you. Thank God for His goodness, for His life-giving Presence in your life.

Prayer

Lord, thank You for the power of Your life and Your ability to change anything by Your Presence. I give You my heartaches and pain. I ask You to transform them into something that brings You glory. Transform my life into a display of Your splendour.

Lord, help me to see Your Presence in my life. Sometimes it is there, but it is hard for me to see it. I only feel my hurt. Transform my wilderness into a garden of Your Presence.

I embrace holiness and pledge myself to walk in Your ways. Give me strength to say "no" to every temptation. Thank You for Your protection. Keep me on the path of holiness.

Breathe Your life into me. I receive the joy that comes from Your Presence. Help me to continue to walk every day, all day in Your Presence.

Jesus, I acknowledge that You came to the earth to bring me life. I come to You now and repent of seeking after false sources of life. I want the life, the full and complete and abundant life, that only You can give me. I need Your Presence in me to birth this life in my heart and soul. I turn to You right now and say "yes" to You.

Holy Spirit come and apply the full power of the cross to my life. Cleanse me so that I will be clean. Come Holy Spirit and fill me with Your peace and life.

In the precious name of Jesus I pray,

Amen.

4

The Nature Of Theology: All I Do Must Be Impacted And Changed by My Love For God And My Access to His Loving Presence.

"Do not conform to the pattern of this world, but be transformed by the renewing of your mind. Then you will be able to test and approve what God's will is – his good, pleasing and perfect will."
(Romans 12:2)

All of life is theological. What I mean by this is that we approach everything we do with an understanding of God and how His world works. That understanding may be totally faulty, but our theology[58] will determine how we view the world around us, how we view God and how we view His activity in our life. Even those who do not believe God exists still have a "theology" that shapes their lives. The importance of this is that our "theology" will influence our reaction to and interaction with

58 "Theology" simply means the "study of God". In this context I am using it to refer to our understanding or knowledge of God or our study of the nature of God and truth. In my understanding, theology involves an encounter with the living God that yields a deep level holistic knowledge of God and truth. It must engage all parts of our being in order to produce transformational change into the image of God.

the Presence of God. As we are impacted by the Presence of God we need to make sure that our growth in our knowledge of and about God is formed and shaped in the right way so that we are truly "formed into the image of Christ". There are some things that must be put in place in order for us to "mature" correctly as we grow in our relationship with God.

Later in this chapter, I will talk about the importance of experience as a component of growing in knowledge, yet we need to make sure that we think about God in the right way so that we are not manipulated by experience into misbelieving the truth. Experience is not truth, even though at times it may substantiate truth. Truth is a person – God. The goal is to integrate our experience into our theology until our experience reflects the truth of God. We do not lower our theology to the level of our experience. This means that we must bring the truth of God into our lives in such a way that we are empowered to love Him and live in obedience to Him. In this book, I am encouraging pursuing the Presence of the Lord and will repeatedly talk about us doing all of those things that cultivate His Presence, yet we must know who this God is whose Presence we are seeking. This is where theology comes in. We must know how to pursue growing in our knowledge of God in such a way that we are transformed by what we learn into Christlikeness.[59] The question then becomes: how do we approach theology so that this happens?

THEOLOGY IS NOT THEOLOGY IF IT IS NOT APPLIED

Theology is not theology unless it is applied. Over the years I have had many students tell me that normally they find theology courses very boring and were surprised to find that the ones I teach are much more interesting than they expected. Usually I respond that, no matter the label on the courses they take, if it was boring, it was not theology. It is

59 See Romans 8:29.

all about application, transformation, and meeting God.[60] Our study of God is intended by God to change the way we live, to transform us little by little into the image of Jesus (Rom. 8:29). This is God's intent. Rightly understood, no Bible College course is more practical than a theology course. It changes how we see reality, how we see ourselves and how we choose to live in the world. It will always have practical ramifications for how we are to live. Yet the truths of God must be received to bear fruit. So, the question is: how receptive are we to being changed?

THEOLOGY AND THE "TACIT" DIMENSION OF KNOWLEDGE

There is a level of learning that only occurs through our *experience* of the material we are learning. This "experiential" component of learning is called the "tacit"[61] dimension of knowledge and cannot be easily transferred from one person to another. For example, no one will ever learn how to drive a car if they only read a book about how to do this. To learn how to drive, you must physically get behind a wheel and drive the car. Our understanding will always be faulty if we do not integrate our experience with what we are learning. There seems at times in the Christian Church to be a deep suspicion of "experience based" theology, yet if there is not an experiential component to our "theology" it is not theology at all. Theology must involve an encounter with the living God and this means there must be an experience with God that produces a deeper theological understanding of God.

Because of who God is, we need to see theology as primarily a relational transaction rather than a content transaction. In other words, it is

---

60 Not only does this apply to theology, but current writers on how adults best learn talk a lot about the importance of application in the classroom in order to cause transformational learning. See M Mezirow, et al, *Learning as transformation: Critical perspectives on a theory in progress.* San Francisco, CA: Jossey-Bass, 2000. If this is important for any classroom, how much more important is it for the theology classroom?

61 This term was first used as far as I know by Michael Polanyi in 1958 in *Personal Knowledge: Towards a Post-Critical Philosophy,* University of Chicago Press, Chicago.

through relationship with the living God that we come to understand the content of what we are learning about Him. Our relationship with God informs and shapes how and what we understand. If our relational experience of God, does not form and shape our integration of knowledge about God, our theological learning may become a barrier to truly knowing God instead of a catalyst to a deeper intimacy with Him. The application of what we are learning to the task of loving God (mentioned later) is crucial as there is always an element of knowledge we will never learn except by doing. It is not possible to study God objectively. One must engage with God to learn about Him. One must encounter God in order to truly know Him.

Ultimately, truth is a person not data.[62] You can look at a person and examine them from head to toe, but until you open up dialogue with that person, you will never know them. It is the same with truth. You need to have a relational connection to the truth in order to know it and you must be open to its revelations. When this is not the case, your ability to learn theology is impaired.

THEOLOGY MUST BE TRANSFORMATIONAL

A third point is that theology is really about transformation. Our interaction with God must change us. I tell my students that I hope they did not come to Bible College to get a good Biblical education because this was never God's intention. God never intended us to gather an array of facts in our minds about God, He intended us to live differently because of what we learn. The goal should be Biblical transformation not Biblical education.[63]

---

62 One of the sub-themes of the Gospel of John is irony and there is a deep irony when, during His dialogue with Pilate, Jesus says that He ". . . came into the world to testify to the truth," Pilate responds with "What is Truth?" (John 18:37-38) not understanding that the living incarnation of the "way, the truth and the life" (John 14:6) was standing right in front of him.

63 I actually think the term "Biblical education" is a misnomer. I think it is not possible to get a "Biblical" education because if we are just getting facts about the Bible and storing up knowledge about God, we are not being Biblical in how we are learning. You do not learn about God the way you learn science.

It is about encountering the living God by means of the material we are studying in order to submit more fully to Him and be transformed by that encounter into people who more greatly resemble Christ. Theology calls us towards a divine encounter with someone greater than ourselves who is the foundation of all reality. Without submission to God and without the application of the material to our own lives, theology is not theology.

THEOLOGY MUST BE APPLIED TO THE TASK OF LOVING GOD

A fourth key in us having a transformational encounter with God, with theology or with the Biblical text, relates to why we are doing what we are doing. In a nutshell, it is all about love. We study about God and read the Bible so that we can love the Lord with all of our heart, mind and soul, with our whole being and learn to reflect His love more effectively to the world. The key to transformational Bible study is to pour our study out on the task of loving God in the context of His overwhelming love for us. God will lead us and empower us as we study the Word because He loves us and longs to have a deeper relationship with us. As I have said earlier, the living God is a God of Presence. He wants more of us so that we can have more of him. I remember once hearing a preacher say that we have as much of God as we really want. I think what he was saying was that we do not have more of God because we do not press in and pursue Him, and that God always responds and gives us more of Himself when we pursue Him. Yet I think there is something that the preacher missed. I always hunger and thirst for more of God as a "deer pants for streams of water, so my soul pants for you, my God." (Psalm 42:1). I have found that in my own life the reality is more like the following: the more God has of me, the more I have of Him. My hunger and thirst for Him pushes me to yield more fully to Him. "More, Lord" goes hand in hand with "Yes, Lord". Engaging in theology with the purpose of loving God in the Presence of God empowers it to be transformational.

Romans 12:2 says: *"Do not conform to the pattern of this world, but be transformed by the renewing of your mind. Then you will be able to test and approve what God's will is – his good, pleasing and perfect will."* What makes us so different from the world is what we love. The focus of our love empowers us to not be conformed to the pattern of this world and enables our minds to be transformed and renewed by the action of the Holy Spirit. Then, when we know God because we love Him and are loved by Him, we are more able to discern what His good, pleasing and perfect will is. The transformation and renewal of our minds involves much more than what we "study." If we are not to "conform" to the "patterns" of the world, our values, our perceptions and our worldview must change. I would hold that in order not to conform to the patterns of this world, everything I do must be applied to the task of loving God. My love for God must impact *everything.* All I do must be impacted and changed by my love for God and my access to His loving Presence. This brings unity and cohesion to my life. How much of a Christian am I if my love for God does not sparkle in all I do?

Bernard of Clairvaux was a Catholic leader and monk who lived in the 1100's. He was a godly man who thought deeply of the things of God and was actively used by God to bring renewal to the monastic movement of his time. He was even known to have a healing ministry. In one of his books, he writes of the "four degrees of love"[64] that he felt all Christians must move through. The *first* of these was to love oneself for self's sake. We love what brings our self pleasure, and we think it inconceivable that we would be asked not to do what gives us pleasure. This is the love expressed by the natural unregenerate human and is purely selfish. This is where most people in the world live. The *second* degree of love is to love God for the self's sake. Here we love God because it benefits us.[65] We call upon God when we are in trouble and start to love Him because He loves us and helps us. Little by little we learn to know the Lord and start to see

---

64 Described in *The Love of God and Spiritual Friendship by Bernard of Clairvaux*, edited by James Houston, Multnomah Press, Portland Oregon, 1983, pp. 154-161.

65 Psalm 50:15: *"Call upon me in times of trouble: I will hear you and you will praise me."*

His goodness.[66] This gradually is meant to lead to the *third* degree of love: loving God for God's sake. Here we become enraptured with the goodness of the Lord and now, no matter if He does or does not help us, we simply love Him for who He is. We praise Him for his essential goodness and not because He has done anything for us. Here also, we will begin to do all those things that are difficult and hard to do because we love Him and He demands it, and we start to love what God loves.[67] Gradually we start to love what God loves for His sake and not for our own. This culminates in the *fourth* degree of love: loving self for God's sake. Here we have left the selfish reasons for loving ourselves and now we delight in ourselves because God delights in us. The problem is, for many of us, we never progress to the third and fourth degrees of love, yet this is the goal of the Christian life: To love God totally and purely and allow Him to change our 'loves" until they reflect His.

To show how this works: Jesus told us that the two greatest commandments for us to follow were to love God with all our heart, mind and soul and to love our neighbour as ourselves (Matt. 22:37-39). In the first degree of love we may love our neighbour if we see that it benefits ourselves although we may be convinced to constrain our love of self for the sake of our neighbour. Here we have little interest in loving God. In the second degree of love we start to love God because we become convinced that it benefits us. If we love Him, He will help us. We may love our neighbour because God will bless us if we do so. In the third degree of love, we will love God for His own sake and our love for Him starts to penetrate beyond selfish motivations. We have tasted of the Lord and know that He is good[68] and so we long for more of Him. Now, we sacrifice to draw

---

66 Psalm 34:8: *"Taste and see that the Lord is good; blessed is the one who takes refuge in him."*

67 1 Peter 1:14: *As obedient children, do not conform to the evil desires you had when you lived in ignorance. (15) But just as he who called you is holy, so be holy in all you do . . . (22) Now that you have purified yourself by obeying the truth so that you have a sincere love for each other. Love one another deeply from the heart.* In this passage, our holiness is reflected in the love we show to others.

68 Psalm 34:8; 1 Peter 2:3.

closer to him. Now, we love our neighbour because this cultivates our love of God. We love our neighbour because this delights Him. In the fourth degree of love, we love what God loves. Now we love ourselves because God loves us and we love our neighbours because God loves them – and we recognize that this is what we were created to delight in. At this level, we realize that what we love reflects on God so we endeavour to whole-heartedly love only what He loves in the way He loves.

In terms of theology, we do not grow in our knowledge of God (theology) to benefit ourselves (first degree) or because God will bless us if we do (second degree), we do so because we love the Lord and we do not want to think wrongly about Him (third degree). We want to know all about the one we love and be changed by Him to become all He wants us to become. It is about Him and learning to love what He loves and delighting in what brings Him pleasure (fourth degree). It is about growing and changing until we become the type of people that He wants to spend time with just as we want to spend time with Him. Our love for God empowers us to be transformed by His love into the image of Christ. This is the goal for theology.

BY DISSECTING WE DESTROY WHAT WE ARE STUDYING

One of the problems often seen in theological literature is that theologians seem to overlook or forget that when we *dissect* something into its component parts in our study of God, we risk killing a right understanding of the living entity we are trying to study. In other words, getting overly analytical in theology can destroy our ability to truly comprehend the living person who is the object of our study – God Himself. By analyzing God, we risk making Him dry, boring, and static. We cannot understand theology at the level of our mind alone, we must pursue it with *all* aspects of our being in order to be transformed by the theological encounter that is inherent in theology. Theology needs to engage more than just the redeemed mind. It needs to encounter God while preserving the mystery of God's nature.

Part of the problem is that in the Western world we tend to gravitate towards a Greek or Roman view of the world that is highly analytical and oriented around the physical world. We call it the "scientific" worldview. The result is that we dissect God and human nature and by doing so both oversimplify these and misunderstand how one relates to the other. For example, in the theological literature, I have seen discussions about whether humans are made up of two parts (body and soul) or three (body, soul and spirit) and arguments about which one is true. My response is, "Neither is true and yet both are true." We are more than what is meant by the above terms. As humans, our bodies, souls, spirits, wills, intellects, emotions, hearts and minds are all aspects of what it means to be who we are; all of these need to be submitted to God and integrated together to produce wholeness. Often one of these will blur and overlap with one or more of the others. This is more like the Hebraic worldview which is holistic and dynamic. Sin can impact and distort and twist any one or more of these areas. In order to be transformed our view needs to be holistic. If we have not had an emotional response to the truth, we probably have not encountered it. Much Bible study material seems to have the assumption that once our spirit is alive (or "born again"), all we need to do is to think rightly about God and transformation will happen. Not True! We must allow the truth to penetrate and transform our wills, our emotions, our hearts, our minds, our desires, and our dreams (just to mention a few areas). All of these and more must be captured by the truth. Only thus can the truth set us free.[69]

It is true that when the spirit is dead, the mind is darkened.[70] When a person comes to Christ, his/her spirit comes alive through this encounter with "Life" itself and now the believer has the possibility of thinking differently *if* that person allows the Holy Spirit to change how they think and how they relate to what they think. Unfortunately, too many believers do not allow the Spirit to transform their minds, so they end up thinking just

69 John 8:32.

70 Ephesians 4:17-21.

like the world around them. Spiritual vitality must be the foundation of our understanding of the world. The dynamism of life must be preserved in theology through the dynamism of encounter. The heart is where the root of transformation begins.[71]

THEOLOGY MUST CHANGE ALL ASPECTS OF OUR LIVES

Fifth, one of our modern heresies is that we have reduced the Word of God to being only something that changes the way we think. We have taken out the "tacit" dimension of learning mentioned above. This trivializes the Word of God which must impact and change all of us – our body, mind, heart, desires, will, soul and spirit. We learn about God so that we can encounter His Presence and grow closer to Him. All else is vanity. Now that we are in the New Covenant, we must allow the Holy Spirit to write on our hearts the truths of God. Soft hearts are so much more powerful than hard hearts since they produce godly people. The mistake our world often makes is that it thinks forceful people are strong people. It takes more strength to be humble and teachable than it does to be stubborn.

SOFT HEARTS EMPOWER US TO ENTER OUR DESTINY

Theology and the study of the Word of God allows us to hear God's voice. The question becomes: "Will we listen to that voice?" A repeated refrain from Hebrews is: *"Today, if you hear his voice, do not harden your heart."*[72] Hard hearts produce unbelief and rebellion as was evident in the history of Israel at the borders of the Promised Land.[73] All that the people

71 Proverbs 4:23.

72 Hebrews 3:7, 15; 4:7. These are referring to and quoting Psalm 95:7: *Today, if you hear his voice, do not harden your hearts as you did at Meribah, as you did that day at Massah in the wilderness."*

73 The historical background to the references in Hebrews.

of Israel had to do to enter the Promised Land was to believe and trust God. They chose not to believe what God was saying to them and their unbelief excluded them from their destiny. This is true today. Unbelief, which stems from a heart resistant to the voice of God, will always keep us in the wilderness when God's desire is that we enter into the Promised Land of plenty. Embracing a soft heart, a heart receptive to God's voice, empowers us to enter into the "Promised Land." The source of the abundance and favour in the Promised Land was not the land itself, it was the Presence of the Lord in that place. There are always giants and fortresses[74] that need to be overcome when we are obedient to the voice of God, but each of these are no hindrance when God is with us. A soft heart keeps us in God's Presence and allows us to experience the wonder of the deliverance He will accomplish on our behalf. When we fix our eyes on the "giants" in the land, we are making our hearts open to fear[75] and unbelief; we predispose ourselves to developing hard hearts, and yet these are what will exclude us from the blessing of God's Presence. When we fix our eyes on the sufficiency of God, and act in obedience, it is inevitable that the giants will fall. The tragedy is that once we start resisting the voice of God, slowly our ability to hear His voice disappears. This is the implication of the verse from Hebrews mentioned above. Sooner or later, the crust of disobedience around our heart prevents God's voice from penetrating. There is no guarantee that if we hear God's voice today and refuse to listen to it, we will be able to hear it tomorrow. The wilderness is not a good place to live your life.

When we say "yes" to the Holy Spirit, it keeps our hearts soft.[76] The more we cultivate the Presence of the Lord, the softer our hearts become. Contrary to the "tough guy" John Wayne model of the warrior, the man who is a spiritually "mighty" warrior knows how to weep and allows him-

74 The reason given by the Israelites for not going into the Promised Land in Numbers 13:28-33.

75 See the "*. . . we seemed like grasshoppers in our own eyes. . .*" (Numbers 13:33).

76 See Ezekiel 36:26.

self to be moved with compassion for the hurting. It takes tremendous courage to keep your heart soft before the Lord.

When we say "no" to the Holy Spirit, it hardens our hearts.[77] The true nature of our faith becomes evident in our obedience or lack of it to the voice of the Lord. What we need to realize is that saying "no" to the challenging voice of the Lord will keep us from entering into God's best for us.

Summary

Growth in our theological understanding of God is about transformation into more mature Christians who reflect the nature and character of God more completely. To be transformed in the right way, we must always be applying the Word of God to the task of loving God as we press into a real experience of His Presence. The core theological task is always to love God with all we are and love others with His love so He can be glorified through our lives.

In summary:

1. We must apply what we know about God to our lives in order for theology to change how we live. God intends that we be changed by what we learn into the image of Christ.
2. There must always be an experiential component in theology for us to grow in our knowledge of God. We learn through encountering the living God.
3. Theology is about transformation, not education.
4. What empowers transformation is to make growing in our ability to love God the key theme of our lives. We love God in the context of His love for us and His involvement in our lives.
5. The goal of theological encounter is loving God and delighting in all those things that bring Him pleasure.
6. We must be careful not to reduce the Word of God to an intellectual experience. The heart is where the root of transformation occurs.

77 See Zechariah 7:12.

7. All aspects of our lives must be transformed. Godliness is about God shaping the deep parts of our lives and changing us so that all of us reflect Him.
8. Cultivating soft hearts before God empowers transformation.
9. Soft hearts usher us into the "Promised Land" of God's Presence. Hard, unsubmissive hearts, keep us in the "wilderness".

Entering Into His Presence

Spend some time worshipping the Lord and asking God to show you any place where you are resisting the application of truth to your life. If God shows you anything, repent of it and ask Him to help you to apply His truth to your life. Ask God to unite your heart to love Him in all you do.

Embrace the Presence of the Lord in your life. Ask God to help you always to keep your heart soft and malleable. If necessary, repent of any unbelief or any times you have chosen self-preservation over obedience.

Ask God to help you keep your eyes on Him despite the "giants" in your life. Thank the Lord that He will take care of those "giants" as you pursue obedience to Him. Thank the Lord for the power of His love for you.

Spend time committing yourself to loving God in all areas of your life and invite Him in to transform your "loves" so that they will reflect His.

Prayer:

Lord, I love what You show us about Yourself. Help me to grow in my ability to apply all of Your truth to my life. Come, I invite Your Presence with me right now. Change me and form me into Your image. I love You. Help me to love You in all I do.

I repent if I have over-intellectualized Your truth. Let Your truth penetrate all parts of my life, even to the deepest parts of my soul. Help me to always honour Your Word and to live in obedience to it.

Keep my heart soft before You. Thank You for making sure that all of the "giants" and "fortresses" that keep me from Your best for me will fall before You as I love You and as I am obedient to You.

Help me to pour out my life on loving You. Be the center of my life. Make my life about You. I want to delight in what You delight in, and love what You love. I want my heart to be transformed by encountering You. You alone are life and I desperately need You to take more of me so that I have more of You.

In the precious name of Jesus I pray,

Amen.

5

The Presence of God Is Not Always Safe.

We will talk later about how to increase the Presence of the Lord in your life, but the key is this: God's Presence is a person not a thing. It is by the person of the Holy Spirit that God is present to us. The first essential is to treat the Lord as a person and not to depersonalize His Presence. And when God is present, anything becomes possible. God is always good. Yet at times His Presence can be both tremendously healing and terribly shattering. God is the Holy One of Israel. We dare not come into His Presence lightly or carelessly. We cannot come into His Presence without dealing with His holiness.

GOD'S PRESENCE HEALS!

I learned that God's Presence heals in the summer of 2013 when I went with Youth Power Invasion[78] to Brazil with my youngest son. He was 13 at the time. The team was composed of about 100 youth aged

---

78 Youth Power Invasion is one of the annual ministry trips taken each year by Randy Clark and Global Awakening. They normally go to Brazil and see many amazing miracles and salvations. I took my son because I wanted him to be exposed to the reality that God heals today. I would highly recommend it.

13-29 and about 20 adults. In the two weeks we were there, there were thousands of people healed, including cripples, deaf ears, blind eyes and even some tumours disappeared! There were also almost 1000 salvations! It was incredible and life changing!

The ministry team members were not big-name evangelists, but "just" the youth, many of whom had never seen anyone healed before. The second night, we were at an evangelistic campaign and praying for the sick. On either side of me were youth. As they were praying, they were seeing healing after healing. Yet with me? Very little seemed to be happening. Yet I was the missionary! I started to get uptight, after all we were there to pray for people and many of those we prayed for were desperate for healing. As I struggled, I felt God tell me to relax, that it was not about me, that it was His love and His Presence that heals. I tried to relax and told God He needed to show me how to pray. The next person who came had a bad pain in his belly. It was so painful that it hurt to touch it even lightly. I invited the Holy Spirit to come and prayed that God would come with His love and Presence to heal this man. The man was touched by the Presence of the Lord in a powerful way and was totally healed. He kept poking his stomach, hard, with more and more amazement at how there was now no pain. He told me that he had had this condition for 15 years but now there was absolutely no pain! I learned a powerful truth. It is God's Presence that heals!

This event was a key moment in what God had been teaching me about staying in His Presence and connected healing in my mind firmly with His Presence. Even though I had been born and raised in Africa with missionary parents who served there 49 years.[79] Even though I had received Christ as an 11 year-old and grew up hearing stories of miracles and healing. Even though I was first a science and math teacher in

79 My father wrote a book I would highly recommend giving many of his experiences and stories from his 49 years as a missionary entitled: *I Sat Where They Sat.* Arnold Bowler. Castle Quay Books. Pickering, Ontario, Canada. 2011. It is available through amazon.com in kindle or paperback.

Canada and then later a missionary with a doctorate teaching in Bible Colleges in West Africa, I still wanted more.

Before arriving in West Africa, I had myself seen several miracles, especially after graduate school when I attended the Langley Vineyard[80] where God was doing some amazing things. I was always hungry for more and attended various conferences on renewal including some by John Wimber, Blaine Cook, Rita and Dennis Bennett, and Reinhardt Bonnke. They were all impactful. My wife, Judy, and I both believed that healing was for today and would often pray for the sick and, at times, see people healed. Yet we did not pursue it with passion.

When we arrived as new missionaries in West Africa, we carried with us the conviction that God still healed today and would pray for people as opportunities came up. The very first Sunday I preached in West Africa a lady was healed of an ankle problem. However, this was somewhat rare. Part of my problem was that I felt it was presumptuous, even arrogant to think I had the "gift" of healing. Yet the key was right in front of me: from graduate school on, I loved books like *The Practice of the Presence of God* by Brother Lawrence and sought to live in His Presence. In 2003 we arrived in a Muslim country with a hunger for God to break through in this land where so many people do not know the beauty of Jesus. We knew that, in the Muslim country we lived in, we could not persuade people into the kingdom of God. It had to be through Supernatural power. I saw in the Scriptures that Jesus told us to heal the sick[81] and how Paul and the apostles evangelized with "signs and wonders."[82] Then, we heard of Heidi Baker in Mozambique who was seeing thousands of Muslims coming to Christ through a similar "signs and wonders" evangelism. Could we see the same where we were? A friend of mine who worked with Youth For Christ was seeing amazing things in Guinea Bissau where many people were coming to Christ with accompanying miracles. I had read books on

80 In Langley, British Columbia. It was the first Vineyard Church in Canada.

81 Mathew 10:8. Luke 9:2,6; 10:9.

82 Romans 15:19; Acts 2:43; 4:30; 5:12; 6:8; 14:3; 15:12; Hebrews 2:4.

how Christianity had expanded in the past through powerful movements of the Holy Spirit and saw how my own Pentecostal denomination[83] had a rich spiritual heritage of signs and wonders[84] that I needed to recapture and walk in. I knew I had to experience and see these kinds of things to learn about them.[85] So, I grabbed my older son with a friend of his and headed down to visit my friend in Guinea Bissau. During our time there we saw many people saved and healed as we preached the Gospel. It was quite an incredible time. After this, my wife, Judy and I started taking courses through Global Awakening with their Christian Healing and Certification Program. It was an awesome faith building experience. Faith started to stir and we started to pursue healing and praying for the sick more vigorously. In a sense, we were starting to re-connect with our own spiritual heritage that we had allowed ourselves to drift away from. Gradually we started to see changes. Whereas in the past we had maybe seen 10 people healed in a 7-year period, we now saw about 50 healed the first year we were pursuing this. As we continued to pursue healing with the addition of prayer and fasting, the number of people we saw healed increased to about 100 in a year period and then 200 the next year. All the while I was struggling with my own insecurities. I kept hungering for more of God and for the ability to impact the Islamic nation where I lived with Christ.

It was then I went to Youth Power Invasion in Brazil and God crystallized this critical point: it is all found in the Presence of the Lord. Pursue and love the Lord's Presence and be obedient to what His voice is saying. Love as He loves. Seek to grow in the empowering Presence of the Holy Spirit so you can more effectively impact those around you. Pursue the Lord not the phenomena. Make it about Him more than anything else.

83 The Pentecostal Assemblies of Canada.

84 I also read several books on the Azusa Street revival that started most Pentecostal denominations.

85 A reference to the "tacit" dimension of knowledge. It is not about head knowledge but about "doing."

Cultivate the Presence of the Lord in your life, you never know where it will lead you!

Do we really want more of God? How hungry are we? What are we willing to sacrifice to get more of God? Many people do not have more of God because they do not want to say "no" to themselves. Yet we always have to put something of ourselves off in order to draw closer to God.[86] When we let go of ourselves in order to get more of God, we always get a great deal! Yet we also need to understand that while the Presence of God will transform us, this often comes about through Him shattering us.

THE STORY OF TWO MEN FROM ISAIAH 6

One of my favorite stories in the Bible is Isaiah 6 which introduces us to two men, Uzziah and Isaiah, who each started well as teenagers, yet ended their lives very differently: one in disgrace, the other in honour as a martyr. I have touched already on the lives of these two men in chapter three, but it is worth visiting them again in more detail. Both of them had a powerful encounter with the Holiness of the Lord in the Temple of Solomon. The difference between the two was how they responded to the powerful Presence of God. It serves as a great lesson to us. If we truly want more of the LORD in our life, are we willing to embrace the cost? What will we do with the Holiness of God? When God comes in power to us it shakes the foundations of our lives. Will His coming destroy us or empower us?

The text from Isaiah 6:1-8 is as follows:

> *1 In the year that King Uzziah died, I saw the Lord, high and exalted, seated on a throne; and the train of his robe filled the temple.*
> *2 Above him were seraphim, each with six wings: With two wings they covered their faces, with two they covered their feet, and with two they were flying. 3 And they were calling to one another:*

86 As was mentioned when discussing Moses' interaction with God at the burning bush in Exodus 3 in chapter two. See also Joshua 5:15.

"Holy, holy, holy is the LORD Almighty; the whole earth is full of his glory."

4 At the sound of their voices the doorposts and thresholds shook and the temple was filled with smoke.

5 "Woe to me!" I cried. "I am ruined! For I am a man of unclean lips, and I live among a people of unclean lips, and my eyes have seen the King, the LORD Almighty."

6 Then one of the seraphim flew to me with a live coal in his hand, which he had taken with tongs from the altar. 7 With it he touched my mouth and said, "See, this has touched your lips; your guilt is taken away and your sin atoned for."

8 Then I heard the voice of the Lord saying, "Whom shall I send? And who will go for us?"

And I said, "Here am I. Send me!"

This passage incorporates one of the most powerful revelations of God in the entire Bible. Isaiah's encounter with the manifest Presence of God re-shaped his life and launched him out as one of the most visionary and powerful prophets of the Old Testament. It puts Isaiah in very rare company – he saw the Lord and lived. Yet he was never the same from that point on!

Two things stand as the backdrop to this passage and explain why this encounter with God's Presence was so transformative for Isaiah: One, the nature of the Temple where this encounter took place, and two, the significance of the life of Uzziah for Isaiah.

The Temple where this was taking place was the Temple built by Solomon. It was a gloriously beautiful Temple crafted with artistically carved timbers plated with gold, silver and precious jewels. At the time of Uzziah's reign, the nation of Judah was powerful and strong; the Temple had not yet been plundered. It is probable, however, that only a few years after this event, under Ahaz the grandson of Uzziah, the Temple was sacked. Solomon dedicated the Temple with great pomp and ceremony[87] with a powerful prayer of dedication. God responded; burning up the offering of Solomon with fire from heaven and filling the Temple with a cloud of glory, so intense that the priests could not stand. Moreover, God also responded verbally to Solomon in a personal visitation with an amazing promise recorded in 2 Chronicles 7:15-16. *"Now my eyes will be open and my ears attentive to the prayers offered in this place. I have chosen and consecrated this temple so that my Name may be there forever. My eyes and my heart will always be there."*

This statement by God is a defining moment for the whole nation of Judah. From this point on, God has promised He *will hear every prayer* offered in this Temple, His name will be attached to this Temple *forever*, and His eyes and His heart will *always* be on this Temple. This cemented the Temple as the centre for the life of the entire nation. If you had any problem, any trouble, any need, all you had to do was get to the Temple because you knew that the living God would hear you and act. There was nothing like this Temple in all the earth. In THIS Temple, you *knew* you could encounter the living God, and yet you knew that this was not always safe.

Now let's consider Uzziah, the first of our two men. By mentioning him in verse 1, Isaiah is purposefully bringing the reader's attention to this man as a reference point. Uzziah became the King of Judah when he was 16 years old,[88] roughly the same age as Isaiah in this passage. He reigned for 52 years, and was the second longest reigning King of Judah. He started well. He was an able and proficient leader, a great organizer and builder and, as a general, won most if not all his battles. Under his rule Judah became one of the most powerful nations in the region, controlling the largest territory since Solomon. He would be the last of the great rulers of Judah. When he followed the Lord, he did well, and the entire nation prospered.

---

87 2 Chronicles 6-7.

88 His story is told in 2 Chronicles 26 and 2 Kings 15.

Then, in a moment filled with pride and hubris, he made a huge mistake. It was in year 37 of his reign. He had fought a great battle and his armies had routed the enemy. Flushed with success, he came back to the Temple in Jerusalem and went to the Temple to offer sacrifices of praise and thanksgiving to God. Since the High Priest was not there, Uzziah became impatient; he pridefully and arrogantly proceeded to offer the sacrifices to God himself, something forbidden for him to do as the King. The High Priest, Azariah, discovered what Uzziah was doing and arrived with 80 other priests to confront him. Since Uzziah was a powerful King and mighty warrior, Azariah was afraid. Yet, with great courage, Azariah confronted the King with his disobedience to God. Uzziah responded in anger and neglecting a key fact – God, the living God, has promised that his eyes and ears will *always* be on this Temple. He will not readily suffer His name to be sullied by the unsanctified sacrifices of an unconsecrated man with blood on his hands fresh from a battle. Uzziah stands before the Lord in the Temple, furious at being caught "red-handed" in his sin while holding an incense censer. Leprosy then breaks out on his forehead as the judgement of God falls on him. The uncleanness in the heart of Uzziah became manifested in the unclean disease of leprosy on his body. It was his pride that was the issue.[89] As a successful man he was unable to humble himself when God through Azariah confronted him. Uzziah encounters the Holy Presence of the Lord, then refuses to repent and admit that he was wrong. As a result, this great man spent the last 15 years of his life isolated in his palace, unable to ever again enter the Temple of God or to enter the Presence of the Lord. In a sense he died that day, and Jotham his son ruled in his place[90] for the last part of his rule. He lost everything he considered important. He became an object lesson for all future generations on the terrible destructiveness of pride. How we respond when God's Presence with His truth and Holiness confronts us, is extremely important. God is not a God to be trifled with. His Presence

89 2 Chronicles 26:16.

90 2 Chronicles 26:21.

will shake the foundation of our lives when we embrace it, so how will we respond? Will we be an Uzziah?

Isaiah probably started his prophetic ministry and received his "call" in Isaiah 6 at about 16, the same age as Uzziah was when he became King.[91] It is conjectured that Isaiah was a member of the royal family, since in Isaiah 37-39 he seems to have easy access to them. His prophetic career was long: it spanned a chunk of the reign of Jotham,[92] all the reigns of Ahaz and Hezekiah, and ended during the reign of Manasseh.[93] He likely died by being sawn in two.[94] His career might have been as long or longer than the reign of King Uzziah. His prophetic career was also spectacular. He suffered persecution under Ahaz and Manasseh, led one of the most powerful renewal movements the nation of Judah ever experienced under Hezekiah,[95] wrote passages of Scripture that became the most quoted Old Testament passages in the New Testament and showed powerful prophetic insights into the nature of the coming Messiah and

---

91 His exact age is not clear, he might have been younger or older than this, but indications are that he was young.

92 2 Chronicles 26 indicates that once Uzziah became a leper, Jotham was over the King's house judging the people (vs. 21). It would not be possible for him to be over the King's house as a 10 year old. 2 Chronicles 27:1 indicates that Jotham was 25 years old when he became King and he ruled for 16 years. Examining the numbers and age of Jotham many commentators think that Jotham's rule overlapped with Uzziah's and so the year King Uzziah died could have been as much as 15 years into the "reign" of Jotham. When Uzziah became unable to rule effectively, Jotham could have become a co-regent with him to rule in his place. This was a common practice to ensure continuity between fathers and their sons. Isaiah was possibly only a prophet for one year under Jotham.

93 2 Chronicles 28:1 indicates that Ahaz ruled for 16 years and 2 Chronicles 29:1 that Hezekiah ruled for 29 years. Even if he died near the beginning of the reign of Manasseh, his prophetic career would have lasted almost 50 years. Some suggest he prophesied for more than 60 years.

94 See Hebrews 11:37. The legend according to Rabbinic sources is that during the reign of Manasseh, Isaiah as an old man was running from soldiers of Manasseh and came across a hollow log in the forest. He crawled into the log to hide and was discovered. The log was then plugged up and carried into the presence of King Manasseh where it was sawn in two thus killing Isaiah. It is thought that Hebrews 11:37 is a reference to the death of Isaiah.

95 See 2 Chronicles 29-32 and Isaiah 36-39.

His sacrifice for the world. Of all of the Old Testament prophets, Isaiah was the one that seemed to prophetically see Jesus the most clearly.[96]

Yet, for Isaiah it all began in chapter six when he saw the Lord, heard His voice and entered into his calling from the Lord. What we see in this passage is instructive for us in how the Presence of the Holiness of the Lord releases us into our calling.

Isaiah as a young man came into the Temple. Why was he there? It is not normal for a 15-16 year old boy to hang out in the temple. I think he was there because he wanted to seek God's Presence. Knowing, like every Israelite that God was in that place and that He heard every prayer offered there. I think he had some big questions he wanted God to answer, perhaps he was struggling with what he should do with his life, and he was smart enough to realize that he needed to find the answers from God. Notice that Isaiah also came there alone. The reality is that if you truly hunger for more of God – you must do it alone. It is between you and God. Others can hinder or support you, but the journey towards the deeper Presence of God is your journey not theirs. Isaiah could have been anywhere – but he chose to be there, in the Temple. He chose to place himself where he knew the Presence of the Lord was.

Imagine you were there in the shoes of Isaiah. You come into the Temple to pray and seek the Lord. You look around at the beautiful temple, at its majesty and are awed. You reflect on the life of Uzziah who has just died. You remember the story of Uzziah and how he was struck down with leprosy because he had sinned in the Temple in the Presence of the Lord and how his heart was unclean before the Lord. You look around and realize that you might be standing right where Uzziah was when he was struck with leprosy. Then the heavens open up and you see the Lord - and are terrified that what happened to Uzziah will happen to you! You

96 Some commentators argue that Isaiah 40-66 were penned by a different prophet. Even if you agree with this, passages such as Isaiah 35 are still powerfully prophetic of the Messiah. The fact that terms such as the "Holy One of Israel" are sprinkled throughout the entire book as a key name for God suggest one author – especially as this term ties in so powerfully to what occurred in chapter 6 of Isaiah.

see the Lord, are confronted by His holiness, and in the process realize just how terribly unclean your own heart really is. You, like Uzziah, have brought sin into the temple! You are no better than Uzziah and you know how Uzziah's life was destroyed in a moment in that very place. How terrifying it would have been for a you!

Looking at Isaiah, there are three things he encounters in his vision of the Lord. Isaiah sees the kingly *majesty and authority* of God, and as he does so, encounters the *glory* and *holiness* of the Lord. Isaiah sees the Lord sitting on a throne in the heavens "high and exalted." This emphasizes God's kingly rule. God is exalted above all earthly kings and rules from the heavens. He has all authority, and His decrees are final. He is the one with whom all of us will have to deal, whether on this earth or in the after-life, and He is the one who will decide Isaiah's fate after he has brought his own uncleanness into His Presence in the temple.

Second, Isaiah sees God surrounded by *glory*; the train of the robe of God fills the temple, and the angels worship Him. Closely connected to God's glory is the third thing Isaiah encounters: he sees and experiences the *holiness* of the Lord. The angels cover their faces since they cannot even look at the face of God it is so pure and filled with majesty. They cover their feet as the place they are standing is holy. And as they worship before the Lord, they shout out a proclamation of the holiness, might and glory of the Lord: *"Holy, holy, holy is the LORD almighty: the whole earth is full of his glory."* Three times the Holiness of the Lord is repeated. The word for "Lord" here is Jehovah – the one who is the foundation and source of all reality, the one who is the ultimate cause of all things and the one who is defined by Presence (from chapter two). He is Jehovah Almighty. He has all might and power. He is the Holy One of Israel. The glory of this creator God also leaks into His creation - the whole earth reveals the glory of the Lord. This is not just a metaphor but also a statement of fact from angels who see clearly spiritual realities often hidden to us. All around us the world sparkles with the glory of God if we could but see it. We will talk about this in chapter 7: there is tremendous power in the spoken word, especially when it lines up with the truth of the nature of God. It is not enough for Isaiah just to see this vision, the angels proclaim its reality and as they shout out the truth of the holiness and might and glory of the Lord, the power of this proclamation shakes the very foundations of the temple and Isaiah encounters this truth in the deep levels of his heart.

This three-fold encounter with the living God shatters Isaiah. He is undone. When he sees this vision of the Lord and hears the proclamation of the angels, the truth of his own heart is revealed to him and he realises that he is unclean. Isaiah cries out: "*Woe to me! I am ruined! For I am a man of unclean lips, and I live among a people of unclean lips, and my eyes have seen the King, the LORD Almighty.*" It was important in the ancient Middle East to show grief at funerals and the most common cry of grief heard at a funeral was "woe, woe to me. I am ruined. My life is over because ----- has died." What Isaiah is doing is entering into the grief of his own imminent death. He thinks he is on the edge of death because he, as a sinner who is unclean before the Lord, has seen the Lord.[97] The word he uses to describe his condition is also key – he is a man of "unclean" lips. Uzziah was a leper. In the culture of the time, a leper was one who was "unclean" and was meant to cry out "unclean, unclean"[98] to all who came near to them so they would stay away. With the connection in verse 1 to Uzziah who died as an "unclean" leper because he had brought his own "unclean" heart into the temple, Isaiah seeing himself as "unclean" is significant. How terrifying it would be for a young man to contemplate that the whole rest of his life he could be a leper because he had come before the Lord lightly with unconfessed sin! If he did not die through this encounter with God, he could end up living a life much worse than death. For Isaiah has "seen the King, the LORD Almighty." He has seen the King of Kings and Lord of Lords. He has seen the one who has all power and authority, and, . . . he is unclean! One way or another, Isaiah's life will never be the same.

---

97 In Exodus 19:21-22 we have a warning for the Israelites to not get too close to the Lord since if they look at Him unworthily, they will die.

98 Leviticus 13:44-45.

We need to know who we are dealing with when we pursue the Presence of the Lord. He is absolute love. He is absolute goodness. Yet we cannot avoid His Holiness when we pursue His Presence. His Holiness is part of His goodness[99] and love and profoundly blesses us when we embrace its confronting nature.

We do not know the exact nature of Isaiah's sin, only that it involves his lips. Was he a liar? Did he have a foul mouth? Was he sarcastic? Was he a mean-spirited man whose hard heart came out through his mouth? All we know is that he saw very clearly when confronted with the holiness of the Lord that his lips were unclean and that he was no different than all the people around him. Often we fool ourselves into thinking that we are not as bad as others so that what we do is OK, but we cannot fool God. When we truly see His Holiness we realize that there are no shades of grey, compared to His purity, our sin is as black as black can be. How much are we a part of our culture? How much have we compromised our integrity and fooled ourselves into thinking we are not so bad? How do we use our lips? Do we use our lips the way the culture around us says is OK, or do we use them as God would have us use them? The truth is that we will tend to sin in the same ways as the people around us. What Isaiah saw here was that not only was he unclean, but all of those around him were also unclean in the same way. The whole society he was part of was broken like he was broken.

Perhaps your problem is not your lips. Is it your eyes? What do you look at? What about your ears? What do you listen to? Whatever it may be, we often bring into the Presence of God the sins of our society that we participate in. This is not a safe thing to do, but God's love does not leave us without an answer if we are open to it.

---

99 According to Andrew Murray in *The Power of the Blood of Jesus,* Marshall Pickering, Basingstoke, UK, 1963 on page 41: "Holiness is that attribute of God because of which He always is, and wills, and does what is extremely good; because of which also He desires what is supremely good in His creatures, and bestows it upon them." In other words, holiness is undiluted goodness.

Isaiah had probably forgotten what Uzziah had also forgotten – that this temple was the place where God's eyes and ears were always attuned, that He had promised to hear *every* prayer offered in that place. For Isaiah this is good news: God hears Isaiah and responds. The God who Isaiah saw in the temple was not only King, and glorious and holy, but He was also Saviour. God hears Isaiah and sends an angel to him. The angel takes a coal from the sacrificial altar which was burning in the temple, comes to Isaiah, and touches it to Isaiah's lips – the very source of Isaiah's problem. The angel says to Isaiah, *"See, this has touched your lips; your guilt is taken away and your sin atoned for."* There is no atonement for sin without a sacrifice and the angel takes the coal from the place where the sacrifice[100] had been made and ministers to Isaiah right at the point of his need. His lips were unclean, now his lips are cleansed, his guilt is taken away, and his "uncleanness" is dealt with. Now the future opens up again for Isaiah. As it does for us when we receive the ministry of the Lord at our point of need.

Isaiah could have responded in several ways to the revelation of his uncleanness. He could have denied it. He could have responded in pride and anger as Uzziah did (and we see that did not do him much good!). What he does do, is respond in honesty, admitting the true state of his heart, and in humility accepting the ministry of the angel God sent to him. As he does so, Isaiah goes from death and disgrace to life and hope. In this encounter with God Isaiah learns a truth about God that penetrates to the very core of his being. He learns that he is a sinner living in the Presence of a Holy God; that the entire nation around him has the same problem that he had; that God has the answer for their sin just as He had the answer for Isaiah's sin; and that God can totally transform a liability into something that sparkles with the power of the Spirit of God. Isaiah's basic problem was unclean lips, yet after receiving the ministry of

100 Leviticus 17:11 – it is through blood sacrifice that atonement is accomplished. We see this ultimately in Jesus. The altar here would have been the altar inside the temple near the entrance where the blood was splashed for the sin offering. It may have been the altar that Uzziah tried to sacrifice on.

the Spirit of God, Isaiah becomes one whose lips are powerfully anointed to declare the prophetic words of God.

After being undone by the power of the Holiness of the Lord and then undone by the unexpected loving ministry of the Lord to the very core of his need, Isaiah hears God talking from His kingly throne saying, *"Whom shall I send? And who will go for us?"*[101] Overcome with love for God, Isaiah cries out: *"Here I am. Send me!"* By doing so, Isaiah starts to enter into his destiny in the Lord. I do not think it is an accident that the key to Isaiah's calling is the proper use of what he had previously misused – his lips. It is the same with us. We may easily misuse our gifts; just as those all around us misuse theirs. Allow God to cleanse, consecrate and sanctify those gifts so that they can be powerfully used by God to impact the nation. The key to being used powerfully by God in the right way is not the development of your gifts according to what the society around us values, it is the consecration and cleansing of those gifts by the Holiness of the Lord so that we can be sent back to those around us who desperately need the same ministry from the Lord that we have received.

We need to know that God is the King of Kings; we are not. God is full of power and majesty; even the greatest of us have not even one iota of His glory. He is completely holy; we are unclean and yet He gladly ministers to our uncleanness when we embrace the ministry of His Holiness with humility and honesty. As we embrace His Holiness and allow Him to shatter the foundations we have built our lives on and reform them according to the lines of Holiness, we enter into our calling. Once we see how much God has done for us, we become willing to 'go' for Him. We need to know that there are people all around us who struggle with what we have struggled with and as we let God minister to us, we become someone who can help them. When we embrace God's Presence, we become transformed by His love into an agent of His mercy and grace. We become the answer those around us need.

---

101 The self-discussion of this overheard conversation and the use of "us" in verse 8 is one of the evidences of the Trinity in the Old Testament.

Isaiah ended up having a powerful ministry but it was not easy. He experienced both intense persecution under Ahaz and Manasseh and yet, with Hezekiah, was key in a powerful revival. This encounter gave Isaiah the strength to endure and persevere. Your encounters with God will do the same. We even see the themes of Isaiah's whole ministry come out of this time with God. For example, God is called "Redeemer" thirteen times in Isaiah[102] and only four times in the whole rest of Scripture.[103] In addition, God is called the "Holy One of Israel/Jacob" seventeen times in Isaiah[104] versus only four times in the rest of the Scripture.[105] Do you see Redemption and Holiness in Isaiah's encounter with God? This "Presence of God encounter" in the life of Isaiah wrote truths on his heart that resonated through everything he did afterwards and gave him the strength to endure. It will be no different with you.

Both King Uzziah and Isaiah started their careers around the age of 16. Both had long careers and accomplished a lot. Both spent time in the Temple. Both were confronted by God in the Temple and had powerful, life-changing encounters with God there. Both had the very foundations of their lives shaken up by this event. One reacted wrongly to his encounter with God and ended his life in disgrace. The other reacted rightly and became a man God used powerfully to impact the nation, saving it from invading armies and bringing renewal.[106] As you press into the Lord with honesty, courage, and humility, who knows what the impact of your God-consecrated life will be?

---

102 Isaiah 41:14; 43:14; 44:6, 24; 47:4; 48:17; 49:7, 26; 54:5, 8; 59:20; 60:16; 63:16.

103 Job 19:25; Psalm 19:14; 78:35; Jeremiah 50:34.

104 Isaiah 5:19; 12:6; 17:7; 29:19, 23; 30:11, 12, 15; 43:3, 14; 45:11; 47:4; 48:17; 49:7; 54:5; 55:5; 60:9. Interestingly enough, 8 of these are from chapters 1-39 and 9 from chapters 40-66 and the unity of this term is one suggestion for one author for the entire book of Isaiah rather than two.

105 Psalm 71:22; 78:41; 89:18; Jeremiah 51:5. In addition, Mark 1:24, Luke 4:34 and John 6:69 call Jesus the "Holy One of God" a title that is slightly different but shows His identification with the "Holy One" of the Old Testament.

106 Isaiah 36-39.

Summary

While the Presence of God is good for us, we must never be glib about entering into His Presence. It is true that we were designed to thrive in His Presence. Knowing Him is the key to our growth and transformation into His image. He is always good. Yet His Presence is not always safe for the sinner. His holiness can confront and shatter us, but must be embraced in order to enter into greater intimacy with Him. Repentance, honesty, humility and living at the foot of the cross are key aspects that we need to hold on to so that we are changed by His Presence rather than being destroyed by it.

In summary:

1. God's Presence heals. God changes us in amazing ways and brings us into deeper levels of life when we have an authentic encounter with Him.
2. God is calling to each one of us to press deeper into Him. Daring to draw closer to God is not always something we do at our convenience. He may need to confront us and change us at the deep levels of our being in order for us to be released into His calling for us.
3. What we do with a revelation of the Holiness of the Lord and whether we honestly and humbly embrace the accompanying revelation of our sin will determine our future.
4. We see in Uzziah an example of a man whose pride did not allow him to be humbled by an encounter with the Lord. His pride ended up destroying his life and isolating him from all he loved.
5. Isaiah placed himself in a position to encounter God and when God revealed Himself, Isaiah's humility, courage and honesty resulted in him becoming a man God could use powerfully to impact a nation.
6. Isaiah learned from the lesson of Uzziah and did not repeat his mistake.
7. As Isaiah confessed his sin, he realized that he was surrounded with people who were sinners just like him. As God ministered to Isaiah

at the point of his sin, he realized that God had the same heart and same redemption ready for others.

8. God touched Isaiah at the point of his sin and turned his life around so that his problem (unclean lips) became the source of his ministry (prophetic lips). God can do the same with you. The answer others need is found in your own encounter with the Lord.
9. As you embrace the shattering encounter with the Holiness of the Lord with humility, courage and honesty, you will begin to enter into your destiny as you say, "Yes" to God's call to you.

Entering Into His Presence

Place yourself in a place to encounter the Lord. Put on some worship music and spend some time soaking in the Presence of the Lord. Tell the Lord He has permission to do whatever He wants. Are there unresolved issues of pride and ego? Be honest with the Lord and ask Him to show you any areas of sin.

Ask the Lord for a revelation of His power, might, glory and Holiness. Does the story of Isaiah stir up any fear? Confess it to the Lord. Choose to trust in the goodness of God. The Holiness of the Lord is never separated from His love or His goodness. It might be helpful to simply go through various parts of your body and consecrate them to God. For example, consecrate your lips to the Lord and ask Him to use them for His Glory. Confess any related sins. Then go on to your eyes, ears, etc. Just spend time with the Lord and ask Him to wash you once again with His blood, cleansing every part of you.

Dedicate yourself to the Lord again. Ask the Lord if there is anything specific you need to confess and consecrate to Him. Realize that Jesus has already accomplished your redemption, no matter what your specific sin might be. It is done! Receive again the ministry of the Holy Spirit in that area where you need a fresh touch of His redeeming love.

Receive the love of the Lord for you. Give your love to the Lord. Tell the Lord that you, like Isaiah, are open to any ministering angels He might send your way, yet keep your focus on the Lord.

Tell the Lord you will do what He wants you to do and go where He wants you to go. Keep saying, "Yes" to the Lord over and over again until it resounds in your heart. Tell the Lord that the basic stance of your heart will always be "yes" to Him.

Prayer

LORD Almighty, Holy One of Israel, I confess I need Your touch. Your Holiness fills me with fear and yet I know it is never separated from Your goodness and love for me.

Lord of Hosts, show me Your Holiness. King of kings, show me Your glory. Let Your revelation rise up within me until it touches all parts of my life.

Lord God, let me be able to join the angels' chorus shouting out: *"Holy, holy, holy is the LORD Almighty: the whole earth is full of his glory."* Write that revelation the angels had on my own heart. Touch me deeply like You did Isaiah so that I am never the same again. Lord, give me the same type of life-changing encounter.

Lord, I confess that I am a sinner, yet I know that You are the answer to my need. Show me Your redemption. Show me Your power to save.

Lord, help me to confess what I need to confess and receive from Your hand what I need to receive. I need You and You are the only answer I need.

Lord, show me those around me that are just like me. Show me those that You want me to minister to in the same way You have ministered to me.

Lord, I love You. Fill me with a passion for You that is so much deeper than my need to preserve myself. Let me be one who embraces Your Holiness.

I will go where You want me to go and stay where You want me to stay.

In the precious name of Jesus I pray,

Amen.

Part II:

The Eight Dimensions of God's Presence

So where can God be found? How do we nurture our relationship with Him? This is what is discussed in the next few chapters. In the Scriptures, you can find at least eight dimensions of the Presence of the Lord. Each of these explain aspects of how God makes Himself available to us in the world and gives us pointers to how we can access His Presence. These "dimensions" flow from one into another and over-lap. Some are accessible to non-Christians, but some are only available to Christians. There will always be a mystery in how it all works since we are talking about God who will always be "unfathomable" and not fit our "boxes".

I have been asked, "Why do you say 'More, Lord' or 'Come, Holy Spirit', isn't God always present?" What we are really asking for at those times is for an intensification of the Presence of the Lord. Yes, He is always present, but not always in the same way. An analogy that might be helpful is water vapour. Water vapour is all around us, but not always in the same intensity or form. We breath water vapour in the air around us. It is in our lungs. Yet we normally never see it unless it is cold. If we increase its intensity, we might see the water droplets that appear when we breathe on a mirror, or the dew drops on grass in the morning. Increase its intensity some more and we get the clouds in the sky. Increase the intensity again and we get fog, then drizzly rain. Increase it again and we get normal rain. Increase the intensity yet again and we get a tropical downpour, then streams, creeks, rivers and finally the vast expanse of lakes and oceans. All of these examples are water vapour but in different concentrations and forms. In the same way, God is always present, yet His Presence is not always accessible in the same way. He is with us all the time but we may never know it. Yet His Presence with us can increase to such an extent that it appears like a cloud and we cannot even stand in His Presence, falling like dead men/women before Him.[107]

As Christians, the greatest possession we have is the Presence of the Lord in our midst – it is what makes us different from everyone else. As indicated earlier, one of the key characteristics of the living God is that He is a God who makes Himself present to His people. In Genesis we see His intimate involvement with creation, how He walked with Adam and Eve in the cool of the evening, and how, when they sinned, He immediately started a plan to bring mankind back into intimacy with Himself. As we look at the dimensions of the Presence of God in the world, may our intimacy with Him grow.

THE EIGHT DIMENSIONS OF GOD'S PRESENCE IN THE WORLD

Part II discusses the eight dimensions of God's Presence in the world, yet the flow of this discussion is "interrupted" by two chapters. Between the third dimension, the Presence of God in His Word, and the fourth, the Presence of God in the corporate gathering of those who are "born again," there is a transition. The first three dimensions are accessible for the non-believer, but the fourth and following dimensions are not. In these levels, the Presence of God can only come to us through Jesus Christ since He fundamentally changes how we relate to and access the Presence of God. Chapter 8 discusses how Jesus is the Gateway into deep-

107 2 Chronicles 7:1-3; Revelation 1:17; 4:9-11.

er intimacy with God and how His death on the cross has changed everything about how we access the Presence of God. We need to understand this in order to fully enter into the Presence of God as described in later chapters.

In addition, the fourth and fifth dimensions of the Presence of God depend on us understanding what it means to be the Temple of the Lord. Chapter nine explores the Biblical foundations of what the temple of God is so that we can understand how, as both the gathered Church and as born-again believers, we become the dwelling place for God's Presence in the world. After discussing the Old Testament prelude to the New Testament temples of God, we continue with our examination of the eight dimensions of God's Presence in the world in chapter ten.

The eight dimensions of the Presence of God developed in later chapters are sketched out below. Key verses are in the footnotes.

(a) **The General Presence of God in the World.** This is normally referred to as the omnipresence of God.[108]

(b) The second dimension of God's Presence is **The Sustaining Presence of God in the World**. God's Presence is the glue that holds everything together.[109]

(c) The third dimension of the Presence of God is **The Presence of God in His Word.** There are at least three components to this: the Presence of God in His Spoken Word,[110] in His Written Word[111] and in Jesus as the Word of God made flesh.[112]

---

108 Psalm 139:7-12.

109 Colossians 1:16-17; Psalm 139:9-10; Hebrews 1:3; 2:10; Revelation 4:11.

110 See Genesis 1.

111 Hebrews 4:12: This may be either the spoken or written word of God. 2 Timothy 3:16-17: This is the written word of God. Isaiah 55:10-11: This can apply to all three of these- the prophetic word, the written word and Jesus.

112 John 1:1-5, 14. Jesus is the Word of God made flesh to accomplish the will of God on the earth.

(d) Fourth is **The Presence of God in the Corporate Gathering of the Church.** This is similar to the next dimension since we, collectively as well as individually, are Temples of the Holy Spirit.[113]

(e) The fifth level is **The Indwelling Presence of God in those individuals who are born again**. God comes to us to make us individually His dwelling place.[114]

(f) The sixth level is **The Presence of God in Worship.** God shows up powerfully in worship.[115]

(g) The seventh level is **The Presence of the God in Love**, particularly when people are loved authentically with "agape" love.[116]

(h) The last level is **The Presence of the Glory of the Lord.** This is when God is so powerfully present that His Presence appears visibly like a cloud.[117]

HOW DO WE GET MORE OF GOD?

The question is, how do we get more of God? First, we need to realize that greater intimacy with the living God only comes through Jesus Christ. He is the Gateway into the deeper Presence of God so we must press into Jesus to find more of God. Second, we need to cultivate in our lives those traits that nurture the Presence of God such as submission, humility, obedience, holiness and reverence for His Presence. Then, as you go through this book, add Presence to Presence. Do as much as you can to enter each of the "dimensions" of God's Presence. Read and honor

---

113 1 Corinthians 3:16-17; Ephesians 2:21-22; 1 Peter 2:4-5. See also Matthew 18:20.

114 John 14:17; 1 Corinthians 6:19; See also Matthew 28:20 and Romans 8:9-11.

115 Psalm 22:3: *"Yet you are holy, you who are enthroned upon the praises of Israel."* (NAS)

116 1 John 4:7-8, 12, 16.

117 In 1 Kings 8:10-11 the temple is filled with a cloud of glory when the temple is dedicated. In 2 Chronicles 5:13-14 the temple is filled with the glory of the Lord during worship also at its dedication.

the word of God, spend time with others in worship, turn your heart to Him every time you think of it, thank God for how He is sustaining you in ways you do not know about, and be obedient to what God is saying to you. Give God more of yourself and you will find more of Him. Raise the level of your expectation of what God wants to do in you and through you as you come more deeply into His Presence.

6

The First Two Dimensions Of The Presence Of The Lord.

"Where can I go from your Spirit? Where can I flee from your presence? If I go to the heavens, you are there; if I make my bed in the depths, you are there." (Psalm 139:7-8)

"He is before all things, and in him all things hold together." (Col. 1:17)

"The Son is the radiance of God's glory and the exact representative of his being, sustaining all things by his powerful word. . . " (Heb. 1:3)

In this chapter, we deal with the two more "general" dimensions of the Presence of the Lord: the omnipresence and the general sustaining Presence of the Lord which are both accessible to non-Christians as well as Christians.

THE OMNIPRESENCE OF GOD IN THE WORLD

This first dimension of the Presence of the Lord is the most basic one. Often called the omnipresence of the Lord it simply involves the truth that the Lord is everywhere present. It does not mean that all things are part of god (pantheism) or that all things are gods (polytheism). It means that He is always present and accessible.

The passage often referred to as evidence of this in the Scriptures is Psalm 139 although more properly this passage refers to the Presence of God's pursuing love no matter where you go and also of His complete knowledge of us. If God's love is present with us, though, then He Himself is also present since His love for us cannot be separated from who He is.

> *You have searched me, LORD, and you know me. You know when I sit and when I rise; you perceive my thoughts from afar. You discern my going out and my lying down; you are familiar with all my ways. . . .*
>
> *Where can I go from your Spirit? Where can I flee from your presence? If I go up to the heavens, you are there; if I make my bed in the depths, you are there. If I rise on the wings of the dawn, if I settle on the far side of the sea, even there your hand will guide me, your right hand will hold me fast. . . .* (Psalm 139:1-3, 7-10)

This passage shows that no matter where we go, God and His love are always there. There is nowhere you can go where God and His love are not. He is available always. He is present always. He sees and hears every detail of our lives. He knows us completely. Just because we do not feel like He is present does not mean that He is not. Paul once described the living God as the one in whom *"we live and move and have our being"* (Acts 17:28). What we need to do to actualize the reality of His Presence is to turn our hearts and minds towards Him, pausing to do so if necessary. We need to recognize His Presence[118] and look for it to perceive it. Thankfulness is often a doorway that empowers us to see the Presence of God. Instead of looking for what God has not done, we look for what He *has* done for us and are grateful. By having this perspective, we begin to

---

118 This is the basis of the classic devotional book by Brother Lawrence, *The Practice of the Presence of God,* Shambhala Publications, Boston, Massachusetts, 2005.

be able to see that He has always been active in our lives and has done more than we thought.

THE ROLE OF UNBELIEF

The truth is that if we are not open to belief in the reality of God, we will not see the Lord even when He is present. Openness to the revelation of truth makes us able to perceive it when it manifests itself. Belief enables us to perceive the Presence of God while unbelief causes us to ignore or misunderstand it. If we are reluctant to go where the sign is pointing, we will not see what the sign is pointing to. This is seen repeatedly in the Bible. For example, in John 6, Jesus prays over a few loaves of bread and miraculously feeds 5000 men (plus others, see John 6:1-15) and then has an extended discourse on how He is the true "bread of life" sent down from Heaven to give life to the world. The miracle in close proximity to this discussion demonstrates tangibly that He is the "bread of life". This is one of the eight miraculous "signs" recorded by John that point to the truth that Jesus is the divine Son of God. Yet immediately after this miracle, the same people who were present during it say to Jesus, *"What sign will you give that we may see it and believe you?"* (John 6:30).[119] Their refusal to accept who Jesus was made them blind to the truth the miracle demonstrated and also to the obvious signs of the Presence of the Lord on Jesus (which showed Him to be the "anointed one", or "Messiah").

Unbelief can blind us to even the most blatant and obvious signs of the Presence of God. In John 11:1-53 we have recorded what is arguably one of the most powerful miracles in the Bible. Lazarus has been dead

119 In John 6:14 this miracle is specifically called a "sign" the same word later used by the skeptics in verse 30 when they ask Jesus to give them a "sign". They had already been given a "sign" and had refused to believe it. This is one of the "ironies" in John. Similarly in Matthew 15:29-38 Jesus heals many people and then feeds 4000 men plus others with only a few bread and fish and immediately after this, the Pharisees in Matthew 16:1-5 ask Jesus to show them a "sign" to prove who He was – but Jesus had just healed many people AND fed 4000 plus people miraculously!

for 4 days and is buried in a tomb, yet Jesus with just the spoken word, calls him forth out of the tomb. Everyone is astonished and some come to believe in who Jesus is through this powerful "sign" (John 11:45). At the same time, some of the people standing there who saw Lazarus raised from the dead were so mired in unbelief that they refused to believe and instead plotted to kill Jesus (John 11:46-53). They were even so upset people were coming to faith in Jesus through this miracle that they plotted to kill Lazarus as well (John 12:10-11)! Even the most obvious signs of the Presence of God all around you will not convince you God is real *if* you are not open to this truth. Similarly, in the story of the rich man and Lazarus in Luke 16, Jesus concluded the story by saying, *"If they do not listen to Moses and the Prophets, they will not be persuaded even if someone rises from the dead"* (Luke 16:31). Unbelief kills our ability to see God. Nothing will convince you if you do not want to be convinced.

This applies to both Christians and non-Christians. If a non-Christian really has openness to the Lord and tries to look for the activity of the Lord in their lives, they will see it and find the Lord. The truth is that He is always present if we have the eyes to see Him. If a Christian carries unbelief in their heart, they will find it hard to see the clear Presence of the Lord all around them. I related the story earlier of my son and I going to visit a missionary friend in Guinea Bissau and during our time with him, we saw many miracles. In one night alone, I saw five backs healed. People who could not bend down at all before prayer, were touching their toes and twisting and turning without pain after prayer. It was quite amazing. At one point we went out to some islands off the shore of Guinea Bissau and preached the Gospel and saw a number of people respond to the Gospel message and several people healed, including a man who walked freely without a cane he absolutely depended upon before prayer.[120] We also went one evening into a hospital and prayed for the sick and saw a woman healed from pain associated

120 I tell more of the details of this story in the next chapter.

with a difficult labour.[121] It was an exciting time, yet I found myself struggling to believe that people were really being healed. My rational, logical, Western-trained scepticism was getting in the way of faith. I wanted to see the obvious tumour shrinking and the twisted limbs straighten out, but I realised that I needed to believe in order to see. God may be "omnipresent", but that does not always mean that His Presence is easy to see. He is there none-the-less. Unbelief makes us spiritually blind.[122]

The question is, do we have the willingness to obey the implications of "seeing" the Lord? People sometimes do not want to "see" the Lord since they do not want to embrace the implications of Him being real and do not want to change. Yet change is necessary for all of us, particularly in order to be transformed into the likeness of Christ which is part of our destiny (see Rom. 8:29). To become like Jesus means we change everything about ourselves that does not resemble Him until He becomes more visible in and through us. God's Presence is deeply confronting to all we build our lives on that is not Him.

THE ROLE OF SIN

Something else that prevents us from seeing the Lord is sin. We were created by God to thrive in holiness in relationship with Him. Yet one of the tragedies of the Fall in Genesis 3 when Adam and Eve sinned was that it separated them from God and caused them to hide from His Presence.[123] Then, as mentioned in chapter 1, after Cain killed his brother

121 My son and I with an interpreter were praying for her. Since she was a woman we were careful to not touch her, just held our hands towards her as we prayed. She had a lot of intense pain in her lower back and abdomen. When we asked if she felt God doing anything, she said, "Yes, where the hand is on my back is very hot." My son and I looked at her back where she said the hand was and at each other. *No one was touching her where she felt the hand and the heat!* As we continued to pray, the "hot hand" continued to touch her, the pain gradually left and she was able to walk freely with no pain whereas she could not move at all without incredible pain before the prayer.

122 This is the point behind the great irony of John 9. By the end of the chapter, you understand that the highly educated Pharisees who claim they "see" are much more blind spiritually than the illiterate blind man who had been healed by Jesus.

123 Genesis 3:10.

the worst thing about his punishment was that he would no longer be in the Presence of the Lord and that he would be *"hidden from the Lord's presence."* (Gen. 4:13, 16). Have we lost the sense of how tragic this is?

Sin raises up within us a desire to hide from the One who is the very source of our life. It also hides His Presence from us. Second Corinthians 3:14-16 talks about a "veil" that covers the hearts of people that is only taken away when someone turns to Christ. Jesus opens up our eyes to see spiritual realities more clearly. We will see the ever-present God with more clarity when we honestly and humbly deal with any sin issues in our lives. Sometimes we claim unbelief when the real issue is sin. At times, we do not want to "see" God because of the implications of this for our life and we do not want to let go of a sin pattern. Even those who say they are Christians will have a hard time truly "seeing" the Lord if they refuse to deal with a favorite sin. Sometimes what happens, even for Christians, is that in reality our wills are more sovereign in our lives than God is. James speaking to believers says: *"Come near to God and he will come near to you."* Then he continues, *"Wash your hands, you sinners, and purify your hearts . . . Humble yourselves before the Lord, and he will lift you up."*[124] God is always near, yet we may need to prepare our hearts in order for His Presence to come to us more fully.

THERE IS NO SECULAR/SACRED DIVIDE IN LIFE

If God is everywhere all the time, there can be no distinction between sacred and secular. We often make a false dichotomy and separate life into secular and sacred spheres. But if God is always near us and always present, every place we are becomes the possible arena where God will interact with us. His Presence makes *everywhere* sacred. Every *moment* becomes potentially holy. We must recognize this to appreciate the sacredness of every moment of each day. I have met "Sunday" Christians who live like the world on weekdays but like a Christian on Sundays because they fail to realize that no day is more sacred than any other since

124 James 4:8-10 and James is writing to believers.

God is always with us. Perhaps they are also failing to realize that God sees every part of their lives and they are never out of His sight. If we do not want to take God to the bar or to the movie we are seeing, perhaps we should not go there at all.

Recognizing the Presence of the Lord in every aspect of our lives will start to change us. As we attune our hearts to recognize God's Presence everywhere we go, we start to carry his Holiness everywhere we go. And we start to become *"holy as God is Holy"* (1 Peter 1:15-16) in our lifestyles.

While non-believers can call out to the Lord and discover that He is never far from them, this truth is particularly powerful for Christians. Through the cross of Jesus Christ and the work of the Holy Spirit, we have clear access to the heavenlies (Eph. 2:18). While barriers will still exist between God and mankind for the non-believer, for the believer these have been taken away in Christ. Believers have a potentially greater ease of access to the Presence of God because of the cross. The key is that we must apply the cross to our lives so that we can access the intimate Presence of God through Jesus.

THE IMPORTANCE OF DREAMS

God is a God who speaks. He is also a God who passionately loves His creation and longs for people to be freed from the hurt, destruction and pain of sin. He is always calling people to come to Him. One of the ways in which the ever-present God speaks is through dreams. This is one implication of the General Presence of God in the world. There are many examples of God speaking through dreams in the Bible, from the six dreams of the Joseph narrative in the Old Testament[125] to the dreams of Joseph in the New Testament[126] as well as others.[127] God also does not

125 Genesis 37-41.

126 Matthew 1:20; 2:13, 19, 22.

127 Genesis 28: 12-17 (Jacob); Daniel 2 and 4 (Nebuchadnezzar); Matthew 2:12 (the three wise men); Matthew 27:19 (Pilate's wife).

stop speaking in dreams with the coming of the Holy Spirit in Acts 2[128] as we see from Paul's dream/vision of the Macedonian man.[129]

Everybody has dreams but not all dreams come from God. I would suggest that there are at least four types of dreams. First, many dreams arise out of the surface levels of our sub-conscious. Things bubble up and manifest in our dreams that are related to what we are going through and experiencing. For example, knowing we have a test the next day and being anxious about it, we might have a dream that we arrive at the exam with no pen, or calculator or even without clothes on. At this level, the dream reveals our anxiety about the exam. A dream might also relate to a movie we saw, a discussion we had, or a problem we are working on. Usually this type of dream connects fairly obviously to our lives, they may come with insight or they may be completely forgettable. Often with this type of dream, we remember we had a dream but may have a hard time remembering the details.

The second type of dream is more profound. I would describe this type of dream as welling up from the deeper, hidden levels of our sub-conscious that we are not in touch with and which may reveal something to us that we did not know before. It is similar to the first, but connected more deeply, beyond the surface layers, to our inner being. With this type of dream, God can be involved as He reveals to us something we need or something that would be good for us to know about ourselves or others. Here we can have the deeper levels of our subconscious stirred up by events in our life and God is often active in the process. These dreams are somewhat revelatory and can have various levels of profundity. These are dreams that are helpful to keep track of since they are connected deeply to our inner life.

128 In fact, Peter uses a prophecy from Joel 2:28-29 to connect the coming of the Holy Spirit to God speaking *even more* in dreams and visions in Acts 2:16-21.

129 Acts 16:9-10. It is also possible that the Holy Spirit directed them in where to go in the preceding verses through dreams. We know that the Holy Spirit stopped them from going to Asia (vs. 6) and did not "permit" them to go to Bithynia (vs. 7) but we do not know how he did this.

The third type of dream comes clearly as some sort of message from God.[130] In these, God speaks with various levels of clarity. They can be descriptive dreams, prophetic dreams, or ones that come with such power that you come awake in the dream and watch it unfold before your "eyes". Sometimes you feel the definite Presence of God in the dream and sometimes you do not. These are the dreams that are vivid enough to be clearly remembered and you know they are important in some way. This does not mean that they are easy to understand, but they are hard to forget and you carry them with you into the day.[131] Some can have clear meanings and others can be heavily symbolic, yet you have the sense that something important is being communicated in the dream. Many times in our secular world people think these dreams are simply one part of their mind talking to another part of their mind,[132] but often it is God Himself speaking (if you do not believe in God, you will not believe He speaks in dreams).[133] These ones you write down and prayerfully try to figure out.

The last type of dream is dark and can be demonic or evil. These may come out of things we have exposed ourselves to or from how we have played in the "muck" of life. They are the kinds of dreams we want to forget and that leave us feeling unclean, defiled, insecure, depressed or with other negative feelings. The more we have played with the occult, or the new age, the more likely we will have these types of dreams. They can

---

130 These are the ones mentioned above that are recorded in the Bible. They are recorded since God speaks in them and this impacted the lives of the people who had them. Some like Jacob's in Gen. 28:12-17 are quite clear in their meaning. Others like the cupbearer's and baker's in Gen. 40:9-19 are more obscure and need insight to understand.

131 With the baker and cupbearer, they knew the dreams were significant but they could not figure them out and needed the help of Joseph (Genesis 40:5-8).

132 Their subconscious is "speaking" to them.

133 Often I hear Christians say that God no longer speaks in dreams because we have the Holy Spirit now, yet this is not what the Bible teaches and models. Joel's prophecy was about the Holy Spirit speaking through dreams and visions and this was fulfilled not canceled out when the Holy Spirit fell in Acts 2. Paul later seems to pay attention to "dreams and visions" as one of the ways God speaks in Acts 16.

also be part of spiritual attack or spiritual oppression.[134] These ones we need to pray over and against and seek the Presence of God to set us free from what they reveal.

The key is that since God is everywhere present we should not discount dreams as a way that God may speak. Sometimes dreams can be extremely powerful as we see in Genesis 28:12-17 where Jacob receives his calling from God. The Scriptures show that God repeatedly speaks through dreams. This does not mean they are automatically easy to understand, but since God is sovereign and He does speak in dreams, He holds the secret to what He is trying to communicate through the dream. Our attitude needs to be the same as Joseph's was when he encountered the dreams of the Baker and Cupbearer while in prison: *"Do not interpretations belong to God? Tell me your dream"* (Gen. 40:8). If God is speaking through your dream, as you turn to Him He will help you understand what He is trying to say. In addition, God speaks to both Christians and non-Christians through their dreams. The Cupbearer, the Baker, Nebuchadnezzar and even Pilate's wife were not believers, but God spoke to them even so.[135] The living God is a God who speaks. Do not limit how He may speak to you or to those around you.

One of the implications of the General Presence of the Lord in the world is that God is more active in your life than you might have thought. He is more present than you know. He is all around you (Psalm 139:7-12). His love is near to you. He loves you and He has a calling on your life. He is working in your life to help bring you into that calling.

A question that comes up is: how do we become more aware of God if He is actually near to us? To answer this, we turn to Francis de Sales. Francis was a wealthy man who renounced his wealth to become an or-

---

134 Demons are real and we need to be careful of inviting them into our lives.

135 In fact, the reality that God speaks to non-Christians through their dreams is an evangelistic strategy that I know has been used among Muslims. I know of three people, former Muslims, who had dreams of a man with eyes like fire, a white beard, and wearing a white robe with a golden sash who appeared to them in the dream, looked at them and told them to come and follow him (see Rev. 1:13-16).

dinary priest with the Catholic Church in the late 1500's. He developed a passion to help make holiness (i.e. the Presence of God) accessible to ordinary people living ordinary lives. He ended up writing *An Introduction to the Devout Life* which has become a spiritual classic.[136] In it he talks of many things including four ways to place yourself in the Presence of God.[137] The foundation for these "four ways" is the General Presence of God in the world. These four ways are:

(a) Since God is universally Present and there is nowhere in the world devoid of His Presence, look for signs of His Presence in your own life and determine to meet that Presence wherever you go;

(b) For the believer, call to mind that God is not only in the place where you are, but most particularly present in your heart and mind which He lights up with His Presence.

(c) Fix your mind on the thought that Jesus in His ascended humanity looks down from heaven on all mankind, but particularly on those who seek Him. He watches over us from heaven even though we may not be aware of it;

(d) Use your imagination to imagine that Jesus in his humanity is always with you as a friend in your life. Talk to him and converse with him as you would a friend.

De Sales suggests that you use one or other of these to place yourself in the Presence of God before you pray. Use one at a time and not all at once. Use them briefly and simply and you will find that your awareness of the Presence of God will grow.

136 *An Introduction to the Devout Life* by Francis de Sales, TAN books, Charlotte, North Carolina, 2013.

137 As described in the article: *How to place yourself in the presence of God according to Francis de Sales* by Philip Kosloski, June 4, 2018, on the website Aleteia (aleteia.org), accessed May 10, 2019.

THE SUSTAINING PRESENCE OF GOD IN THE WORLD

The second dimension of the Presence of God is the Sustaining Presence of the Lord. Not only is God always present, but He is also active in sustaining and holding creation together. Not only did God create the universe and all in it, He remains actively participating in nature and continues to help keep it running.

Both Hebrews and Colossians link God's sustaining Presence with His creation of the world:

> *. . . but in these last days he has spoken to us by his Son, whom he appointed heir of all things, and through whom also he made the universe. The Son is the radiance of God's glory and the exact representation of his being, sustaining all things by his powerful word.* (Heb. 1:2-3)

> *The Son is the image of the invisible God, the firstborn of all creation. For in him all things were created: things in heaven and on the earth, visible and invisible, whether thrones or powers or rulers or authorities; all things have been created through him and for him. He is before all things, and in him all things hold together.* (Col. 1:15-17)

In both passages we see that Jesus was the creator of all things and immediately, in the next verse, that Jesus is "sustaining all things" or that "in him all things hold together". Since He is Lord of all and the creator, He has the unique ability, knowledge and power to sustain what He has created. He is the glue that holds all things together. Every atom of creation, every atom of our being is touched by the sustaining Presence of the Lord.

There are at least three reasons why God sustains His creation. First, since He is Lord of all, He is the only one capable of sustaining creation.[138]

138 The divinity and Lordship of the creator is emphasized where his sustaining activity is mentioned.

Second, creation was formed for God,[139] and so He has a desire to continue His involvement in creation so that He can continue to enjoy it. Third, God loves what He has created[140] and remains active in His creation because of this love. God in His nature cannot abandon what He has created, especially when He delights so much in it. The sustaining Presence of the Lord means that He is always lifting up, nurturing, caring for, undergirding, and even healing His creation.

Sin destroys and disintegrates.[141] Broken relationships, sinful actions, murder, disease, sickness, all of these came into the world when Adam and Eve sinned. Sin blocks the full expression of the Presence of the Lord. Without God's sustaining Presence there would be a lot more cancer, a lot more tumours, a lot more sickness, a lot more murder, etc. The question is not why we get sick at all, it is why we are not sicker than we are. We have as much health as we have due to the blessing of the sustaining Presence of the Lord. We are more blessed than we know.

What this means for us is that God is far more present and active in our lives than we know or are aware of. He is always active sustaining and caring for His creation, which includes you and I!

This sustaining love of the Lord is not partisan. God sustains all of creation. He sustains and cares for both believers and non-believers. He loves everyone. As Jesus says in Matthew 5:45: ". . . *He causes his sun to rise on the evil and the good and sends rain on the righteous and the unrighteous.*" No matter who you are, you will experience God's loving provision and care. You may not know it or acknowledge it, but God's sustaining care is nevertheless active in your life. This means also that God is active in the lives of non-believers more than they or we realize. Yet, when we choose to accept the reality of His sustaining Presence, we have a greater ability to see and even benefit from it.

---

139 Hebrews 2:10: " . . .*it was fitting that God, for whom and through whom everything exists . . .*"

140 Genesis 1 – repeatedly calls creation "good" and "very good".

141 Romans 6:23. Death involves the release of chaos and disintegration into those places touched by sin.

Psalm 139:10 talks about how even in the remotest part of creation, the hand of the Lord still guides and "holds us fast". The Sustaining Presence of the Lord includes His guidance and protection for those who love him. He is not only present in His creation, His care is available and imminent to His creation, particularly to those who choose to accept His care and protection

We need to learn to look for the activity of the Lord in the undergrowth of our lives. In order to see this, we must nurture thankfulness and gratefulness. We need to look for how God is sustaining and nurturing us, rather than for how we think He has not sustained us or what we think He has not done. He is more active in our lives than we think He is.

Passages such as 2 Thessalonians 2:6-7 which talk about how God is holding back the "lawless one" or antichrist until the right time suggests that part of God's sustaining presence involves restraining evil. We do not realize how God's sustaining activity in the world changes the presence and activity of evil. The world would be a much darker place without God's sustaining Presence. People often ask how God can be loving if there is so much evil in this world. This is actually the wrong question. The more correct question is why is there so little evil in the world, or, why does evil not dominate even more than it does? Humans are clearly capable of great evil! The answer is that God, in His sustaining love, is preventing the evil released into the world by the rebellious sin of Adam and Eve, from having its full effect. And part of the reason there is as much evil in the world as there is, is that the children of God have not pursued His Presence as they should and have not released His love more to those around them. God's love active in and through His people is one of the ways God restrains the manifestation of evil. Christians are to be "salt" and "light" in the world.[142] When we disobey God, we prevent His goodness from being manifested and fail to keep the "rot" of society and the "darkness" in it at bay.

---

142 Matthew 5:13-16.

THE SUSTAINING PRESENCE OF COMMUNITY

God is a relational God who created us in His image as relational beings. What this means is that God often chooses to use supportive human relationships to sustain and nurture those He loves. One of the manifestations of the Sustaining Presence of the Lord is healthy community relationships where real care happens. God created us as relational beings who need to be sustained emotionally, as well as psychologically, and since He uses the obedience of His people to accomplish His will, He will use humans to express His sustaining love for others and for creation. In contrast to this, evil is often released by humans who are unable to love because they have not themselves experienced authentic love. God uses healthy community relationships to nurture and sustain healthy societies. Loving others is part of how we are "salt" and "light" in the world.

SUSTAINING BY HIS POWERFUL WORD

Hebrews one verse three indicates that Jesus sustains all things *"by his powerful word."* Just as God created our world through what He spoke, He continues to sustain that world through the words He continues to speak. In particular, He sustains creation through the Word He speaks through and by His Son. Jesus is the Word made flesh[143] sent into the world to accomplish the will of God.[144] This suggests that part of how God sustains the world today is when Jesus speaks again through His Church. This is part of how the Church is "salt" and "light" in the world. The sustaining Presence of God spills out from the Church to impact, strengthen and care for the world as the Church is faithful to God's love for creation. In the garden of Eden, Adam was set apart and called by God to be a steward of creation.[145] That task for Christians is renewed as we are set free from sin so that we can love as Christ loved and "be" his visible representatives on the earth. Part of how God sustains the world is through the obedi-

143 John 1.

144 Isaiah 55:11.

145 Genesis 2:15.

ence of His people who care for and sustain and nurture the world God created and loves. This is why "*. . . the creation waits in eager expectation for the children of God to be revealed. For the creation was subjected to frustration . . . that the creation itself will be liberated from its bondage to decay and brought into the freedom and glory of the children of God.*" (Rom. 8:19-21). Creation itself is set free from its "bondage to decay" as the children of God come into their inheritance and the sustaining and loving Presence of God is released to the world through them.

GOD LOVES BOTH CHRISTIANS AND NON-CHRISTIANS

The omnipresence of the Lord and His sustaining Presence in the world also means that His call to both non-believers and believers is always there. He so loves us that He will never leave us alone and His love is always calling us to Himself. God knows that we need Him more than we know this. The question is always: will we listen for the voice of the Lord in our life? Will we be open to hearing His call to us? Will we slow down enough to hear His call? Just because we do not take the time to really listen for the Lord does not mean that He is not calling to us. People can often think God does not exist because they do not take the time to truly listen for His voice in their lives, yet it is there.

The omnipresence of the Lord and His sustaining Presence in the world means that there is no excuse for those that refuse to listen to His call to them. God loves us enough to call us into His life. He also loves us enough to not force Himself upon us.

Non-Christians do not realize how active God already is in their lives, loving them and calling them into His goodness. They do not realize how terrible their world would be if the living God was totally absent from their lives.

I have heard people railing at the idea that a loving God can judge people to hell, but they do not realize that part of the judgement of God is merely releasing us into the fruit of our choices with respect to the Presence of God. As mentioned in the introduction, when we reject God, hell is simply entering into the absence of His Presence which we have never experienced before. All that makes life pleasant and wonderful is taken from us as we enter into the fruit of our rejection of God. In Him we have life (John 17:3, 20:31), we do not have it apart from Him. That is how He designed us and formed us: to thrive in His Presence. Apart from His Presence is only the agony of death and unceasing torment. Separation from Him is simply the complete separation of our lives from all that is good.

Heaven is entering into the fullness of the Presence of the Lord that we only taste in part on the earth. He is totally and completely all we need. He is life itself and being with Him in Heaven is to experience the fullness of His life for all eternity. This is why the gift of God to us through Jesus Christ is called "eternal life."

Summary

Through both the General Presence of God in the world and the Sustaining Presence of God in the world, God makes Himself available to the seeking heart, whether this is the believer or non-believer. He loves His creation and immerses Himself in loving and sustaining it. He is always close, closer than we realize. Yet we need to turn our hearts and ears to listen to His voice in order to hear Him. It is not always easy to hear the God who speaks.

In summary:

1. The omnipresence of God in the world means that there is nowhere we can go where God's love is not. God is near to us every moment of every day.
2. Faith or belief opens us up to see the reality of the Presence of the Lord all around us. Unbelief and sin blind us to seeing the reality of His Presence.
3. An implication of this is that, since God is always present to us, His Presence makes every moment sacred. There is no such thing as a division of the world into secular and sacred spheres. All of life is sacred since all of life can be the arena in which He encounters us.

4. God is both creator and the sustainer of His creation. He is active today in loving and bringing His life-giving Presence to all parts of His creation.

5. God is more active in our lives than we know. He is doing more than we see.

6. God's sustaining love is non-partisan and is available to both Christian and non-Christian. His love is always available to us and is already at work in our lives even though we may never see it or acknowledge it.

7. The sustaining Presence of God restrains the full effects of evil from being felt in the world. The world would be a much darker place, a much more evil-filled place, without the active, sustaining Presence of the Lord.

8. God uses healthy community relationships to sustain us and His creation.

9. One way God sustains the world when we express God's love for the creation and act as good stewards of it.

10. Part of what the sustaining Presence of the Lord means is that God is always calling to us to come into His goodness, yet many people think He does not exist because they do not take the time to listen for His voice.

11. Hell is the agony of the total absence of the Presence of God, something we have never experienced before our physical death. Heaven is entering into the fullness of the blessing of the Presence of the Lord, also something we have never fully experienced before our physical death.

Entering Into His Presence

Put on some worship music and tune in your heart and mind to the Presence of the Lord around you. Ask the Lord to show Himself to you. Ask Him to touch your eyes to really see spiritually what He is doing in the lives of you and your family. Thank God for His Presence with you. Ask forgiveness for not being more open to His Presence. Ask God to show you specific things that might be blocking your ability to see His Presence. Apply Francis de Sales' four ways to become aware of the Presence of God around you.

As you go through your week, take time to pause and turn your heart and mind towards the Lord. He is with you always. Try to live in His Presence moment by moment. Imagine the Presence of Jesus with you. Talk to him as you would a friend.

Take time to thank the Lord for how He sustains you and your family. Ask Him to show you how He has been sustaining you. Be open to the wonder of what God has been doing for you that you never knew about.

Take the time to quiet your heart to listen to the voice of the Lord. He is calling to you right now. What is He saying to you? Do you sense His love for you? He created you to thrive in His Presence and He has more for you than you realize.

Tell the Lord you want to be filled up with His Presence here on the earth so that you are ready to enjoy His Presence for all eternity in heaven.

Prayer

Thank You, Lord, for Your Presence all around me. I ask that You would open my eyes to see Your Presence. Show me where You are in the undergrowth of my life. I need to see You. I want to see You.

Thank You, Lord, for Your love for me. Help me to see all of the little things You do that I am not aware of. Forgive me for thinking You do not love me and that You are not loving me right now at this moment. I choose to accept that You are near to me right now.

Thank You, Lord, for Your sustaining love for me and my family. Thank You for the health I have and for Your constant provision in my life. Help me to see what You are doing for my family and me right now. Thank You for protecting me from evil. Empower me to be obedient so that I do not make myself vulnerable to evil. I want "Yes, Lord" to be the expression of my life.

Help me, Lord, to show Your love to those around me. They need Your love as much as I do, and I want to show them Your love.

In the precious name of Jesus I pray,

Amen.

7

The Presence of The Lord In The Word of God.

"All Scripture is God-breathed and is useful for teaching, rebuking, correcting and training in righteousness." (2 Tim. 3:16)

"For the word of God is alive and active. Sharper than any double-edged sword, it penetrates even to dividing soul and spirit, joints and marrow; it judges the thoughts and intentions of the heart." (Heb. 4:12)

"...so is my word that goes out of my mouth: it will not return to me empty, but will accomplish what I desire and achieve the purpose for which I sent it." (Isa. 55:11)

The Word of God is sent forth by God into the world to accomplish His will. It does this by carrying the living and active Presence of God at various levels in the "words" that are "spoken" or "sent out" by God. There are at least three components to the Presence of God in His Word: The

Presence of God in His Spoken Word[146], in His Written Word[147] and in Jesus as the Word of God made flesh.[148] We will start with the Presence of God in His Spoken Word because this brings a background for correctly understanding the power of the Presence of God in His written Word – the Scriptures. We will finish with looking at Jesus as the Word of God made Flesh.

THE SPOKEN WORD HAS INHERENT POWER:

God has so structured reality that words have creative power. The power of the declared word is directly proportional to how well the words spoken reflect the will of the living God who alone has all power. This is supremely seen in Genesis 1 where God speaks and the universe and all living things erupt into existence at the power of God's spoken word.

> *'And God said, "Let there be light," and there was light. ...' (Gen. 1:3)*

> *'And God said, "Let there be a vault between the waters to separate water from water." So God made the vault and separated the water under the vault from the water above it. And it was so.' (Gen 1:6-7)*

> *'And God said, "Let the water under the sky be gathered to one place, and let dry ground appear." And it was so.' (Gen 1:9)*

> *'Then God said, "Let the land produce vegetation: seed-bearing plants and trees on the land that bear fruit with seed in it, according to their various kinds." And it was so' (Gen 1:11)*

> *'And God said, "Let there be lights in the vault of the sky to separate the day from the night ...". And it was so.' (Gen. 1:14-15)*

146 See Genesis 1.

147 Hebrews 4:12: This may be either the spoken or written word of God; 2 Timothy 3:16-17: This is the written word of God; and, Isaiah 55:10-11: This can apply to all three of these- the prophetic word, the written word and Jesus Himself.

148 John 1:1-5, 14. Jesus is the Word of God made flesh to accomplish the will of God on the earth.

'And God said, "Let the water teem with living creatures and let birds fly above the earth across the vault of the sky." So God created the great creatures of the sea and every living thing with which the water teams...' (Gen 1:20-21)

'And God said, "Let the land produce living creatures according to their kinds, ... ". And it was so.' (Gen 1:24)

'And God said, "Let us make mankind in our image..." And so God created mankind in his own image...' (Gen 1:26-27)

Just pause a minute and reflect on how much power was released by God when He spoke into the dark, formless, empty void of the universe (Gen. 1:2). Wow! God speaks and moons and stars are formed. God speaks - seas and oceans are formed. Dry lands, plants, trees, sea creatures, birds, land animals, and, finally, mankind appears, almost all of it with the power of God's voice. If God's voice alone can form and shape the cosmos, what else can He do?

If we look at principles that come out of the creation story, we can see that words that God speak have power, power to form and destroy. People argue that God is not like us, surely His voice carries more power than ours? True - He is after all God, yet creation bears the stamp of its creator. As Proverbs 18:21 indicates: *"Death and life are in the power of the tongue (NASB)."*[149] Words do have power both to invite people to live or to die. There is a grade school jingle I always hated: "Sticks and stones may break my bones but words can never hurt me." I, as is true for many, have felt the hurt that words cause. The truth is more like: "Sticks and stones may break my bones, but words can shape my destiny." We need to recognize the power of the tongue and use it responsibly to call forth God's best for those around us.

We intuitively know the power of the spoken word. In a courtroom context, words may produce conviction or innocence. I remember when my wife and I adopted our youngest child from Russia, we had to make

149 See also passages like Jeremiah 5:14: *"I will make my words in your mouth a fire. . ."*

a court room appearance before a judge. She heard from the various representatives the case for adoption and whether it was the court's opinion that we would make good parents for David. Finally, the judge slammed down her gavel and pronounced that the adoption was granted. With those words we were now the excited parents of a new child. Backed up by the power of the state, the judge's words had real power.

We also know the power of words such as "I do" to unite a man and a woman together in marriage. In some cultures, simply saying the words "I divorce you" to your wife three times is enough to produce a divorce.[150]

Yet the power in words is more than just the idea that certain words trigger the power of the state. This is where the power of the testimony, of the prophetic, of prayer and even the power of preaching comes in.

THE POWER OF TESTIMONIES OF WHAT GOD HAS DONE

I mentioned earlier how a few years ago, I traveled to Guinea Bissau to join my friend who did evangelism characterized by "signs and wonders" as I was eager to grow in this area. I was excited at the chance that my son might be able to see God do some great things during our time there. At one point we were on a small island off the coast of Guinea Bissau doing evangelism with praying for the sick. One night, there were about 30 people that responded to the message with the same number wanting prayer for healing. In the dark by the light of a headlamp, my friend with my son ended up praying with a man who had problems walking and who could not walk at all without the help of a stick he used as a cane. After praying for a while, my friend encouraged the man to try to walk without the cane to see if God had touched him. He protested, "No, No! You do not understand! I cannot walk without this cane!" My friend kept asking him to try walking without it: after all, they had asked God to heal him and he wanted to find out if God had done something in response to their prayers. Finally, the man turned and walked into the darkness with

150 This is one of the practices found within Islam.

the cane, then came walking back into the pool of light without using the cane. He gave the cane to the translator who gave it to my son saying, "I do not need this anymore!" He had been completely healed!

Fast-forward a few months. I was preaching out of John 5 in a church in the city where we lived and was making the point that often God asks us to do impossible things but when we step out in obedience, the power of God honours that obedience and brings the miracle. After making this point, I gave the example of the above story as a modern-day testimony of God healing someone illustrating what I had said. I finished up the sermon and prayed for a release of the Spirit to bring healing. As the service was coming to an end, I noticed an older man walking up the left side of the sanctuary and by the time he got to the front he was waving his arms in the air and smiling. I turned to the pastor and asked what the man was doing. The pastor said, "I don't know." The man asked for a microphone and explained, "When I came to church today, I could not walk without a cane. Then when pastor Bowler told this story of the man who was healed in Guinea Bissau, I felt God tell me that this story was for me. Faith rose up in my heart. I decided to get up and try to walk just like the man in the story. I started to walk without my cane and look I can walk!" He walked back and forth and even did a little jump. A young man ran up and grabbed the microphone, "I just want to tell you that this man is telling the truth. I am his son and he has not been able to walk without his cane for a while now. I tell you - he could not walk without his cane this morning. Look: he is walking!" Everybody cheered. Not a single person had prayed with him. Yet as he heard the story of what God had done a few months before, faith rose up in his heart that God would do the same thing again for him. As he acted in obedience to the voice of God, he was healed. Several weeks later I saw the pastor from that church and asked after the man who was healed. He told me: "He still does not need a cane!"

Psalm 107:20 is an intriguing verse that says God ". . . *sent out his word and healed them; . . .*" While you can make the case that the "word" that is "sent out" by God to bring healing is either Jesus or the preached word, the context suggests that the "word" that is sent out is the testimony of what God has done among His people. Psalm 107:1-2 begins: *"Give thanks to the Lord, for he is good; his love endures forever. Let the redeemed of the Lord tell their story . . ."* (NIV) Then several times the Psalmist instructs the people to tell of the unfailing love of God and of the wonderful deeds he has done for mankind (vs. 8, 15, 21,[151] 31) and ends the Psalm with the admonition to *"ponder the loving deeds of the Lord"* (vs. 43). This suggests that the word that is "sent out" to bring healing is the testimony of how God has demonstrated His love through what He has done amongst His people. The linkage of testimony with faith in the goodness of God empowers the "word" of the testimony to bring healing through releasing His Presence.

A declaration of what God had done in the past creates the opportunity for God to do the same thing again in the present. In a sense the testimony opens a door for faith to walk through and encounter a miracle. If God is truly the same yesterday, today and forever[152] then what He has done in the past is what we can experience from Him in the present as well as in the future. This is part of the power of the testimony: it creates the opportunity for us to experience what others have experienced from God. Part of the power of the testimony is also that it is a declaration to the congregation that reflects God's will and thus comes with particular force. It also links us in our specific setting to what our God has done and is doing elsewhere. Testimonies come with an invitation to enter into them and make them our own, yet few Christians seem to fully understand the power of recalling for others the wonders of what God is doing in the world today. It releases the Presence of God through testimony. It lifts and builds our faith.

I have found that some pastors do not understand the power of bearing witness to what God is doing in a particular service. There are at least four advantages to giving a testimony of what God is doing in the congregation: Testimonies invite others to experience what God is already

151 Notice that verse 20 is just before one of these summary statements.

152 Hebrews 13:8.

doing in their midst; they build faith that God is working in that place; they honour God for what He is doing in the congregation; and they give the congregation an opportunity to give thanks to God.

Just to illustrate the power of the spoken word of a testimony, contrast the following two stories. We were in one church in Canada where there were a number of people healed including a woman who had broken her neck 15 years before in a workplace accident where two vertebrae were crushed. Since then, she had been on disability and in pain every day, unable to turn her neck either to the left, or right and unable to lift her head to look at the ceiling. She came running up to me after the service thanking me for "giving me my life back." She told me the story and shared how she now had zero pain and could freely move her neck all around and look at the ceiling. Also healed at this meeting was a man who had a right knee problem. There were a total of about ten people healed. The pastor was not present, but I emailed him to share what God had done and encouraged him to get people to share what God had done so that faith could be built in the church community. He did not do this and months later people from his church[153] who heard me tell these stories told me they wished God did that kind of stuff in their church! I believe God could have done more of the same if the pastor had shared the testimonies of what God had done. Testimonies encourage the continued activity of God in our midst and nurture the expectation for more.

The second story is from another church a few months later, also in Canada. I had a word of knowledge about God wanting to heal necks. I gave the word but before praying for anyone with this neck condition, my wife told the people in the church that we had increasingly seen people healed during the message (more on this later) without getting prayer and so asked if there was anyone there who had already been healed. We told them to try out their bodies and check to see if God had touched them. One man put up his hand and said he had come into the service

153 By failing to share these stories, the pastor failed to build a communal faith in the congregation that would have created a faith-context where God could have done more.

with a painful neck problem but realized that now he was pain free. Then another man put up his hand and said that when I had said the word of knowledge about God wanting to heal neck problems, he felt an instant release in his neck and was healed. Then a third person put up their hand and said that when she heard the testimony of the second person being healed, her neck was healed as he was giving his testimony! My wife said that God was obviously healing necks so we should pray for any other neck problems. As we checked with the congregation, there were no other neck conditions in need of healing. God had healed all of the neck "issues" sovereignly through the power of a word of testimony without anyone praying for them! When we do not share testimonies, we limit people from experiencing all of what God has for them. People do not need prayer to experience a miracle, they need the Presence of God and testimonies can release people into a faith that produces an encounter with God.

THE POWER OF A TRUE PROPHETIC WORD FROM GOD

In the Old Testament, God spoke and the prophets wrote down His words, calling people into dynamic obedience to the voice of God. A prophetic word of God can change our understanding of and relation to reality and of what God has for us. Like the testimony in the present life of the church, a "prophetic word" invites a response. While the testimony uses the power of the spoken word to invite participation in what God is doing in the world today, the prophetic word uses it to invite a faith response towards pursuing the calling of God on your life. To put it another way, when people are struggling to clearly hear God's calling for them, a prophetic word from God uses the power of the spoken word to invite them to enter their destiny in God. It links the power of the Presence of the Lord to confer identity with the power of the spoken word. This shows also that a "good" prophetic word is birthed in the Presence of God. Again, when the spoken word is in line with the will of God, it arrives with particular force. A "bad" prophetic word is not characterized by God's character and is not birthed in His Presence.

Perhaps an example of a "good" prophetic word might be helpful. After finishing graduate school, I was looking for the church God wanted me to get involved with and had been visiting several, praying for Him to show me the right one. The first Sunday I was at a particular church, the pastor asked if anyone known to the leadership felt they had a "word" from God to share that had been birthed in their hearts by the Holy Spirit. One of the elders got up and said, "There is someone here for the first time. They have been looking and looking and looking and God says to that person: Stop." It hit me like a ton of bricks. I knew God had spoken and wanted me to get involved with this church for the next little while. My time in that church ending up being transformational for me. Note that the person giving the word was a mature leader who had a vibrant relationship with God.

At times our ability to hear the voice of the Lord to us is hindered by our wounded hearts. In my own life, I had very godly parents who gave their lives to missionary service. At one point my father was planting a church every 10 days for a period of 5 years. This meant he was often gone from the home for extended periods of time. My mother would get frustrated with us boys and promise that dad would give us our spankings when he returned. This meant that I often both eagerly anticipated and dreaded my father's return from his trips. I remembered at one point hearing my dad's car arrive after dark, and then dreading the sound of his steps in the hall as he came towards my room to give me my well-deserved spanking. Not surprisingly, I developed "father" issues. It was only after receiving some healing to my heart that I could start to embrace my own calling to be a missionary. I sometimes wonder if Satan uses our wounds to keep us from our calling in God. Wounded hearts keep us from hearing what God is calling us to and so we need brothers and sisters to love us into our destiny. What the "prophetic word" can do is put into the power of words what people cannot hear for themselves for various reasons.

THE POWER OF PRAYER

God has conferred upon us the dignity of being causes. When we pray, especially when what is prayed is linked to the will of God, the world around us is changed and impacted by our prayers. The Bible says that if two *"agree about anything they may ask, it shall be done for them by my Father who is in heaven"* (Matt. 18:19). Part of the reason for this is because God Himself is present[154] with us (Matt. 18:20) and so as we gather together, submitting and aligning ourselves to the loving Presence of God, a unity develops between us and God so that God's will is accomplished when we pray in His name. Prayer activates spiritual realities as God's children pray according to the will of the Father. God can easily act without reference to what people pray but chooses not to do so. Prayer is part of how God's will is accomplished on the Earth. God acts through partnerships with us as we pray even as He does with our obedience. Prayer catalyzes or empowers the activity of God in the spiritual realm to accomplish His will. The context of prayer is the loving relationship between our heavenly Father and His children. In the flow of intimacy, God listens to His well-loved children and at times allows them to influence what He does on the earth.[155] Then He empowers His will to be accomplished as His children are obedient. For example, we see in Exodus 3 that God heard the prayers of His people (3:7), acted in response to those prayers (3:8) to come down to speak to Moses (3:4, 7-10) and then sent him to bring deliverance to them (3:10). Prayer is always more powerful than we think. It activates spiritual forces on our behalf to accomplish God's will.

An example of the power of prayer from my own life is a story about the day my father was almost killed when I was only one year old.[156] If my

154 This also relates to the Presence of God in the Corporate Gathering of the Church developed later in chapters 9 and 10.

155 See Exodus 33:1-3, 14-17 where Moses intercedes for the people and seems to "change" God's intentions, i.e. Moses influenced God.

156 This story is told in more detail in my father's book: *Arnold Bowler. I Sat Where They Sat.* Castle Quay Books. Pickering, Ontario, Canada. 2011.

father had died that day, I would not have a younger sister. The life of my younger sister is a testimony to the goodness of the Lord and of the power of prayer. One day in Kenya, a person came to the door of our house requesting help as two groups of bandits were waging what amounted to a turf war not far from our house. This was in the older days when firearms were less accessible and the two groups were attacking each other with machetes, bows and arrows and spears. The man at the door asked my father to go to the police to get help as he was afraid many people would get killed. He came to my father as he had one of the few cars in the area. My mother had our car so my father told the man that he would go at 4:00 pm when my mother returned from shopping. When my mother was late, my father went to a neighbor, borrowed his VW beetle, and headed for the police station. However, as my father turned a corner on the dirt road, he drove right into the middle of the battle! He stepped on the accelerator and zoomed down the road through the middle of the opposing sides. Just as he got to the center of the field, a man ran up to the car and hurled a spear viciously at his head. My father ducked and heard a clunk but didn't know what had happened. At the police station, he was shocked to see there was a five-foot spear embedded in the thin metal of the door frame on the driver's side. The man had missed my father's head by about an inch and miraculously had not smashed the window or anything else.

Six weeks later, my parents got a note from Canada asking what had happened on a certain date at about 8:00 am since my grandfather had suddenly felt a burden to pray for my father. He knelt down right where he was at work and interceded for him and then went to find another man from their church and the two of them prayed. The burden lifted after about 20 minutes. As they calculated the time change, 8:00 am in Canada was 4:00 pm in Kenya. The time they were praying was the exact time the man was throwing the spear at my father. What would have happened if they had not prayed? My father would likely have died and my sister would never have been born. Prayer in Canada catalyzed spiritual realties to protect my father in Kenya. Our prayers are more powerful than we think.

Paul emphasizes this point when he prays and writes about prayer. For example, in 2 Corinthians 1:10-11, Paul says *"(v.10) . . . he (God) will continue to deliver us (v.11) as you help us by your prayers. Then many will give thanks on our behalf for the gracious favour granted us in answer to the prayers of many."* The people of God are linked to Paul through prayer as they pray for him. We see here that Paul receives favour and is delivered from death by the prayers of the people of God. Since the world is primarily spiritual in nature, when spiritual realities are marshalled and released through prayer, real situations in the physical world are changed. Prayer is not just a bunch of wishful words, but links together the Presence of God with the power of words so that the will of God can be declared and accomplished. If we do not pray, the will of God is hampered from being expressed. What would have happened if people did not pray for my father? Or, if people had not prayed for Paul?

THE PRESENCE OF GOD IN THE WORD OF GOD

God's Word is the revelation of the nature and character of God and records for our benefit the key actions of God in history. God's intent was that people He inspired[157] write down His words and deeds for the benefit of subsequent generations. It is not history, it is revelation, yet because the God it describes is personally involved in the world, it reflects history

157 The normal sense of the verb "to inspire" involves the creative flow of authors and artists as they try to express some aspect of life or beauty. This is not the way in which this term is applied to the Biblical documents. God "inspired" his Word by the movement of the Holy Spirit on the minds and hearts of people who submitted to his leadership. God authored the Scriptures but used the "voice" and personalities of those he worked with. God "breathing" on them implies a greater sense of God's activity in the writing process than just them creatively expressing "god thoughts". The Bible is distinctly different than other types of literature and must be interpreted and understood differently. It cannot be understood or interpreted objectively since it was never written that way. It was written from a faith perspective intended to inspire faith and lead to a deeper relationship with and submission to the God who is its principle character. If your intention is not to submit to the God of the Bible, you will never understand it correctly.

and is linked to it.[158] Because of the purpose of God in giving us the Bible, it has particular power to reveal the nature of God and call people into relationship with Him. What we see in the Scriptures is the power of words joined to the Presence of God Himself. The Word of God is pregnant with the Presence of God.

A key scripture is 2 Timothy 3:16 which says, *"All Scripture is God-breathed and is useful for teaching, rebuking, correcting and training in righteousness."* We see in this passage that the Scriptures are particularly powerful in empowering and facilitating change because they carry the Presence of the Lord in a unique way. The initial implication is that we must read the Biblical text with dependence on the same Spirit with which it was written. Without that dependence we will not correctly understand or apply what we are studying. Yet, there is much more here. The phrasing is similar to when God breathed on Adam in Genesis 2:7 and the breath of God caused Adam to become a living creature. When it says that the Scriptures are "God-breathed" it means that God has placed His Spirit in them causing them to have life. This is why they are useful for "teaching, rebuking, correcting and training in righteousness". The Presence of the Lord in His Word enables it to accomplish what He intends it to accomplish. We are not talking about merely "words", concepts, principles or ideas. There is something much more vital here, something that makes the Scriptures much more effective than any other type of "literature".

When Hebrews 4:12 says: *"For the word of God is alive and active. Sharper than any double-edged sword, it penetrates even to dividing soul and spirit, joints and marrow; it judges the thoughts and intentions of the heart,"* it is not just using metaphors. The Word of God IS really alive and active, made so by the Presence of God. It really does penetrate the thoughts and intentions of our hearts. Part of this is the empowering of the Holy Spirit to facilitate encounter with the living God. When God is present in His Word, all the secrets of our hearts are laid bare and we are

158 In other words, the Bible is an historically valid document, but not an historically complete one.

undone. God's Word even judges us. People who are closed to God and in rebellion to Him can act with violence against the Word of God because of their rebellion to the God whose Presence is in it.[159]

God wrote his Word purposefully and the Presence of the Lord in His Word makes sure it accomplishes what God intends for it. This is what Isaiah 55:11 refers to: "*...so is my word that goes out of my mouth: it will not return to me empty, but will accomplish what I desire and achieve the purpose for which I sent it.*" God sends forth His Word. He breathes it into existence. Then it goes forth, impacting and touching people until it accomplishes God's will. God's Word is rich in His Presence, yet sometimes we struggle to feel the life that is there. When our experience does not reflect the truth, we need to press into the truth until the truth becomes our experience.[160]

Several years ago, I was working full time as a teacher as well as leading a Home group, overseeing our church's Sunday evening training, and teaching one of the courses. I was in the process of getting burnt out. I felt dry and barren. I was still able to teach effectively but in my personal life I felt dead inside. I remember holding my Bible in my hands and crying out to the Lord: "Lord, I need you to bring me life! I know you have so often brought me life through this book, but I cannot feel it right now. I am tired inside. I feel dead inside. The Bible used to be living for me but now it just seems like dry dusty bones." I do not remember if God directed me to Ezekiel 37 or if I just happened to turn there, but what God started to say to me changed my life.

> *The hand of the LORD was on me, and he brought me out by the Spirit of the LORD and set me in the middle of a valley; it was full of dry bones. He led me back and forth among them, and I saw a great many bones on the floor of the valley, bones that were very dry.*

---

159 In our Islamic setting, I once saw a man grab a Bible and tear it up into pieces.

160 Remember that while experience is an important component of knowledge, experience alone is not truth. It has to be exegeted.

He asked me, "Son of man, can these bones live?"

I said, "Sovereign LORD, you alone know."

Then he said to me, "Prophesy to these dry bones and say to them, 'Dry bones, hear the word of the LORD! This is what the sovereign LORD says to these bones: I will make breath enter you, and you will come to life. I will attach tendons to you and make flesh come upon you and cover you with skin; I will put breath in you, and you will come to life. Then you will know that I am the LORD'"

So I prophesied as I was commanded. And as I was prophesying, there was a noise, a rattling sound, and the bones came together, bone to bone. I looked and tendons and flesh appeared on them and skin covered them, but there was no breath in them.

Then he said to me, "Prophesy to the breath; prophesy son of man, and say to it, 'This is what the Sovereign LORD says: Come breath, from the four winds and breath into these slain, that they may live.' So I prophesied as he commanded me, and breath entered them; they came to life and stood on their feet – a vast army." (Ezekiel 37:1-10)

As I read these words, I realized that the Bible had become for me like that valley of dry bones. It had been in the past something living and powerful, a vast army, but not now. I felt like the Lord asked me the question from verse 3, *"Son of man, can these bones live?"* I knew what the answer should be, but I cautiously answered in the words of Ezekiel, *"Lord, you alone know."* Then God said to me from verses 4-5, 9, *"Prophecy to these dry bones! . . . I will make breath enter you and you will come to life. . . . Come breath . . . that they may live."* As God said this to me, I realized that, while I had relied on the Spirit of God, my approach to the Word of God was too intellectual. I was also not living out of His Presence, but out of my own strength. I was "learning" from my study of the Bible, but I was not encountering Him in the process. I realized that I must read the Word of God in order to encounter Him not just learn about Him. I must make my Lord the context of my Bible study. I saw that I must be more intentional in inviting the Holy Spirit into my interactions with the Bible so that the Word He spoke in the past to His people becomes the living Word He speaks to me today. It is the Holy Spirit that connects dry bone to dry bone. It is the Holy Spirit that puts flesh and tendons on the bones. It is the Holy Spirit that puts skin on the whole and it is the Holy Spirit that brings it all to life. The applications, illustrations, testimonies, and stories are all part of how the Holy Spirit puts flesh on the bones and puts skin on it so that people understand and see what Biblical truth is. Yet even the best applications, etc. are nothing unless the Holy Spirit breathes on it all to bring it to life. Again we see a similarity to Genesis 2:7 where God breaths on a lump of clay during the creation of Adam. God is the source of life and He must be our source of life when we come to the Scriptures and theology. Part of this is to interact with the Bible at the level of the heart and emotions and less so at the level of the mind.

It took a while but slowly, step by step, as I allowed the Holy Spirit more room in my study, the dry bones of Scripture came alive again. So, if the Scriptures seem boring or dry to you, "prophesy" to them, invite the Holy Spirit in, that they may live again . . . and look for the applications and testimonies that put flesh on the bones. I found part of the answer was to consciously look for His Presence in the Scriptures. . . and be attentive to His Presence with me as I read;[161] assuming He was eager to show me the depths of His Word[162] and asking Him to show me something new each time I read it. I also found that, in essence, I needed to be on my knees each time I approached His Word. Studying God's Word is about worshipping the God we encounter there. We can lose sight of the fact that we do not control the Scriptures. They are living and active; rich with His Presence and it is His Presence that I long to encounter as I interact with His Word. The power of the Scriptures to instruct, train, teach, transform, and change us is because of God's Presence in it.

161 I.e. I needed to access the General Presence of the Lord with me.

162 Since He wrote the Scriptures and His Presence is in them.

God is calling to each person in the world today, yearning to reveal His amazing love for him or her. Part of God's intent for His Word is that it brings us closer to Him.

Only as we allow the Holy Spirit to breath on His truth will it become the mighty army envisioned by Ezekiel, powerfully able to draw us closer to God and build up truth in our life. As we read and encounter the Word of God, we encounter the regenerative force of His truth.

God is present in His Word, yet we need to cultivate His Presence with us as we read and meditate on it. We need the Spirit of God by which the Scriptures were written to breath on us again as we relate to them so that we understand and apply them correctly. This requires humility, obedience and submission with holiness.

An implication here is that those who do not depend on the Holy Spirit to understand God's Word, and who do not approach it with intent to submit to it, will never understand it. The Word of God is not understood by the intellect, but by the work of the Holy Spirit leading us into God's truth.

Our interactions with the Word of God must be about an encounter with Him. When we encounter God it brings us to something greater than and beyond ourselves. If we do not encounter God in His Word, it will only equip us to reject or refute the truth. It builds an intellectual stronghold that stands against the humility needed to learn and be transformed. It is through encountering God that the integration of truth into our lives will be facilitated since He IS the greater truth we need to come to terms with. This is where the tacit dimension of knowledge comes in. As we encounter Truth, we have the renewed ability to perceive and understand it.

THE POWER OF THE WORD OF GOD IN PREACHING

Transformational preaching comes from linking together the power of the Presence of God in His Word with the power of words well chosen. In particular, the power of the Presence of the Lord in the Word of God can be seen when it is preached or taught in a way that reveals the Lord. It brings us face-to-face with God, and through encounter it produces transformation. Preaching is about more than a nice homily. It is about God being released to love on His people through the medium of the preached Word, and since all of God comes with His Word, anything becomes possible.

If all of God comes with His Word, we should expect the power of God to be released when we preach in such a way that He is clearly seen, and His love manifested. I have heard stories about people like Smith Wigglesworth preaching and people being healed as he preached. If it is not so much about people like Smith Wigglesworth[163] but about God, should we not expect similar things today when we preach and invite people to encounter Him? In our own ministry we have testimonies of more than 20 people healed during the preaching of the Word of God in a one year period. What happens is that faith is stirred up, people see more clearly that God loves them, they reach out to Him and are healed. The creative, healing Presence of God is released in preaching that is faithful to His Word. Healing received is also not just physical healing. God can touch people physically, spiritually, mentally, emotionally and in other ways. It is all about the Presence of the Lord in His Word. If God is truly present in the preached Word, we should expect healing as something that is a normal outcome.

Unfortunately preaching today often touches the minds but not the hearts of people. There are several reasons for this. First, we have reduced it to being a well-crafted homily that is not designed to transform. Preaching is no longer about an encounter with the Living God. In addition, there seems to be little expectation of the power of the Presence of

---

163 It is instructive that Smith Wigglesworth was often late to his meetings because he would stay in his room praying until he felt that God had given him something definite to say, or that he "felt" the anointing. In the same way, in the Azusa Street revival, William Seymour would often sit with a box over his head (a bit eccentric!), praying, until he knew what God wanted him to share. In other words, both of them waited until they had themselves aligned with what God wanted to say before they preached so that God would be powerfully manifested through their preaching.

God being released as preaching occurs. Third, preaching can be ineffective when it is not joined to faithful obedience on the part of the listeners. Hebrews 4:2-3 comments on why the people of Israel fell short and failed to "enter" the Promised Land (the "rest" of God). He says: ". . . *but the message they heard was of no value to them, because they did not share the faith of those who obeyed. Now we who have believed enter that rest* . . ." If we do not hear what is preached with faith and the intention to obey, the message we hear becomes ineffectual and does not empower us to live differently. Related to this, if the preacher does not permit the Word of God to confront, change, challenge, or mold him or her then their message will not do this for their audience. The preaching needs to come out of the preacher's own Word-mediated experience with God. The preacher's relationship with God needs to be dynamic for their preaching to be dynamic. When you have experienced the truth and made yourself obedient to it, you have authority to call others into it. If the preacher has not aligned themselves with God's Word,[164] God will not be speaking what the preacher is speaking and it will lack authority and power. As has been mentioned earlier, when what you say is aligned with what God is saying, it comes with God's Presence. We need to endeavor to make sure that our words are the words God is speaking when we preach for it to have real power. This comes with humility and submission to the Word of God. Also, we often get overly analytical when we approach the Word of God. We dissect the Word of God and forget that when we do so, we are killing what we are examining. Analysis can be helpful but only if it facilitates encounter with God. It is not about data and details, it is about submission to and worship of the living God. Sixth, related to chapter four, preaching can be ineffective when there is a lack of encounter with God or a lack of an application of the material in the passage to the task of loving God and others. We are always meant to "do" something with the Scriptures not just "listen to" them.

---

164 This is part of what it means in 2 Timothy 2:15: *"Do your best to present yourself to God as one approved, a worker who does not need to be ashamed and who correctly handles the word of truth."*

When preaching is aligned with the Word of God it can be extremely powerful. Biblically, we often see proclamation linked with "signs and wonders."[165] In these moments, the Presence of God in the preached Word of God releases the transformative power of God on the audience. We are not just preaching words, but God is speaking through what is preached and actively confirming its truth.

In evangelism, the power of the Word of God comes in the kindling of faith. It is by hearing the preached Word that faith comes to the hearers (Rom. 10:17), their hearts are opened and the Gospel bears fruit. God can empower and bless the preaching of His Word with demonstrations of power,[166] as God calls people to Himself. This is particularly true when we preach Jesus who is the "Word" of God made flesh. Here we join Jesus as THE "Word" with the preached "Word" in alignment with the will of God and the power of the Presence of God is released.

The connection of faith to how the Word of God impacts us is important. In 1 Thessalonians 2:13 Paul says, " . . . *when you received the word of God, which you heard from us, you accepted it not as a human word, but as it actually is, the word of God, which is indeed at work in you who believe.*" This suggests that we need to receive the preached word as a message from God for it to be able to properly work in us. We need to accept its authority. It is not merely something human. Then, as we accept the preached Word for what it truly is, it starts to work its fruit in us. Faith like a catalyst releases the power of the Word of God. We need to wrestle with unbelief and allow the truth to penetrate to the deepest levels of our being until it seizes the core of who we are and then radiates outward to affect all areas of our life. Our faith and belief in the Word of God releases the power of God's Presence in His Word to accomplish the will of God in and through us. Preaching will not have its full effect unless we fully receive it. I was once in a meeting with Gordon Fee, a renowned New Testament scholar, who said that the only proper response to any

---

165 See Romans 15:17-19; Acts 2:43; 14:3; 1 Thessalonians 1:5.

166 Romans 15:17-20; 1 Thessalonians 1:5.

encounter with the Word of God was to be kneeling before the Lord in your heart. We need to allow the power of the Presence of the Lord to be seen again in our preaching and understand that the living God is really speaking to us through it.

Another factor with Paul was that he had a very powerful conviction that what he preached was the word of God and with that conviction came tremendous power. In 2 Corinthians 4:13-14 Paul says, *(v.13)"It is written:" I believed; therefore I have spoken," Since we have that same spirit of faith, we also believe and therefore speak, (v.14) because we know . . .*" Paul spoke out of his faith and conviction. He knew the truth of what he said: he had experienced it. Our belief in the truth of what we say adds power to our words. Our belief also empowers our understanding and reception of the truth. If we do not truly believe what we are preaching, this will rob our preaching of its power. This is not just at the level of a good salesman. In some way, when we believe, truly believe, the power of God is released in what we say to accomplish the will of God through what we say. In other words, His Presence comes through the Word when we preach it with conviction. Part of the power of preaching comes from the faith and conviction you bring to it and how this opens up room for the Holy Spirit to work. In a sense, our faith and conviction allow the Scriptures to become God-breathed again to the audience. Sadly, some preachers today seem to be drifting away from a deep level conviction that the Word of God is truly the Word of God and that it mediates His Presence.

JESUS IS THE ULTIMATE WORD OF GOD SENT FROM HEAVEN FOR US

John in his Gospel purposefully makes a connection to Genesis chapter one: both start with *"In the Beginning."*[167] In Genesis, it is God who exists at the beginning of the world and sends forth His "word" to create

167 Genesis 1:1: *"In the beginning God . . ."*; John 1:1: *"In the Beginning was the Word . . . "*

the world. As God "declares" things, they come into existence. In John, it is the "Word" that exists in the beginning and who is both with God and is God Himself. It is by means of this "Word" that God created everything.[168] Then in John we see that this creative "Word" is again sent forth by God into the world, this time becoming human[169] so that He can in tangible ways reveal to mankind the true nature of the Father.[170] In both it is clear that the "word" is something that is "sent out" from the Father into the world to accomplish the will of God and in fact has power to accomplish that will because of the unity between the "word" that is sent out and the God who sent it.[171]

Jesus is the ultimate "Word" of God sent from heaven to reveal God to us. John 1:1, 14 says that the *"Word was with God and the Word was God. . . The Word became flesh and made his dwelling among us. We have seen his glory, the glory of the one and only Son, who came from the Father, full of grace and truth"*. We see in these verses that Jesus Himself is not just a "word" sent out by God who is anointed to carry the Presence of God but IS Himself God. We also see that this "Word" was sent out or "came from" the Father. This is one reason why Jesus repeatedly emphasizes to the disciples and to others that He has been sent from the Father[172] to the earth with a specific purpose. After he makes it clear that Jesus is this Word sent from heaven, John in 1:18 indicates: *"No one has ever seen God, but the one and only Son who is himself God and is in closest relationship with the Father has made him known."* Later again in John 14:9, Jesus says to Philip: *"Anyone who has seen me has seen the Father. . ."* All of this emphasizes that Jesus is the "Word" sent from the Father to reveal

168 John 1:1.

169 John 1:14: *"The Word became flesh, and made his dwelling among us."*

170 John 1:4-5, 9-14, 18.

171 See also Isaiah 55:11: The word goes forth from the Father and does not return to the Father empty, without accomplishing what God desires and achieving the purpose for which it was sent out.

172 John 5:23, 36, 37; 6:44, 57; 8:16, 18, 42; 10:36; 12:49; 14:24; 17:21, 25; 20:21.

the nature of God to us[173] and to accomplish His will. He is the Truth of God made visible to us. He mediates God's life to us. Just as Jesus reveals God to us, He also reveals to us how the Word of God works. Jesus who is THE Word of God fulfills all that the Word of God does.

In Jesus there is a unity between God and Jesus that is profound. Earlier I mentioned that when you align your words with the will of God and speak out what God wants to say, your words can impact an audience with tremendous power. We see this in Jesus. Several times it is noted that He teaches with unusual authority[174] since He makes sure that He teaches only what the Father would have Him teach.[175] Yet we see in Jesus more than just authority in His teaching, we see a unity between the words of God and the works of God.[176]

In Matthew 4:23 and 9:35 we have summary statements of what Jesus did in his ministry. He went through all the towns of Galilee: ". . *teaching in their synagogues, proclaiming the good news of the kingdom and healing every disease and sickness. . . .*" We often approach passages such as this with our analytical Greek mindset and see these passages as describing three different things that Jesus did as He traveled among the people. Yet, despite being written in Greek, Matthew, Mark and John were all Gospels written by Greek speaking Jews who thought out of a Hebraic mindset.[177] I would suggest that instead of being three separate things Jesus did, what we might be seeing here are three aspects or facets of the same thing.

173 See also the following passages where Jesus does the "works" of the Father and speaks the "words" of the Father: John 5:36; 8:28; 12:49.

174 Matthew 7:29: ". . . *he was teaching them as one having authority, and not as their scribes.*" Mark 1:21-22: ". . . *they were astonished at his teaching, for he taught them as one who had authority, not as their scribes.*" You also see His evident authority in the Sermon on the Mount where He contrasts the teachings of the rabbis with His teachings which are superior (Matthew 5-7) and also in Matthew 22:23-33.

175 See John 8:28; 12:49-50.

176 The implication in John 5 and other passages is that the words of the Father Jesus speaks and the works of the Father that Jesus does are two facets of the same thing and should not be separated.

177 Which is more dynamic and holistic.

We tend to separate what is united in Jesus.[178] When Jesus taught, He proclaimed the Kingdom of God powerfully and God's rule was made manifest by the miracles that accompanied that proclamation.[179] In other words, when the preacher, here Jesus, is united in His message with what the Father is revealing, it comes with unusual power since God Himself is present in His preached Word. This is evidenced by the miracles that arrive in the context of that preaching. God backs up His word being preached with signs that authenticate that word. In the case of Jesus, since His unity with the Father is profound[180] when the word goes forth from Him, miracles broke forth as He preached. The result of His preaching is an expansion of the works of God as many rush to bring the sick and hurting to Him so that they can be healed by the Presence of God through Jesus.[181] The truth He proclaims arrives with the power to heal.

When the Word of God who IS God comes from the Father to speak the words of God, His words have tremendous power and authority. In John 5:24, the one who *hears*[182] the words of Jesus and believes them has *"eternal life and . . . has crossed over from death to life."*[183] In John 11, Lazarus who was dead for four days is raised to life by a word from Jesus. Then we have passages such as Hebrews 1:3 where Jesus sustains creation by "His powerful word." This encourages all of us preachers that our words need to always be in alignment as Jesus was with what God wants to speak. As we do this, the message we preach will not just be words but will arrive with power, with the Holy Spirit and with deep conviction,[184]

178 This was mentioned in chapter 4. See the section, "By dissecting we destroy what we are studying."

179 This is why when Jesus sends out his disciples he sends them out to proclaim the kingdom of God and to heal (Matthew 10:1. 7-8; Luke 10:9).

180 John 10:30; 17:11, 21.

181 Matthew 4:24, 9:36; 8:16. See also Romans 15:19 where Paul proclaims the Gospel with signs and wonders accompanying the preaching.

182 I.e. fully receives what they are hearing.

183 This is like 1 Peter 1:23: *"For you have been born again . . . of imperishable (seed) through the living and enduring word of God."*

184 1 Thessalonians 1:5.

so that *"no word from God will ever fail"*[185] to accomplish what God wants it to accomplish.

The question becomes: "Are we receiving Jesus as the Word of God?" Jesus talks of this in John 6 where He calls Himself the true bread of life[186] descended from heaven and compares Himself to the manna in the desert. He is the Word sent from heaven to accomplish the will of God through belief and trust and the reception of Him as the Truth. Are we acting in our daily lives as if Jesus is the "bread" we cannot live without? Is He truly the source of our life? He IS what gives us life, but this truth needs to be received in order to become our reality.

THE WORD OF GOD AS A "SWORD"

It is important to understand that the Word of God is a powerful weapon in spiritual warfare. There are two reasons for this. First, the Word of God is Truth and truth is always an effective weapon against lies, deception and manipulation (which are key weapons Satan uses in spiritual warfare). Second, since the Word of God is "God-breathed", the Spirit of God animates and renders this truth particularly effective. As mentioned earlier, Hebrews 4:12 indicates that the Word of God is like a sword that cuts, penetrates and divides the interior dimensions of soul and spirit, judging even our thoughts and our heart attitudes. It is no surprise that Paul, when discussing how we need to put on the full armor of God in our battle against spiritual forces and principalities, says we must put on the "sword of the Spirit which is the Word of God."[187] Here the sword of the Word of God is one of the few offensive weapons mentioned by Paul in the passage. In the temptation narrative of Matthew 4:1-11, Jesus recognizes this and uses the Word of God to defend Himself against and resist the manipulations of truth embedded in Satan's temptations.

185 Luke 1:37. See also Psalm 107:20: "He sent his word and healed them." God's word is powerful.

186 John 6:32, 33, 38, 48.

187 Ephesians 6:17.

In the end Jesus' spiritual warfare strategy is successful and chases Satan away to try again later.

There are several passages in the Bible that describe the Word of God in various forms as a "sword."[188] Many of these are closely linked to Jesus. In a passage fulfilled by Jesus, Isaiah 49:2 says: *"He made my mouth like a sharpened sword . . ."* The obedience of Jesus with the anointing on His life empowered His speech as a sword to accomplish the will of God. He spoke with authority, often healing and bringing deliverance by His spoken word alone.[189] The ascended Jesus in Revelations 1:16 as well as Revelations 19:15, 21 is described as having a "sharp double-edged sword" coming out of His mouth. When Jesus speaks, it cuts. As the Word of God made flesh, He fulfills Hebrews 4:12. The Revelations 19 passage is particularly pertinent since it is as the "Word of God" (19:13) that Jesus goes out from heaven to wage war on the enemies of God with a sharp sword coming out of His mouth (19:15), and it is this sword that kills the enemies of God (19:21). Similarly, in 2 Thessalonians 2:8, it is the "breath" of Jesus (a possible allusion to His speech) that destroys and overcomes the anti-Christ. All of this demonstrates that the Word of God is powerful in spiritual battle. The enemies of God are overcome by the revelation of the power of God that comes by means of the spoken Word of God (especially when spoken by Jesus). The right kind of "words" are powerful for the demolition of strongholds[190] and the extension of the kingdom of God. We need to understand the power of the Word of God and use it just like Jesus did. When God speaks through His Word, Satan trembles and flees. Let's make sure that we do not under-estimate the power of the Word of God, particularly when it focuses on Jesus, the Ultimate Word of God made flesh.

---

188 Isaiah 49:2; Hebrews 4:12; Ephesians 6:17; Revelation 1:16; 19:13-21. See also Job. 15:30; Psalm 33:6; Isaiah 11:4; 2 Thessalonians 2:8 where "breath of the mouth" of God could refer to God's powerful speech.

189 See Matthew 8:13 as an example where Jesus heals the centurion's servant from a distance.

190 Ephesians 6:12.

Summary

God is a God who speaks. He uses words to mediate His Presence and call people to Himself. This includes the spoken Word (which includes testimonies, the prophetic, prayer and preaching), the written Word (the Scriptures), and Jesus as the Ultimate Word sent out from God to accomplish the will of God on the earth. Each needs to be received with dependence on the Spirit of God who helps us to apply and understand the Word of God correctly. Since the Scriptures are "God-breathed" there are few pathways more powerful for entering into the real Presence of God or for giving victory in spiritual warfare.

Key points in this chapter include:

1. The spoken word has inherent power. The power of the declared word is directly proportional to how well the words spoken reflect the will of the living God who alone has all power. Life and death are in the power of the tongue.

2. The power of the word of testimony is seen in that it calls us to experience in our specific setting the living God who acts today as He has in the past and as He has in other places. Testimony calls us into an encounter with the love of the living God who wants to make our walk with Him dynamic and powerful.

3. The power of the prophetic word comes in that it invites a faith response towards pursuing what God is calling a person towards. The prophetic word links the power of the Presence of the Lord to confer identity[191] with the power of the spoken word to call us towards God and into our destiny in Him.

4. The power of prayer is another example of the power of the Word of God. God has conferred upon us the dignity of being causes. When we pray, especially when what is prayed is linked to the will of God, the world around us is changed and impacted by our prayers.

191 See chapter 1, page 20

5. The Scriptures are particularly powerful in empowering and facilitating change because they carry the real Presence of the Lord. If we read the Scriptures with an open, receptive heart, they will change us.
6. Since the Scriptures are God-breathed, we must read the Biblical text with dependence on the same Spirit who helped write it.
7. If we are not finding the life of God in the Scriptures, we need to cry out to God to breathe on the dry bones of Scripture to bring it to life again.
8. We must read and study the Word of God with the goal of encountering Him and submitting more deeply to Him.
9. Preaching that faithfully reflects the truths of God and invites people into encountering the living God can be powerfully used by God to heal, evangelize and bring people more fully into an experience of God.
10. Jesus is the ultimate Word of God sent from heaven to bring us life. We must live as if we truly believe this to be true.
11. Jesus taught and proclaimed the Kingdom of God with such unity with the intent of the Father that miracles fruited in the context of His preaching. His proclamation carried the Presence of God to those receptive to receiving it. In the same way we need to press into God the Father and deepen our relationship with Him so that His Presence is also manifested as we proclaim the kingdom of God.

Entering Into His Presence

Start to read and meditate on Psalm 23. As you read it, ask God to make the Scriptures the green pasture of the passage. Quiet your heart and thoughts so that they are the quiet streams of the passage. Try to be still as you read the verses of this chapter and let the Lord speak to you. Tell the Lord how much you love Him and want to meet Him in His Word. Ask Him to show you something in the passage that you have never seen before. Pray through what He is showing you and ask Him what He wants you to change because of what He is showing you. Again, tell the Lord how much you love Him and receive His love for you.

Are you serious about finding the Lord in the pages of His Word? Are you willing to say "Yes" to Him and be changed by your encounters with Him?

If you are, I am praying for you: Lord, by the power of your precious name, I release to those reading these words the ability to find You and Your life in the pages of your Word. I bless them with the discovery of Your loving Presence in Your powerful Word.

Prayer

Lord, I want to make my life about You. Fill Your Word with Your life. Fill Your Word with Your Presence.

Holy Spirit, come and breath on the Word of God so that it is not just dusty, dry bones. Please, put bone to bone, then flesh on the bones of Scripture and breath on it so that it rises up like a mighty army in my life.

Father, I want to meet You in the Scriptures, help me to find You in Your Word.

Jesus, I want You to be my all in all. Empower Your truth to set me free as I encounter it in Your Word. I need Your truth to set me free.

Lord, I love You. I submit to You. I say "Yes"! Change me into Your image. I accept and receive Your love.

Lord, make me more focused on the Word of God, realizing its power to help me and to destroy the strongholds of the enemy. Make me a person of the Word of God. Fill my hand each day with the sword of the Spirit which is the Word of God.

Jesus, open my eyes so that I would see You clearly in the Scriptures. Teach me Your ways.

Lord, unite me with You so that I speak Your words and release Your life to people around me. Let Your Word bear fruit in me and through me for the greater glory of Your name.

In the precious name of Jesus I pray,

Amen.

8

Jesus Is the Gateway to the Greater Presence Of God

Between the last level of the Presence of the Lord in His Word, and the next one, the Presence of the Lord in the gathered Church, there is a transition that needs to be understood. Since the coming of Jesus Christ into the world and His death on the cross, Jesus has fundamentally changed the way in which we access the Presence of God.

The first level, the general Presence of the Lord, is accessible to everyone. All we must do is turn our hearts towards the Lord, who is always near, and we will find Him if we search for Him with all our hearts (Jer. 29:13). A revelation of the reality of God's Presence is never far from the true seeker.

Similarly, with the second level, God sustains both believers and non-believers alike. He is active in the entire world with His sustaining, undergirding love, and does not exclude non-believers from some of the benefits of His Presence – even if they refuse to acknowledge the reality of that Presence. Yet for the believer, through the sacrifice of Jesus Christ, the Spirit of God can come to us and make alive our spirits so that we become more sensitive to the Spirit of God. This means that, as mentioned earlier, we can discern God's Presence in the world, and hear His voice speaking to us more easily. We start to be able to hear the "still, small voice of the Lord" and discern it even amidst the noise around us. We are also able to access the sustaining Presence of the Lord more as we enter more fully into His Presence as Christians. It is possible that we might notice greater recovery from injury or greater benefits to our immune system, for example, since our increased ability to come into God's Presence means an increased ability to access His sustaining grace.

As a person relates to God's Word it is similar. God's Word is accessible to the non-believer and God can use the power of His Presence in His Word to bring non-believers to saving faith. While the non-believer can encounter God in His Word, he will not be able to discern or understand the Scriptures in the right way unless he has the Spirit of God in him guiding and leading "him into all truth."[192] A key aspect of this is whether the reader is open to the reality of the Presence of God or not when he reads the Word. God will not force Himself on anyone. The Word of God can only be correctly understood with reliance on the same Spirit with which it was written. It is only as we come to Christ that the veil over our heart is taken away and we can correctly discern the things of God.[193] Non-believers can access the Presence of God through His Word to some degree, but they cannot understand it fully or correctly because they have not yet submitted to the Spirit of God. The sacrifice of Jesus Christ on the cross changed the way in which we access the Presence of the Lord. For the non-believer there are still barriers in their life to the Presence of the Lord. For the believer, through Jesus Christ, there are now no barriers if he/she rightly understands the work of the cross. Jesus has changed everything.

The non-believer cannot freely access the various levels of the Presence of God discussed in later chapters without coming to them through

192 See John 14:26: *"But the Advocate, the Holy Spirit . . . will teach you all things and will remind you of everything I have said to you."* and John 16:13: *"But when he, the Spirit of truth, comes, he will guide you into all truth. . ."*

193 2 Corinthians 3:15-17: *(vs. 15) Even to this day when Moses is read, a veil covers their hearts. (vs. 16) But whenever anyone turns to the Lord, the veil is taken away. (vs. 17) Now the Lord is the Spirit and where the Spirit of the Lord is, there is freedom."* In context, the freedom the Spirit brings is freedom to discern correctly the things of God.

Christ. They can perhaps sense the Presence of the Lord in each of these areas, and God may use these experiences of His Presence to bring the non-believer to saving faith, but they cannot experience the Presence of the Lord in the same way as do believers.

For the Christian, however, through the sacrifice of Jesus, we now have a new identity that transforms how we relate to God. Part of this is the new birth mentioned above where our Spirits come alive.[194] Through the cross, we are changed. To correctly understand the next few levels of God's Presence, we need to understand more fully the new identity Jesus gave us through His sacrifice and how this new identity gives us greater access to God's Presence.

JESUS MAKES US THE GATEWAY TO HEAVEN

A key passage to look at is the story of Jacob's dream from Genesis 28:10-17. This passage starts with Jacob fleeing his family after he had stolen the birthright of his brother Esau, and, on the way, he stopped to sleep. While he slept, he had a powerful dream in which he glimpsed heaven and the LORD.[195] And he sees a stairway connecting heaven and earth with angels descending and ascending on it. He woke up with a strong sense of the Presence of the Lord and was filled with awe. He thought he had randomly picked this place to stop for the night, but found the LORD was present there – and he did not realize it. This is characteristic of us all. God is often more present to us than we realize since He is always near. Jacob calls this place Beth-El which means "house of God." He says, "*How awesome is this place! This is none other than the house of God; this is the gate of Heaven*" *(vs. 17).*

Jump ahead to the end of John 1 in the New Testament where we have the story of Nathanael coming to Jesus. Jesus had a word of knowledge

194 2 Corinthians 5:17: "*Therefore, if anyone is in Christ, the new creation has come. . . .*" The new creation is also mentioned in Galatians 6:15 and referred to in Ezekiel 36:26.

195 Jehovah or Yahweh is the actual term used here, see chapter 2 for the significance of this name for God.

about him in verse 48. Nathanael was so struck by this that he declared in verse 49, *"Rabbi, you are the Son of God; you are the king of Israel."* Jesus says to him, (vs. 50-51) *"'You believe because I told you that I saw you under the fig tree. You will see greater things than that." He then added, "Very truly I tell you, you will see heaven open, and the angels of God ascending and descending on the Son of Man.'"*

Jesus seems to be making a purposeful linkage between the dream of Jacob from Genesis 28 and what He is saying to Nathanael in John 1. In Jacob's dream, the angels are ascending and descending on a stairway or ladder, whereas in John 1, Jesus says they are ascending and descending on *Him*. In other words, Jesus, himself, is the stairway that connects heaven and earth. Jesus is the one sent by the Lord to carry heaven to earth, and through Jesus we reach up and touch heaven. Jesus makes heaven accessible. Some see this as a prophetic reference to the cross. The cross of Jesus bridges heaven and earth and the death of Christ was so spiritually powerful it was full of the divine activity of angels. Some of this power is seen in the earthquakes that occurred, the darkness that overshadowed the cross and the veil of the temple being torn in two.[196]

Just as the stairway Jacob saw made it possible for Jacob to say God is present on the earth, in the same way, the cross of Christ makes it possible for God to be more fully present on earth. As Christians, the place where Jesus touches the earth is our lives. This is developed more in the next chapters.

Jesus changed everything. Back in Genesis 3, mankind sinned and because of this had no access to heaven except temporarily through the Old Testament sacrificial system. Because of Adam and Eve's sin, God could not dwell fully with mankind as He desired. Our sin was too much of a barrier to intimacy with Him. But the cross of Christ changed this. Now, through the cross of Christ and faith in its work, we all have access by the Spirit of God to God Himself (Eph. 2:18). Now, through the

196 Matthew 27:45, 51-53.

cross, our sins are placed on Jesus and He gifts us His righteousness.[197] Now, we are clean and pure in the sight of God so we can access heaven, and God can dwell with us in our hearts on the earth. So, through the cross, we become the Beth-El of God and we become the gateway to heaven. Through our lives the people around us can access heaven. Yet most Christians do not seem to know what they carry and do not seem to realize what they now have access to through Jesus Christ. We become, through Jesus, mediators of the Presence and the love of the Lord to those around us. Many times, the people around us, particularly non-believers, will not know anything about the truth of who God really is unless we act, on their behalf, as gateways to His Presence. For many the only way they will ever know the truth of who Jesus is will be through Christians who faithfully show them the truth and reality of heaven as it touches the earth through their lives.

JESUS GIVES US ACCESS TO GOD

Due to the sacrifice of Jesus, we now have complete access to God through faith in what Jesus did on the cross. In our own natural state, we were fallen; we had fallen "short of the glory of God,"[198] but Jesus took our sin nature, all of our uncleanness, upon Himself on the cross. Then He gave us His own spotless righteousness.[199] Now, God sees us through the cross as having the righteousness of Jesus and so the sin we used to have no longer keeps us from the His Presence. We were sinners but now we are saints. The cross of Christ has released to us all the forgiveness we need so that all barriers that used to exist between God and us are gone. Now all those who have applied the cross to their lives, have free access by the Spirit of God to the Father.[200] This access is not conditional. At any time of the day or night, we have access to the Lord of Lords and King of

197 2 Corinthians 5:21.

198 Romans 3:23.

199 Romans 5:19; 2 Corinthians 5:21.

200 Ephesians 2:18.

Kings. No matter what our challenge is, we have access to the one who makes every impossibility possible. This is transformational! We have ACCESS to the Father!

In addition, there is a horizontal dimension to what the cross has done. The cross has also destroyed all barriers that existed due to sin between ethnic and cultural groups.[201] Jesus has freed us so that we can forgive others in the same way we have been forgiven. Unity is now possible as we all enter into the same inheritance under God through the cross. Jesus gives us access to others we would previously have seen as outsiders to our group. This is the basis of our corporate identity as the temple of God. We are all one in Christ and are being built together by the Spirit into one common dwelling place for God.[202] One of the great gifts God releases to us through the cross is the new access we have to others who also love God and have embraced the cross. One of the great tragedies we see in the Church is that we continue to allow our sin and flesh to raise barriers between us and our brothers and sisters when Jesus died to make us one.[203]

One implication of the new access we have to the Father is that we now are more sensitive to His voice.[204] Receiving forgiveness and entering into holiness opens up our hearts to hear the Lord. Since the cross gave us access to the Lord, the cross also gave the Spirit of God access to us.[205] The cross has dealt with the barriers we used to have to hearing God's voice and to having the Spirit of God reside in us.

---

201 Ephesians 2:11-17; see also Galatians 3:26-28.

202 Ephesians 2:19-22.

203 John 17:22-23 – Jesus prays: "*. . .that they may be one as we are one – I in them and you in me – so that they may be brought to complete unity. Then the world will know that you have sent me . . .* "

204 John 10:3-5 – the sheep of the Good Shepherd (Jesus) know and recognize His voice.

205 This is part of the point of Romans 8:14-15.

JESUS MAKES US SONS AND DAUGHTERS OF YAHWEH THROUGH THE CROSS

Romans 8:19 says: *"For the creation waits in eager expectation for the children of God to be revealed."* What we do not often realize is that we are part of the creation that is groaning[206] and yearning for God to adopt us into His family.[207] All of creation groans under the evil released by the sin of Adam and yearns to be restored to the Father. Creation was designed to fulfill its destiny and purpose in His Presence. There is something deep in the heart of every person that aches to bask in the pleasure of God's smile simply because we are who we are, without reference to anything we could ever do to earn His pleasure. Jesus did it all. In Hebrews 12:2 Jesus *"for the joy set before him"*—for the joy of seeing us come back into the family of God, for the joy that we would have the same intimacy with the Father that He enjoyed—*"endured the cross, scorning its shame."* Jesus embraced the pain and agony of the cross so that our adoption into the family of God would be accomplished. This is why the Father sent Jesus[208] to be born as a man.

Galatians 4:5-7 and Romans 8:14-17 are two passages that emphasize the intimacy we now have with the Father as His children.

> *"Because you are his sons, God sent the Spirit of his Son into our hearts, the Spirit who calls out 'Abba, Father.' So you are no longer a slave, but God's child; and since you are his child, God has made you also an heir." (Gal. 4:6-7)*

> *"The Spirit you received does not make you slaves, so that you live in fear again; rather, the Spirit you received brought about your adoption to sonship.[209] And by him we cry, 'Abba, Father' (vs. 16) The Spirit himself testifies with our spirits that we are God's children." (Romans 8: 15-16)*

---

206 Romans 8:22.

207 Romans 8:23.

208 Galatians 4:4-5.

209 This is not exclusive to males and includes "daughtership".

Both passages emphasize that the Spirit now confers upon us a new identity as sons and daughters of the Father. He both testifies in our hearts to this identity and brings us deeper into intimacy so that we can call the Father-God "Abba."[210] God sees us as His little children and loves us passionately as our all-sufficient Father. The relationship is not formal, but intimate. This new relationship is also not to have any fear in it, but instead love. We are no longer slaves or servants; we are now sons and daughters. This is astounding! We not only have access to the Father, but we also have the confidence that He has called us,[211] chosen us, and done everything possible to free us to enter into His Presence without fear. We are no longer orphans, but children chosen by God to be in His special family before the foundation of the world.[212] This transition is a key one that allows us to access our inheritance in Christ. Unfortunately, many Christians claim "sonship" yet emotionally and psychologically continue to live as orphans without a deep-level security that they are truly loved.

Both passages also mention that as God's children we now have a different inheritance. We are not second-class family members in the family of God, but equal in status to our older brother Jesus. We are *"heirs of God and co-heirs with Christ"* (Rom. 8:17) and *"since you are his child, God has also made you an heir"* (Gal. 4:7). This means that not only do we have access to God in heaven, but we also have access to the resources of heaven in the same way that Jesus had access to the resources of heaven when He was on the earth. So, how did Jesus access the Father and the resources He had as God's well-loved son? When the sick came to Him, He healed them.[213] When the hungry came to Him, He gathered the loaves of bread He had access to on earth, blessed them, then accessed heaven and fed 4000 or 5000 men plus others.[214] If Jesus did all that He did because

210 Equivalent to "daddy" or "poppa".

211 Ephesians 1:4: we are chosen in Christ before the foundation of the world.

212 See Ephesians 1:4.

213 Luke 4:38-42.

214 Matthew 15:29-39; John 6:1-15.

God was with Him by the power of the Spirit,[215] then we also have access to the same God and to the same Spirit to do the same kinds of things. Jesus is our model of how to act as God's kids in this world. He illustrates for us how to function in our inheritance. We receive that inheritance by listening to the voice of the Father (to which we now have access) and being obedient to what He says.

Submission begets authority. It is by humbling ourselves under the mighty hand of God that we are elevated to high rank and status (I Peter 5:6). It was through being submitted and obedient to the Father even to the point of death that Jesus was elevated to be Lord of all (Phil. 2:6-11). It is through submission and obedience that God molds and crafts us to be the kind of people who can handle tremendous authority. The way up starts by going down. This is often misunderstood. We tend to reject submission as demeaning without understanding that it is actually the route by which our destiny becomes accessible. Both men and women must embrace submission and obedience in order to grow into their destiny. Most Christians do not walk in the authority they have as God's children in part because they have not entered into their authority through submission. They often do not know firmly enough their identity as God's children who have access to the resources of heaven. Faith unlocks the supernatural and is the door through which God's power walks. God acts in response to faith. Yet do we have the humility necessary to operate in the supernatural dimensions of life without it destroying us?

Through adopting us into His family through the cross, and giving us a rich inheritance in His family, God confers tremendous honour and favour upon us. We are His beloved children, chosen in Christ, sought after and pursued by God at great cost to Himself simply because He loves us. We can never give to God anything He does not already have. If we want to see how God loves us, look at how He loved His son Jesus. The declaration from the Father at the baptism of Jesus that Jesus is the well beloved Son in whom He (the Father) is pleased, becomes ours through the cross.

---

215 Acts 10:38; 1 John 3:8.

Here we have the power of the Father's voice to confer the love and acceptance we long for and need. The Father loves us. The cross removes barriers in our hearts so that we can more clearly hear the orchestra of God's love for us. We need His love to find our destiny.

JESUS TEACHES US HOW TO LIVE AS SONS AND DAUGHTERS OF GOD

We do not know what Jesus was told about His birth, but we do know that by the age of 12 He was both proficient in the Word of God and knew clearly that God was His Father.[216] I think that these two things are related. Jesus understood that many of the aspects of His life were fulfillments of the Scriptures and thus identified Him as both the Messiah and the Son of God. Knowing the Scriptures helped Him to know who He was. His purity and sinlessness also kept Him in communion with God. At the age of 12, He amazed the religious leaders with His knowledge of the Word of God and that knowledge would only grow. Yet later, it was not only His knowledge of the Word that was clear, it was His authority with the Word that astounded people.[217] In the Sermon on the Mount, Jesus repeatedly says: "*You have heard it said . . . But I say . . .*"[218] thus showing His confidence that His authority superseded that of the scribes and Pharisees and that His understanding of the Word of God was greater than theirs. Where did this sense of authority come from? It flowed from His awareness of who He was as a Son. He drew His identity from His relationship with God. What God affirmed, He stepped into. Before He launched out in His ministry, at His baptism, God publicly affirmed that Jesus was His well-loved Son who pleased Him. Every child needs this kind of affirmation from their father! This love of the Father and confidence in that love gave Jesus His authority. Later when Satan tried to rob

216 Luke 2:47-49.

217 Matthew 7:28-29; Mark 1:21-22; Luke 4:31-32.

218 Matthew 6:21-22; 27-28; 31-32; 33-34; 38-39; 43-44.

Jesus of His identity[219] by manipulating Him not to trust His Father, Jesus would have none of it. This is important. The strategy of Satan is always to drive a wedge between us and our heavenly Father. He will manipulate and use the circumstances of our lives and the voices we listen to, to sow doubt in our hearts. We must always choose the darkness of faith to the "clarity" of logic. To choose trust over unbelief. A true "son" draws his life from God and chooses to trust Him. Jesus made submission to the will of His Father the touchstone of His life. He only did what the Father wanted Him to do.[220] It was all about maintaining intimacy with His Father at the center of his life.

In His ministry Jesus routinely taught, proclaimed the kingdom of God and healed the sick.[221] Knowing the will of His Father and knowing who He was as a "Son" called by the Father to do His will gave Jesus authority in teaching and over sickness and oppression. He knew what He had been anointed by the Holy Spirit to do. He lined himself up with God's will and through His preached word, released the Presence of God into His environment so that God could be seen and His name glorified. Jesus lived to make His Father known[222] and famous.[223]

Jesus teaches us that when we make our life about intimacy with our heavenly Father and press into His Word, we will grow in our authority as sons and daughters to carry out the will of God on the earth. The Word of God teaches us that God is our Father and teaches us who we are as His special ones. Yes, we need the empowering of the Spirit of God. This is why Jesus told his disciples to stay in Jerusalem until they were "clothed in power from on high."[224] Yet, at the core, it is about our intimacy with the Father so that we can take that "anointing" and use it in the right way to accomplish the will of the Father for a hurting world. It was only

219 This will be developed more later.

220 John 5:19.

221 Matthew 4:23-24; 9:35.

222 John 1:18.

223 Matthew 9:8.

224 Luke 24:49.

after spending three years nurturing His relationship with the disciples that Jesus told them they would be empowered by the Spirit. We never want to be a son or daughter that takes the gifts the Father has given us and uses them in a way that discredits or dishonors Him. If we do not know the Father's love for us and live in it, all of the Gifts of the Spirit will be nothing but noise.[225] When we know that we are deeply loved by our heavenly Father and make our life about making Him famous, His anointing finds the right channels to flow in. God has given us both His Word and the Holy Spirit to nurture us in our identity as "sons" and "daughters." Intimacy with God and knowledge of the Word of God are extremely important in growing in our relationship with our Father.

JESUS GIVES US A DESTINY

Now through Jesus Christ we are no longer cut off from God. We no longer live under the weight of sin. We are free to choose right. He gives us hope for a future that is sure and strong since it depends on the unchangeable nature of God who has done everything necessary to bring us the forgiveness we need through the sacrifice of Jesus.[226] The sacrifice of Jesus shows us the depth of God's love for us.[227] He is for us. Now we have access to the resources of heaven for our own lives and for others. He will not abandon us. We are never alone.[228] Jesus gives us a new destiny.

Jesus in his death and resurrection has broken the power of sin and death over us. First Corinthians 15 is a key chapter that talks of this: (vs 22) *"For as in Adam all die, so in Christ all will be made alive. . . (vs 54) death has been swallowed up in victory. (55) 'Where, O death is your victory? Where, O death is your sting?' (56) The sting of death is sin . . . (57) But thanks be to God! He gives us the victory through Jesus Christ our Lord."* Now we have victory over sin and over death. Sin disintegrates and de-

225 1 Corinthians 13:1.

226 Hebrews 6:18-20.

227 Hebrews 12:1-2 – for the joy set before him he endured the cross.

228 Matthew 28:20 – Jesus will be with us even to the end of the age.

stroys. Now we can live in forgiveness and holiness – and holiness brings life since it keeps us in the Presence of God. Now we have a hope and a future.

JESUS IS THE BREAD OF LIFE

Bread is the theme of John 6. The chapter starts with Jesus feeding 5000 people in a wilderness place with a few loaves and fishes. Later Jesus challenges the Jews not to work for food that spoils but for food that endures for eternal life (v. 27). The Jews then demand Jesus do something like what Moses did when he gave the Israelites manna in the desert as proof that they should believe in Him. This manna was given daily, and they could not save it up (except for Friday when they could get enough that they would not need to search for it on the Sabbath). It was daily "bread" from heaven that fed the people for 40 years in the wilderness. Jesus responds that this manna pointed to something else beyond what happened in the wilderness. It was a prophetic sign sent from heaven by God as a precursor of the *"true bread from heaven"* (vs. 32)[229] that would later come. In John 6:35, Jesus proclaims that He is the bread of life. The rest of the passage is an extended teaching on how Jesus is the *"living bread"* (vs. 51) who came down from heaven to give life to all who would "eat" this bread. The chapter ends with many "disciples" leaving Jesus, upset over what He is teaching and with Peter telling Jesus that they would never leave Him for *"you have the words of eternal life"* (vs. 68).

Symbolically in Scripture, bread is a staple food that is a symbol of what is needed to nurture life. What Jesus is saying to the Jews in this passage is that, just as the Jews were nurtured for 40 years in the wilderness by the manna God sent from heaven, now the true bread from heaven has arrived and people need to feed on Him in order to have all that is needed for eternal life. Jesus as the bread of life is what we need to feed on daily to thrive. The problem is that we often do not live as if we believe

229 Mentioned briefly in chapter 7 when talking about Jesus as the Word made flesh.

that Jesus is truly the bread of life. Christians declare the importance of Jesus in their lives, but there is often a disconnect between their lived and declared values. If Jesus is truly the bread of life, we need to live as if that is true and "feed" on Jesus daily. Living as if Jesus is the bread of life we need every day nurtures the real Presence of the Lord in our lives.

JESUS SHOWS US THE FATHER.

Both Colossians 1:15 and Hebrews 1:3 indicate that Jesus is the visible image of the invisible God. What this means is that Jesus puts flesh on our image of God and makes Him visible to us. To put it another way, Jesus shows us the face of God. He shows us God's response to sin, sickness, and oppression.

The heart of the Father is seen by how Jesus related to the sick and the hurting. When people ask me whether it is the will of God to heal, I tell them to look at Jesus and they will know the answer. Jesus never showed a reluctance or an unwillingness to heal. He healed everyone who came to Him. Faith for healing is about looking at Jesus and when you see Him clearly it is easier to believe.

JESUS IS BOTH GOD MADE VISIBLE AND THE MODEL FOR OUR HUMANITY

There is a paradox here. Jesus is both fully God and fully man. When we want to see what God is like, all we have to do is look at Jesus. The "I am"[230] sayings of John point intentionally to His divinity. The miracles Jesus did do not actually point to who He is as God, they point to who

230 There are two types of "I am" sayings in John. Those with a subject predicate include when Jesus said, "I am the good shepherd", "I am the bread of life", "I am the resurrection and the life", "I am the way, the truth and the life", etc. He cannot be what He says He is without being God (or a crazy man). The second type are those with no subject predicate and in these Jesus applies the Old Testament "I am" divine name for God to Himself, very specifically calling Himself God. For example, see John 8:58: " . . . before Abraham was born, I am!" and John 8:24: "You will die in your sins unless you believe that I am" or John 8:28: "When you have lifted up the Son of Man, then you will know that I am." These are not always clear in the translation you may use.

He is as the Messiah, the "anointed one" of God, sent into the world to do His will and accomplish deliverance for God's people.[231] His purity, His holiness, His manner of life, His teachings, the fact that He could say at the end of His life that Satan *"He has no hold over me"* (John 14:30), His fulfillment of the whole of the Levitical sacrificial system,[232] His revelation of the Father (John 1:18), His ability to be tempted yet without sin (Heb. 4:15), all of these point to His absolute divinity. Philippians 2:6-11 tells us that Jesus put off his Godly prerogatives and put on human nature, becoming submitted to the will of the Father to the point of death. His essential nature stayed the same. He never stopped being God, but He chose to function on the earth with a reliance on the anointing of the Holy Spirit as the model for our humanity.

God anointed Jesus with the Holy Spirit and power and He went about doing good and healing all who were under the power of the devil, *"because God was with Him"* (Acts 10:38). It does not say He healed people because He was God, it says He healed people because He was anointed with the Holy Spirit and power and that God was with Him. John the Baptist indicates that it was the coming down of the Holy Spirit on Jesus in bodily form as a dove and *remaining on him*[233] at His baptism that proved Jesus was the coming Messiah. When God is with us, we can do incredible things by the power of the same Holy Spirit. Jesus maintained His intimacy with the Father and His anointing by the Holy Spirit through prayer, obedience and holiness just like we are to. First John 3:8 says that the reason the Son of God appeared was to destroy the devil's work. We are also to destroy the devil's work through the power of the Holy Spirit and obedience to God in the same way that Jesus did. Jesus is our model for life and ministry. We need to understand the power of

231 One of the clear indications of this is Luke 7:18-23. When the disciples of John the Baptist come to Jesus to essentially ask if he was indeed the Messiah John prophesied, Jesus referred to Isaiah 35 and cited the miracles they could see happening in his ministry. They left content since the miracles proved Jesus was indeed the promised Messiah. They did not think they proved he was God.

232 The main point of the Epistle of the Hebrews.

233 John 1:32-34.

the obedience that we see in Jesus. Like Him, we listen to the voice of the Father and do what He is doing (John 5:19). Fasting helps us to clarify, or discern, what the Father is doing and saying and is one practice that we need to do regularly. Fasting is something Jesus also did.[234] We need to relate to the Father as Jesus did as the model for our humanity.

Summary

Jesus is the doorway through which we access the Presence of God in a more intimate way. He changes everything. Now we have greater access to God, and more intimacy with Him. Jesus makes it possible to be accepted and adopted into the family of God, and he shows us how to live as children of God. He is our model, our pattern and our destiny. We can only truly access the next levels of God's Presence through Jesus.

The key points from this chapter are:

1. Jesus connects heaven to earth and makes us, through the cross, the gateway to heaven for those who do not know Him.
2. Jesus gives us access to the Father and access to all of the incredible resources of heaven.
3. Jesus destroyed all barriers that previously existed between God and us when He died on the cross. Jesus now gives us intimacy with the Father.
4. Jesus makes us sons and daughters of Yahweh. We are no longer slaves but children of the King of Kings. We are no longer orphans but chosen and sought out by God to be in His family as privileged children.
5. Submission begets authority in the kingdom of God. The root of Biblical authority is humility not power.

---

234 Jesus did fast for 40 days in the temptation narrative (Matthew 4:1-11) but did not seem to fast as often as the Pharisees did. His disciples seemed to not fast during the time Jesus was with them, but Jesus indicated that they would fast after he was gone (Matthew 9:14-15; Mark 2:18-20). We also see Christians later fasting (Acts 13:2; 14:23).

6. Jesus gives us a destiny. Now we have victory, hope and a future.
7. Jesus is the bread of life. We need to access Jesus each day and imbibe His presence as truly essential for us to live each day.
8. Jesus shows us the Father. When we see Jesus, we discover the hidden mystery of the nature of God. In Jesus we see God's response to the darkness, sickness and oppression in the world.
9. Jesus is both God made visible for us, and the model for our humanity. Jesus shows us how to destroy the works of Satan by the power of the Holy Spirit. He shows us how to relate to the Father and listen to His voice in obedience.

Entering Into His Presence

Put on some worship music and let yourself dwell for a few minutes in the Presence of God. Thank the Lord that Jesus has died for your sins and cleansed you with his blood so that you can have access to God and all the resources of heaven. Ask the Lord to show you how to be Beth-El, the house of God, on the earth. Hear the Holy Spirit speaking to you and calling you the "son" or "daughter" of the living God. You are now in the family of God and have access to His Presence.

Take a few moments to examine your heart and let the Holy Spirit show you where you have not been submissive to His voice. Determine to say "yes" and to grow in submission to God so that His authority can be more greatly expressed through your life.

Turn your mind and imagination to Jesus. He makes the invisible nature of God visible to you. How does Jesus change the way you may have seen God in the past? Ask Jesus to send the Holy Spirit to anoint you so that you can be his hands and feet in the world.

Prayer

Jesus, thank You for changing everything! Thank You for embracing the cross so that I would be forgiven and the power of sin and death would be broken in my life. Thank You for giving me a hope and a future.

Help me to have an ever-increasing understanding of what the cross has done for me and how it has set me free.

Jesus, thank You for giving me access to the Father. Help me to understand what that means and how to access the resources of heaven for myself and others. Teach me, Holy Spirit, how to walk more fully in what Jesus has won for me.

Father God, You have chosen me in Christ before the foundation of the world. You loved me and wanted me to be in Your family so much, You sent Your Son to die for me, to destroy every barrier that existed between You and I. Thank You for doing this. I do not deserve it.

In the powerful name of Jesus, I come against that belief or feeling of being a second-class child in Your family, of being an orphan cut off from being loved by my Father. Any "orphan spirit" that plagues me I tell to go in the name of Jesus. In the name of Jesus, I come against rejection and command it to go from my life, never to return. Lord, I receive Your love and acceptance of me. I am loved. I am accepted.

Lord, I want to grow in submission to You. Show me how to abandon myself to You so that I can walk in Your authority to love those You love. Help me to be Your hands, destroying the works of Satan in this world. Empower me by Your Spirit to do Your works, to carry Your freedom to others.

Jesus, I want You to be the daily bread I eat each day. Be my life. Feed me with Your Presence. I need You. I need Your life. I need to walk in Your holiness. Show me how to do this more.

Father, I carry Your name. Make me worthy of such a high calling. Teach me what it means to be Your son (or daughter).

I declare in the name of Jesus that I am loved by my heavenly Father. Father, Daddy, I receive that love right now. I give You all my fear and anxiety. I receive Your peace right now.

I declare in the name of Jesus that I am forgiven. I receive the washing and cleansing of the blood of Jesus right now. Right now, in the name of Jesus, I have access to the throne room of God.

I declare right now that my sins have been placed on Jesus and now, Jesus, I receive Your righteousness. I am pure in the sight of God. So - in the name in Jesus I receive the favour of God on my life. I receive the pleasure of my Heavenly Father on my life.

In the precious name of Jesus, I pray,

Amen.

9

The Presence of God in the Temple of God: The Old Testament Prelude to the New Testament Temples of God

We as Christians are here on the earth to be world changers. It is not about us so much as about what we become through Jesus. God created humans to be the crowning point of creation, formed to love and nurture creation with the love God has for it. Adam and Eve sinned, thus falling short of their potential under God, yet God brings us back into our original destiny through Christ. Through Jesus, we now have access to God and can walk in His favour, releasing His love to the world. God believes in us and in what we can become in Christ.

God knows we are more than we think we are. He sees us as the gateway to Heaven for those around us who do not have access to God and the things of Heaven. God sees us as having just what the people around us need in order to be blessed by God. We, through Jesus, become the means by which God loves the world.

In the last chapter, we saw how Jesus made us the gateway to heaven for others; here I will talk about how the place where heaven touches earth is Beth-El, the dwelling place of God. Going back to Genesis 28:10-18 for a moment:

'Jacob . . . stopped for the night . . . and lay down to sleep. He had a dream in which he saw a stairway resting on the Earth, with its top reaching to heaven, and the angels of God were ascending and descending on it. There above it stood the LORD, and he said: "I am the LORD, the God of your father Abraham, . . .

. . . . All peoples on earth will be blessed through you and your offspring. I am with you . . . "

When Jacob awoke from his sleep, he thought, "Surely the LORD is in this place and I was not aware of it." He was afraid and said, "How awesome is this place! This is none other than the house of God; this is the gate of heaven."

Early the next morning Jacob took the stone he had placed under his head and set it up as a pillar and poured oil on it. . .

He called that place Bethel . . .' (Genesis 28:10-13, 14-15, 16-19)

This dream is a prophetic call to Jacob of what God was initiating for the future through him. The one who speaks is "Yahweh", the creator God who is the source and foundation of all reality. He speaks from heaven with all His kingly authority (vs.13) and He declares His heart to bless the world through Jacob and his offspring (vs. 14). God always seeks to bless the earth through people who say "yes" to Him. This is possible because God will be with Jacob and will watch over him (vs. 15). God sends angels from heaven to earth to carry out His will, and, in the dream, the gulf between heaven and earth is bridged by a ladder or stairway. The place where the ladder touches earth is an awe-filled, Presence-of-God-filled place (vs. 17). It is "Beth-El" or the "house of God" and this becomes the gateway to heaven. From this "gateway" heaven becomes accessible to mankind.

This was a life changing moment for Jacob. He hardly seems to realize its significance: he only knew he had just had a powerful encounter with the living God. Before this point Jacob was a schemer, a cheater - definitely not a good man. Yet from this point on, he starts to change until he became the father of the nation of Israel. Notice how Jacob set up a memory stone to make sure he never forgot this life-changing encounter with God. When God comes down to touch us in a significant way, we need to find a way to remember these moments so they can continue to impact us.

For Jacob this was an "awe" moment where he knew God was present. It shook the foundations of his life. I remember a similar moment at a conference where at the end of a meeting, as the speaker invited the Presence of God to come, a lady at the front started laughing loudly. God was obviously doing something. Later when she had calmed down enough to be coherent, they had her come to the front and tell what had happened. She explained that she had a foot problem and as she entered the auditorium that night, she felt God tell her He would heal her foot. She took out her phone and snapped a photo of her foot. When the Holy Spirit came, she suddenly felt intense heat in her foot and knew God was healing her. She was overwhelmed with the power of God. They put the photo of her foot up on the screen – showing a 60-degree bend (or more) in her foot about halfway down the arch of the foot. When they asked how her foot was now, she pointed to it, and they put that image on the screen. It was perfectly normal! God, in about 30-40 minutes had totally transformed her foot better than a surgeon could have done. As I saw the two photos on the screen, awe filled me! God was here! God had come in His powerful Presence in the corporate gathering of His Church.

Moments like this need to be remembered just like Jacob made a point to remember his "awe" moment. After these "encounters" with the "reality" of God, our perception of what God did will inevitably be challenged. We tend to be forgetful people and like Jacob need memory stones. This is one of the reasons God repeatedly had the Israelites set up monuments to remind them of significant events in their corporate life when God broke through for them.[235]

235 As examples see when God defeated the Amalekites (Exodus 17: 8-16), when God gave the Ten Commandments (Exodus 24:4), the crossing of the Jordon River (Joshua 4:1-7; Deuteronomy 27:2-6), Jacob's dream and Bethel (Genesis 28:18, 22; 35:14-15), and when God rescued Jacob from Esau (Genesis 33:20).

It is remarkable that God tends to choose unlikely people to be the ones He will use to change the world. God chooses them, not based on who they are, but based on who they can become. In a sense God chooses them based on the identity He sees in them and calls them to rather than because of who they think they are. When you say, "Yes" to God, as Jacob did, you start to enter in to exactly what and who you are. If you ever feel like you are not the person God can use in a great way, that may be the sign you are exactly who God *can* use!

When we link this passage to what Jesus said in John 1:48-51 (see previous chapter), we see that Jesus calls himself the ladder or bridge between heaven and earth. Through Jesus, heaven becomes accessible once more. The place where Jesus touches earth and where His Presence is continually felt becomes both the house of God on earth and the gateway to heaven. And, of course, this is fulfilled at the cross.

GOD IN CHRIST FORMS THE NEW TEMPLE OF GOD

To develop this thought, through the cross, God in Christ forms the new temple (or dwelling place) of God on the earth in the community where the cross touches the earth in the lives of people. This is possible because through the cross of Christ, all sin barriers, the "dividing wall of hostility" between God and mankind and between different groups within mankind are destroyed (Eph. 2:14).[236] Now, true reconciliation is possible. Now, true intimate relationship with God and others is possible. God's purpose through the cross ". . . *was to create in himself one new humanity out of the two,*[237] *thus making peace and in one body to reconcile both of them to God through the cross by which he put to death their hos-*

236 Not too long ago, 100 people were killed in the Paris bombings and people are wondering how the growing tensions in the world can be overcome. Apart from the cross, the growing "wall of hostility" between "us" and "them" cannot be overcome.

237 In the context Paul is referring to Jews and Gentiles, those that were previously part of the people of God ("us") and those that were excluded ("them"). God's intent is to destroy all hostility and bring peace through the cross.

tility" (Eph. 2:15-16). How is this new unity possible? By bringing to all people through the cross a new access to the Father by one Spirit (Eph. 2:18) and by forming all peoples into a temple of God, a dwelling place for God to live on the earth by His Spirit.

> *"Consequently, you are no longer foreigners and strangers, but fellow citizens with God's people and also members of his household, built on the foundation of the apostles and prophets, with Christ Jesus himself as the chief cornerstone. In him the whole building is joined together and rises to become a holy temple in the Lord. And in him you too are being built together to become a dwelling in which God lives by his Spirit." (Ephesians 2:19-22)*

Reconciliation is possible because God Himself comes to dwell on the earth through His people and where God is, anything becomes possible.

The place where the cross intersects the earth, where the realities of heaven and of Jesus touch the earth, is the church, the new community that came into being through the cross of Christ. The sacrifice of Jesus Christ made us "Beth-El", the "house of God", so that we would become the gateway to heaven. The heart of the Father is that all mankind would have access to the same things that His children have access to through the cross. As God says in Genesis 28:14, all mankind **will be blessed** through Jacob and his descendants. Yet to understand the glory and beauty of what is going on here we need to understand the five distinct types of temples of God found in the Bible. This also empowers us to understand and enter into the next two levels of the Presence of God in the world discussed later.

THE FIVE TEMPLES

There are five distinct temples of God mentioned in the Bible. I am not talking about the "temples" as historical physical entities but as five distinct types or kinds of temples. The first Temple we see in the Bible is the Old Testament place of worship where the Jewish nation gathered to worship Yahweh. This temple was started by Moses as a temporary tabernacle that traveled with the Israelites, then later constructed in a more permanent form in Jerusalem by Solomon and then dedicated by him. The temple was periodically destroyed and rebuilt as the fortunes of the nation of Israel waxed and waned; being rebuilt at least twice – once under Ezra and Nehemiah and a second time by Herod. All of these historical temples were central to the Levitical sacrificial system and really represent one distinct temple "type." We have the most details for this temple as it was designed to help us understand the significance and importance of each of the others. It was always intended by God to be temporal, transitory, and prophetic in nature; a type and symbol for what was to come. The other four are fulfillments of the significance of this temple of God.

The second temple is the New Testament temple of the gathered community of believers. When the new community of God is gathered, God dwells in a unique way in that corporate setting.

The third temple is the New Testament temple of the individual believer. Both the individual Christian and the gathered community of Christians are temples of the Holy Spirit and of God. They are distinct from one another, yet they overlap. They are both formed as temples through the cross of Christ. The first temple was temporary and, once it had fulfilled its purpose, was no longer needed; however, both the second and third temples are eternal. They are inaugurated on earth when one believes in Jesus, accepts the forgiveness that comes through the cross of Christ and receives the sanctifying Presence of the Holy Spirit, but they continue into eternity.

The fourth temple is the heavenly Temple that is the archetype, model, and example of the true Temple of God. This Temple has existed from the moment the first worshipping being was created by God and will exist to all eternity. In a sense this temple is the "first" temple as it is the source of the true worship of God, yet it is placed here as the "fourth" as it is the temple to which all redemptive history points and is heading. It is formed in heaven by the Presence of the eternal God and exists apart from creation. As one goes from the first temple to the second to the third and finally to the heavenly temple, one sees an intensification of intimacy with God and an increased ability to enter into His Presence.

One can argue that there is a "fifth" temple, which is simply God Himself who fills the heavens and then comes to dwell on the earth in the New Jerusalem. When describing this, John writes in Revelations 21:22-23: *"I did not see a temple in the city, because the Lord God Almighty and the Lamb are its temple. The city does not need the sun or the moon to shine on it, for the glory of God gives it light, and the Lamb is its light."* In the New Jerusalem, the entire city becomes a consecrated place filled with the glory and light of God so that as people enter the city, they are immersed in the powerful Presence of God, a place set apart for the worship and adoration of the King of Kings and Lord of Lords. No one who has not consecrated themselves to holiness can enter this Living Temple of God. Revelations 21:27 says, *"Nothing impure will ever enter it, nor will anyone who does what is shameful or deceitful, but only those whose names are written in the Lamb's book of life."* It is a special place, a uniquely holy place, where those surrendered to the Lord dwell.

What makes each of the temples the "temple" of God is the Presence of God in it. Just as foreigners were excluded from the Old Testament temple on earth, non-believers cannot enter the heavenly temple where God's Presence dwells. The wonder of this temple image is that Yahweh, the source and basis of all reality, has decided to link Himself to a time and place out of His overwhelming love for humanity and desire for intimacy with them. God will never force anyone to accept His Presence, but for those who do, He invites them to become His temple on earth and to join Him in His eternal Temple in heaven. It really is all about "Presence".

THE HEAVENLY TEMPLE OF GOD THAT IS OUR DESTINY

The heavenly Temple of God is the archetype and pattern for the first three temples. For 40 days God hovered over Moses and Mount Sinai with tremendous power, shaking the ground with peals of thunder and flashes of lightning. As God gave Moses the Ten Commandments, He revealed to him the pattern of the heavenly Temple that was meant to be built by the people as an earthly place of worship.[238] Moses was so immersed in the Presence of the Glory of the LORD during this time that his face shone with the Glory of God, scaring the other Israelites.[239] What was he seeing? Was he seeing the heavenly Temple mentioned in Revelations 15:5-6, 8.[240] Did he hear the "song of Moses" being sung around the throne of God?[241] Did he prophetically hear the sounds of those from all nations of the world worshipping the LORD?[242] Did he prophetically see Jesus our Great High Priest in the temple?[243] It would have been clear to Moses when he came down from the mountain that the temple he was to initiate on the earth was just a shadow, a symbol, and a foreshadowing of that heavenly vision.[244] It was extremely important that this "copy" of the heavenly sanctuary be accurate since it was illustrative of the higher things of heaven.[245]

This heavenly Temple of God was not only the pattern for what Moses initiated with the Israelites when they built the Tabernacle, it is also part of the destiny of all believers. We see a glimpse of this again in Revelation 15.

> *"And I saw what looked like a sea of glass glowing with fire and, standing beside the sea, those who had been victorious over the beast and its image and over the number of its name. They held*

238 See Exodus 20:18-21; Deuteronomy 5:22-33; Hebrews 8:5; 12:18-29.

239 Exodus 34:29-35.

240 See also Revelation 11:19 where the heavenly temple is "opened" and 13:6 where one of the sins of the Antichrist is that he blasphemes the name of God and his dwelling place.

241 Revelation 15:3-4.

242 Revelation 15:4.

243 Hebrews 7:11-28; 8:1-13.

244 Hebrews 9:23-24 – it mentions that while the "copies" of the heavenly things were sanctified with the blood of bulls and goats, the heavenly things were sanctified by the greater sacrifice of Jesus and how Christ entered the heavenly sanctuary to minister as a priest before God. See also Hebrews 10:1.

245 Moses is repeatedly told to be extremely accurate in copying the heavenly pattern he was shown. See Exodus 25:9, 40; 26:30; 27:8.

harps given them by God and sang the song of God's servant Moses and of the Lamb:

"Great and marvellous are your deeds,
Lord God Almighty.
Just and true are your ways,
King of the nations..."

After this I looked, and I saw in heaven the temple – that is, the tabernacle of the covenant law – and it was opened." (Rev. 15:2-5)

The Temple of the LORD will be opened in heaven and all nations will worship the LORD there. Both the throne of God and His Temple in heaven will be at the core of that worship.[246] The Temple of God is not only the place where the Presence of the LORD is, but also the place where God Himself is enthroned amidst the praises of His people. And, wherever God is enthroned in people's lives on earth it serves as a precursor of this heavenly Temple (see also Col. 2:17). It is about the Lordship of His Presence.

THE OLD TESTAMENT TEMPLE OF GOD IN JERUSALEM

The foundation for how we as sinful people can enter into the Presence of God is found in the Old Testament. The Old Testament Temple and the associated Levitical sacrificial system had several purposes. Primary in its purpose was the cultivation of the truth within the people of God that the key attribute of Yahweh was holiness and that He needed to be

246 Revelation 4:1-6; 11:16-19; 15:2-5. In Revelation 4:5 "From the throne came flashes of lightning, rumblings and peals of thunder"; while from the *temple* of Revelation 11:19 "came flashes of lightning, rumblings, peals of thunder. . . ". In Rev. 4:6 in front of the throne was a "sea of glass, clear as crystal"; In Revelation 15:2 John says he "saw what looked like a sea of glass glowing with fire" near the heavenly temple (vs. 5, 6, 8). This suggests that there is some overlap between the heavenly *throne* of God and His heavenly *Temple*. Of course, Isaiah in Isaiah 6:1 saw God's heavenly throne IN the Temple. Perhaps he was seeing a vision of God's heavenly throne in the heavenly Temple as His reign extended from the earthly temple into the heavens.

approached with purity. It was only after dealing with the gap that existed between the sinfulness of mankind and the holiness of God that one could approach Him. This gap was bridged through the sacrificial system of the Old Testament and occurred through making God's people holy. Only when they were holy could they come into His Presence. This was the secondary purpose of the sacrificial system: to provide a means by which mankind could approach and be in the Presence of the living God safely. The Temple was the place where this encounter between God and mankind took place. It was in this special place, built of materials sanctified and set apart for God, that one could enter, after having done all the prescribed sacrifices to make oneself pure, and meet the LORD. It was a place of Holiness and a place of encounter.

The Temple was born out of God's passionate love for His people and His desire to bless them with the full fruit of His Presence. It was also born out of the passion of God's people to be with and love their God. At the creation of the earth in the Garden of Eden, fellowship between the Holy God and mankind was ruptured by the sin of Adam and Eve. God wanted to get this intimacy with us back. He knew that we needed that intimacy in order to be fulfilled. The truth was that even though God longed for mankind to live in His Presence, if people were not sufficiently sanctified for this encounter with God, the encounter could destroy them. The sin issue, the sin barrier in this relationship, must be dealt with. Under the leadership of Moses, a major step forward was made as God instituted a system that would sufficiently sanctify the sinner for brief periods of time so that they could meet the Holy One of Israel without being destroyed.[247] During the time of Moses God had Moses construct a temporary "temple" which became called both the "Tabernacle"[248] and

247 This is not because God always "judges" sin but that holiness destroys sin. It is like the vacuum of space and a balloon filled with air. When you place the balloon in a vacuum, the vacuum does not "judge" the balloon, it just destroys it because one cannot exist in the presence of the other. In the same way, sin is destroyed in the presence of Holiness unless the sin has been removed or dealt with before the encounter.

248 See for example Exodus 40:33, 35, 36, 38 (in verse 35 it is called both the "tent of meeting" and "tabernacle" in the same verse; see also 39:32).

the "tent of meeting."[249] The first name came out of the temporary nature of this "temple," the second came out of the reality that this place became famous as being the place God would meet with Moses and talk to him "face to face."[250] Later Solomon constructed a more permanent meeting place in Jerusalem and the Old Testament "Temple" of Yahweh came into existence.

To understand this aspect of encounter and "meeting" that related to the Old Testament temple it is helpful to look at several passages. The first passage is Exodus 33:7-11:

> *Now Moses used to take a tent and pitch it outside the camp some distance away, calling it the "tent of meeting". Anyone inquiring of the LORD would go to the tent of meeting outside the camp. And whenever Moses went out to the tent, all the people rose and stood at the entrances of their tents, watching Moses until he entered the tent. As Moses went into the tent, the pillar of cloud would come down and stay at the entrance while the LORD spoke with Moses. Whenever the people saw the pillar of cloud standing at the entrance to the tent, they all stood and worshipped, each at the entrance of their tent. The LORD would speak to Moses face to face, as one speaks to a friend. Then Moses would return to the camp, but his young aide Joshua son of Nun did not leave the tent."* (Exodus 33:7-11)

In this passage we see that the precursor to the Temple in Jerusalem was about meeting God. This was seen as an incredibly special privilege that many people yearned for yet very few could experience. Moses was one of the special few. When Moses went to this special tent, all the people would get up, go to the doorways of their own tents and watch in awe as Moses entered the tent and God responded by meeting with Moses personally. This moment was so incredible that people would worship the LORD when they saw Him coming to meet Moses. Then in the context of

249 See for example Exodus 33:7; 40:30, 32, 35.

250 Exodus 33:11.

that encounter, Moses and God would talk "face to face" like friends. The level of intimacy seen here is astounding. Moses is one of the very few people who had this deep level of encounter with God and lived. Part of the reason is that he was such a humble and meek man[251] that he was able to enter the Presence of the LORD with a fairly pure heart. His meekness made him into the kind of person that could be the friend of God. One of the things this passage teaches us is that we should never take for granted our cross-granted ability to enter into God's Presence. The intimacy we have available to us through the cross is far greater than what Moses experienced. May we always be filled with the same awe we see among the Israelites in this passage.

Moses was a man who understood the importance of the Presence of the LORD. There are several passages where Moses and God dialogue about the value of the Presence of God with the nation of Israel. After the sin of Aaron in making a golden calf for the Israelites to worship, God is angry and tells Moses He has had enough.

> *"Then the LORD said to Moses, "Leave this place, you and the people you brought up out of Egypt and go up to the land I promised . . . I will send an angel before you to drive out the Canaanites, Amorites, . . . Go up to the land flowing with milk and honey. But I will not go with you, because you are a stiff-necked people and I might destroy you on the way." When the people heard these distressing words, they began to mourn . . .* "(Exodus 33:1-4)

Then begins this amazing dialogue between God and Moses:

> *"" . . . You have said, 'I know you by name and you have found favour with me.' If you are pleased with me, teach me your ways so that I may know you and continue to find favour with you. Remember that this nation is your people."*

251 Numbers 12:3 – Moses was the "meekest" or "humblest" man on the face of the earth.

The LORD replied, "My Presence will go with you, and I will give you rest."

Then Moses said to him, "If your Presence does not go with us, do not send us up from here. How will anyone know that you are pleased with me and with your people unless you go with us? What else will distinguish me and your people from all the other people on the face of the earth?"

And the LORD said to Moses, "I will do the very thing you have asked, because I am pleased with you and I know you by name."" (Exodus 33: 12-17)

" . . . *"Lord," he said, "If I have found favour in your eyes, then let the LORD go with us. Although this is a stiff-necked people, forgive our wickedness and our sin, and take us as your inheritance.""* (Exodus 34:9)

There are several things that surface here. First, the sin of the people had so angered God that He was on the verge of cutting off access to His Presence. Moses and the whole nation knew this to be disastrous and they began to mourn at hearing this. Second, it is in the context of meeting the Lord that Moses can "know" Him. Growing in knowledge of the Lord through the instruction of the Lord in the context of one's relationship with Him is what Moses longs for. Moses wants to know God, not just about Him. He wants God's interaction with his life to teach him what God is really like. Third, we see that what Moses is really asking for is that the Presence of the Lord be with him and the people of God. Even when God promises an angel would go with them rather than His Presence, Moses is not happy. He really wants God Himself to be with them. God also does not say to Moses, "OK, I will teach you about me." Rather, He says, "My Presence will be with you." It is the Presence of the LORD that instructs us - the tacit dimension of knowledge. Fourth, "rest" is one of the fruits of the Presence of the Lord with Moses and the nation. When the Presence of the Lord is with Moses and the nation, he and they will have "rest." This connection between rest or peace and the Presence of the Lord is extremely significant. Later when David, a "man after God's own heart"[252] wants to build the Temple of God in Jerusalem, God does not allow him to do this[253] since he is a man of war and, instead, it will be for his son to do who will be a man of peace.[254] Those who build the Temple for God's Presence must be men of peace since God's Presence brings peace.[255] True peace and rest are not possible outside of the Presence of the LORD. Fifth, Moses knows that the Presence of the LORD with him and the nation is a sign of God's favour on them. It is *the* distinguishing characteristic that sets apart the people of God from *every other nation* under the sun. This implies that the Presence of the LORD with His people is obvious to others. The Presence of the LORD is noticeable and bears obvious fruit. Finally, God grants His Presence to Moses and the nation because He is pleased with them and "knows" them (especially Moses). This shows the high value of Godly leaders interceding on behalf of those they lead. Again, there is a relational implication here. God "knows" Moses because they are friends; they talk with one another; they spend time together. Moses also knew that sin could tear apart the intimacy of his relationship with God if God did not take initiative in dealing with it. Moses takes advantage of his access to God to intercede for those around him. Without God choosing to forgive them, it would not be possible for God's Presence to go with them. An angel, while still powerful, was inferior to having the real Presence of the living God with them.

Thus, we see that God is a highly relational God who wants to "know" us as friends. He wants to grant us His Presence, which comes with tremendous blessing, because He loves us and we have His favour. We also see that the distinguishing feature of the people of God is that they have

252 1 Samuel 13:14. You would think that being a "man after God's own heart" would make David worthy of being the one to construct the Jerusalem temple but being a man of "peace" or "rest" was more important.

253 1 Chronicles 17:1-17.

254 1 Chronicles 22:8-9.

255 Later the Epistle to the Hebrews builds on this and talks of how we must enter into the "rest" of God (see Hebrews 3:18; 4:1-11).

God's Presence in their midst. We enter into our identity as God's people when we value and cultivate His Presence; we start to drift from our true identity when we do not value the Presence of God in our midst. Sin is one of the factors that has the most potential for destroying the power of the Presence of the LORD with His people.[256]

THE GLORY OF SOLOMON'S TEMPLE

Later, in the time of Solomon, the "tent of meeting" is finally replaced with a more permanent building. This Old Testament temple was extraordinarily beautiful. The amount of gold and precious jewels used in its construction is mind-boggling. Second Chronicles 3:8 indicates that six hundred talents of fine gold were used in constructing the Most Holy Place of the temple! This is around 21 metric tons of gold with a value of over 1.22 billion dollars US in one room alone of the temple! Wow! And this does not count the value of all the other gold and precious stones used in the construction of the temple. It was one of the great wonders of the ancient world!

It was no wonder that Solomon, at the dedication of the temple, said to the LORD, *"I have built a magnificent temple for you, a place for you to dwell forever"* (2 Chron. 6:2). Yet there was a greater temple to come. Even Solomon asks in 2 Chronicles 6:18 asks, *"But will God really dwell on earth with humans? The heavens, even the highest heavens, cannot contain you. How much less this temple I have built!"* He realized that God is so much greater and larger than anything we can make for Him. Nothing is worthy of HIS worth! All the same, this temple was truly a magnificent temple!

The dedication and consecration of the Old Testament temple was a tremendous event. The people of Israel gathered together and Solomon stood on a platform before them and prayed for the blessing of the LORD

256 See Numbers 35:34: *"Do not defile the land where you live and where I dwell, for I, the LORD (Yahweh), dwell among the Israelites."*

on the temple. In chapter 6 of 2 Chronicles, Solomon prays a powerful prayer:

> *Yet, LORD my God, give attention to your servant's prayer and his plea for mercy. Hear the cry and the prayer that your servant is praying in your presence.*
>
> *May your eyes be open toward this temple day and night, this place of which you said you would put your Name there. May you hear the prayer that your servant prays toward this place.*
>
> *Hear the supplications of your servant and of your people Israel when they pray toward this place. Hear from heaven, your dwelling place; and when you hear, forgive."* (2 Chron. 6:19-21)

Upon hearing this prayer, God responds. The priests have already started the sacrifices for the forgiveness of their sins and the sins of the people, but when Solomon finishes praying *"fire came down from heaven and consumed the burnt offerings and sacrifices, and the glory of the LORD filled the temple."*[257] God had heard the prayer of Solomon and the fire of God and the glory of the LORD descended on the temple. The power of the Presence of the glory of the LORD is so strong the priests cannot enter the temple and all the people fall on their faces in worship, declaring the goodness of the LORD.[258]

Now, as worship is stirred up, Solomon and the people of Israel respond, sacrificing 22,000 head of cattle and 120,000 sheep and goats,[259] an absolutely staggering number of animals offered in sacrifice. The people

257 2 Chronicles 7:1. This is one of five times in the Scriptures where the fire of God falls and consumes sacrifices offered to Him. The five are here, the offering of Samson's parents at the prophecy of the birth of Samson (Judges 13:20), at the inauguration of the Aaronic priesthood and the Tent of Meeting (Leviticus 9:24), David's sacrifice which he offered to God to stop the plague on the people (1 Chronicles 21:26), and Elijah and the prophets of Baal (1 Kings 18:38).

258 2 Chronicles 7:2-3. In Leviticus 9:24 when the fire of God consumes the sacrifice at the inauguration of the Aaronic Priesthood, the people also worship – shouting for joy and falling facedown on the ground.

259 2 Chronicles 7:5.

worship the LORD, singing of His goodness for seven days![260] I doubt any other temple in the history of the world has had such a powerful and costly inauguration.

God is not finished and visits Solomon at night in his palace saying in 2 Chronicles 7:12-16:

> *"I have heard your prayer and have chosen this place for myself as a temple for sacrifices. . . . Now my eyes will be open and my ears attentive to the prayers offered in this place. I have chosen and consecrated this temple so that my Name may be there forever. My eyes and my heart will always be there."* (2 Chron. 7:12, 15-16)

This statement by God fundamentally changed the nation of Israel[261] and made this temple the center of its national life. The living God for the first time placed His Presence permanently in one location, a beautiful temple in Jerusalem built by Solomon. The ache of every human heart for the Presence of God can now be met in this place. God's eyes, ears and heart are now permanently inclined towards the prayers offered there. This so marked the nation of Israel that even now, the one remaining wall of Solomon's temple still in Jerusalem is called the Wailing Wall. Jews from all over the world come to this place, part of the ancient temple of Solomon, to cry out to the LORD and to weep and wail for His mercy upon their lives. This assurance that God would truly hear every prayer prayed in this place is absolutely incredible!

There was no temple like this temple. It was constructed with the best of the best and was dedicated with an incredible amount of pomp and cost. The glory of the living God poured down upon the temple at its dedication. An unprecedented amount of intimacy with the living God is promised through this temple, yet this temple was still only preparatory for something to come. Stephen in Acts 7:48-49, while recounting the history of Israel echoes the comment by Solomon on the greatness of God and how He cannot be contained by any temple saying, *"However,*

260 2 Chronicles 7:6-8.

261 Mentioned in chapter 3 briefly. This is why pilgrims came to Jerusalem in hope.

the Most High does not live in houses made by human hands. As the prophet says: "Heaven is my throne, and the earth in my footstool. What kind of house will you build for me? says the Lord. Or where will my resting place be?"" Even the most beautiful and wonderful temple does not measure up to the beauty and wonder of our God. The question is: what kind of "house" will ever be good enough for Him? The implication is one not made with human hands! Through the cross that is exactly what God brought into being.

This exquisite Old Testament temple was never intended to be permanent. The gold, the beauty, the rituals associated with it, all pointed to something greater. It revealed the relational passion of the living God for humanity and His desire for us to come into His Presence. And it showed the cost of coming into that Presence and that God would provide a way to make it happen. After the cross, it was inevitable that this wonderful temple would be destroyed, never to be rebuilt since through the cross God had finally provided for Himself a better temple, a better means to empower loved humanity to come into His Presence. This incredible temple was no longer needed once Jesus died on the cross. It should have been no surprise that the temple was destroyed in AD 70, less than 40 years after the death of Jesus, and has not been rebuilt since.

This new temple would produce a deeper intimacy than that experienced by Moses. It would be inaugurated by a better sacrifice[262] than 22,000 head of cattle and 120,000 sheep and goats. It would be inaugurated by the sacrifice of the Holy Son of God Most High. It would be a more magnificent temple than one decorated with millions of dollars' worth of fine gold and precious jewels. It would be a temple cleansed by the blood of Jesus, adorned with the beauty of humanity released to be the light of God in the world, sparkling with the powerful Presence of God and of His love for a lost world. It would be filled with a more intimate Presence of the living God, whose ears and eyes would be permanently inclined towards His people. There would be an even greater confidence that the

262 See Hebrews 9:23 and Hebrews 10:4, 10, 14, 18.

living God heard the prayers of His people since He Himself would dwell in them. This temple not made with human hands would be a temple fit for the creator to fill. This new temple would be the means for God to finally call a lost humanity back into His arms. This new temple would be the fulfillment of everything represented by the Old Testament temple. This new temple would be a place where every cross-washed believer on earth could connect to heaven and join in the worship of God occurring in the heavenly temple.

Summary

A temple is a special place consecrated and set apart to be a place to worship God. In the Old Testament, the temple was to be a place where the people of God could come to pray, seek the face of God and worship Him. It was also to be a place where God's blessing would flow out to the nations. Through the Old Testament temple and tabernacle, we gain a greater appreciation of how, through the cross of Jesus, we become the new temples for God's Presence. Despite the magnificence of the Temple of Solomon, we as new temples formed through the sacrifice of Jesus have greater worth and value in God's eyes.

Key points from this chapter include:

1. We as Christians are designed to be world changers. As we come to Christ and enter into the meaning of his death and crucifixion, we become a sanctified place where God can dwell. We become a place where heaven touches earth.

2. God has always wanted to dwell on the earth with mankind. This is why He has set up temples where He is worshipped and where His Presence dwells.

3. There are five main temples of God in the Bible: The Old Testament Tabernacle which became the Temple of Solomon; the New Testament Temple of the corporate gathering of the Church; the New Testament Temple of the individual believer; the Heavenly Temple which is the pattern for the earthly temples; and, finally, God Himself who comes to dwell on earth in the New Jerusalem.

4. The Presence of God is the distinguishing characteristic of each of the temples of God.
5. The Old Testament Tabernacle was a place where God met and talked with the leaders of Israel. It was a place of encounter and worship where God's glory resided.
6. Solomon's temple was an incredibly beautiful temple adorned with gold and precious stones, yet its beauty and cost are nothing compared to the beauty of the Lord. It was His Presence in it that gave it value.
7. Yet, despite its splendour and cost, it was never intended to be more than a temporary temple until, through Jesus, God would establish a greater and more permanent temple not "made with human hands."

Entering Into His Presence

Put on some worship music and spend time in the Presence of the Lord. Invite His Presence to come and saturate your heart. If needed, repent, so that there are no barriers between you and God. Thank Him for forgiving you through Jesus.

Take some time to read Solomon's Prayer of Dedication of His temple in 2 Chronicles 6:12-21. Read it slowly and prayerfully, imagining that you are the temple that Solomon is praying over, and that you are the temple being dedicated. Imagine that you are the long planned for temple that David and Solomon worked towards.

Now read 2 Chronicles 7:12-16. Imagine again as you read God's response to Solomon's prayer, that you are the temple God is referring to. What does it mean personally to you that you are the temple of God?

Prayer

Lord, like Solomon, I want to acknowledge that there is no God like You in all the earth. We can search the whole earth and even the highest heaven and never find Your equal. You are the King of Kings and the Lord of Lords.

You are my King, my Lord.

Thank You, Lord, that You are a God of Presence, who loves to reveal Yourself to mankind. Thank You, Jesus, that You died so that we might come into Your Presence, washed clean of all sin by Your blood.

I stand like the Israelites at their tent doorways worshipping as You came down to meet with Moses in the Tent of Meeting. Help me to have the same awe as I come now into Your Presence. May I never take it for granted.

Lord, make me a consecrated place set apart to worship You. May my worship of You spill over to bless others. May others see the glory of Your Presence in me and in my life.

In the precious name of Jesus, I pray,

Amen.

10

The Presence of God in The Corporate Gathering of Believers

Throughout the Bible, God is forming a community of people who are characterized by His Presence in their midst. The Presence of God among His people is intended to be the basis for how God will bless the nations and draw all men to Himself. Through Jesus, God's plan to establish His Presence among His people comes to fruition. The cross makes both of the New Testament Temples of God possible.

THE TEMPLE OF THE CORPORATE GATHERING OF BELIEVERS:

While more permanent than the Old Testament temple was, the temple inaugurated by the sacrifice of Jesus on the cross still points to a future fulfillment and destiny for every believer. Every believer will one day be fully in the Presence of God in heaven, surrounding the throne of God and worshipping in the heavenly Temple. Yet the blessing of that future moment and time is brought into our present experience through the cross of Christ.

The first New Testament temple is the Presence of God in the *corporate gathering* of the Church. This is the fourth dimension of the Presence of God in the world: the Presence of God in the gathered Church. It is about God's Presence making a whole community a temple where He can be known and worshipped. This is closer to what we see in the Old Testament where an entire nation was to be characterized by His Presence.

Three passages clearly show that God fills the corporate gathering of His people making them collectively His temple. These are Ephesians 2:19-22, 1 Peter 2:4-5, 9-10 and 1 Corinthians 3:9-11, 16-17. In the Western world we over-emphasize individualism to such an extent that we often interpret these passages as applying to the individual Christian. While the individual believer is filled with the Presence of the Lord, there is a very vital truth that God fills the corporate gathering of His people in a way that He does not fill individuals (the "you" in the passages below are in the plural form).

> *"Consequently, you (pl.) are no longer foreigners and strangers, but fellow citizens with God's people and also members of his household, built on the foundation of the apostles and prophets, with Christ Jesus himself as the chief cornerstone. In him the whole building is joined together and rises to become a holy temple in the Lord. And in him you too are being built together to become a dwelling in which God lives by his Spirit."* (Eph. 2:19-22)

> *"As you (pl.) come to him, the living Stone – rejected by humans but chosen by God and precious to him – you also, like living stones, are being built into a spiritual house to be a holy priesthood, offering spiritual sacrifices acceptable to God through Jesus Christ .... But you are a chosen people, a royal priesthood, a holy nation, God's special possession, that you may declare the praises of him who called you out of darkness into his wonderful light. Once you were not a people, but now you are the people of God; once you had not received mercy, but now you have received mercy."* (1 Peter 2:4-5, 9-10)

The emphasis in the Ephesians passage is that we collectively are part of God's people and members of His household, therefore we, through Christ, are formed into a holy temple to be the dwelling place for the Spirit of God. The new intimacy we have with God because of the cross of Christ results in the Presence of the Spirit living in us corporately. We see the same in the 1 Peter passage: as we come to *the* living Stone, Jesus, we, as living stones, are being built into a spiritual house for the Lord. Through the Spirit of God, we are transformed into a chosen people, a royal priesthood, a holy nation, a chosen possession of God set apart to declare His praises. Our collective identity as people of God has been changed through the cross. We now, as living stones, have been built into a living temple that God can inhabit for the greater blessing of mankind. We become God's chosen possession, and we become a nation of priests[263] (under Christ our High Priest) who mediate God's love to others, set apart as worshippers of the living God. We become the new "people" of God characterized by His Presence. The linkage of worship with this "new" temple of God is important as this has always been one of the principal activities of the temple priests. Now through the cross we have a new level of intimacy with the Lord and can relate to Him clearly and access the blessings of heaven more easily. This is part of the fulfillment of the blessing prophesied over the line and lineage of Jacob.[264] Since the Presence of God can now fill the corporate gathering of His people, no matter where they are, the blessing of the Lord can now impact the wider world in a new way. With the death of Jesus, God's Presence and blessings are no longer tied to one specific physical location or nation. Now the entire world can have access to the Presence of the Lord through the new temple God has formed for Himself.

So, what does it mean for us corporately to be the new temple hosting the Presence of God? Paul in 1 Corinthians 3:9-11,16-17 writes:

> *"For we are co-workers in God's service; you (pl.) are God's field, God's building.*

263 One of the implications of passages such as Joshua 3:1-17 is that since the Priests carry the Arc of the Covenant which symbolized the Lord's Presence and went in front of the people into the Promised Land, one of the roles of the priests, besides mediating between God and mankind, is to carry the Presence of the Lord so that others can follow them into the "Promised Land" God has for them.

264 See the Genesis 28 passage and Jacob's dream.

> *By the grace God has given me, I laid a foundation as a wise builder, and someone else is building on it. But each one should build with care.(vs. 11) For no one can lay any foundation other than the one already laid, which is Jesus Christ . . .*
>
> *Don't you (pl.) know that you yourselves are God's temple and that God's Spirit dwells in your midst? If anyone destroys God's temple, God will destroy that person; for God's temple is sacred, and you together are that temple."*

First, those that seek to "build" the church must build the Church on a foundation that rests on Jesus Christ the cornerstone. To build the Church on anything else is to skew the development of the Church and to inhibit the fullness of the Presence of the LORD in it. Jesus must always be the center of our disciple making. Second, the corporate life of the Church must cultivate and be characterized by the Presence of the Holy Spirit who is "in your midst". The gathered community of God's people is a sacred place because God is there. Third, since the gathered community of God's people is a holy temple, rich in God's Presence, the sanctity of the Church gathering must not be destroyed or *"God will destroy that person."* God highly values His Presence in the Church. To attack the Church is to attack what God jealously watches over. Anyone doing this is playing a dangerous game.

The reality of the Presence of the LORD in the gathered community of believers also impacts corporate prayer. Jesus says in Matthew 18:18-20:

> *"Truly I tell you, whatever you bind on earth will be bound in heaven, and whatever you loose on earth will be loosed in heaven.*
>
> *Again, truly I tell you that if two of you on earth agree about anything they ask for, it will be done for them by my Father in heaven.* ***For where two or three gather in my name, there I am with them.***"[265] (emphasis added)

265 Some translations have "there I am in the midst of them." (See NAS and KJV)

John adds in 1 John 5:14-15: *"This is the confidence we have in approaching God: that if we ask anything according to His will, he hears us. And if we know that he hears us - whatever we ask - we know that we have what we have asked of him."*

Here we see in the Matthew passage that the prayers of the gathered community of believers, even if only involving two or three people, are powerful because the Presence of the LORD is with that gathered group of God's people. God's Presence increases the efficacy of prayer. This is why God gives the Church the ability to bind and loose. We have true authority when we gather in the Presence of God to carry out His will. He is with us, in our midst. There are times when corporate prayer and worship are more powerful than individual prayer. There often seems to be a catalytic effect increasing God's Presence and power when the Church gathers in conferences or other settings.

From the John passage we see how power in prayer comes through praying according to the will of God. As we do this, He gives us what we ask for. Here we see the necessity of aligning our prayers with the Presence of God who is in our midst and praying that God's will be accomplished. His Presence is with us, we must be sensitive to that Presence and then pray according to what is He doing amongst us and through us.[266] He hears us, more importantly, we also need to hear Him.

We ramp up our understanding of the power of corporate prayer when we realize that God will use it to accomplish His will. In the Old Testament, God's Presence was linked to the Temple, and He committed Himself to hear and answer every prayer prayed there.[267] How much more will He listen to and respond to prayers prayed in corporate gatherings of believers which is His new temple formed by the shed blood of His Son? We can have confidence that when we pray together, God hears and sees us just like He did when the Israelites prayed in Solomon's temple. And

266 This is in line with what Jesus himself did. He only did what the Father did and so was able to accomplish great things. God heard Jesus because he prayed according to the will of the Father and Jesus received what he prayed because of this (John 5:19).

267 2 Chronicles 7:12ff.

as we seek His will together and pray accordingly, we will see Him do amazing things.

The nature of our life together influences how powerfully God can inhabit the gathered community. Are we cultivating holiness and purity as we come together? Are we cultivating love for one another? We are to love the Church as Christ loves the Church. We need to deal with and correct sin in the corporate setting if necessary. There needs to be a culture of grace where repentance and confession are safe when we have sinned against others in the body of Christ. Some sins which have a "corporate" dimension such as slander, backbiting, criticism, jealousy, gossip, and even sexual sins are particularly destructive of community and so must be dealt with in order to preserve the Presence of the LORD in our midst. This is why Jesus, Paul and John all emphasized the need to "love one another"[268] since love and holiness cultivate the Presence of God in the gathered community of believers.

THE HOLY SPIRIT AND THE GATHERED COMMUNITY OF BELIEVERS

The corporate experience of the spiritual gifts is intended by God to build up His Presence in the gathered Church. God needs to be strong in US *together* and not just strong in ME individually. One of the means God uses to build up and edify His Presence in the Church, His temple, is through the expression of the gifts of the Spirit which are to draw us closer to Him. Paul indicates that we are to excel in and pursue those gifts that build up our corporate life together.[269] Each of the gifts of the Spirit have a context in which they are most appropriately used. Prophecy, for example, is mentioned in 1 Corinthians 14 as one of the gifts that builds

268 John 13:34: *"A new command I give you: Love one another."* Romans 13:8 *"Let no debt remain outstanding except the continuing debt to love one another."* 1 John 4:7 *"Dear friends, let us love one another. . ."* 1 John 4:12 *"No one has ever seen God; but if we love one another, God lives in us. . ."*

269 1 Corinthians 14:1,3, 6-12.

up and edifies the Church.[270] It is *meant* to be used to strengthen, encourage and comfort people in the Church and make us stronger together in Christ.[271] It helps us to nurture His Presence amongst us and can even be used to bring others into an awareness of the reality of the Presence of God and lead to repentance and salvation.[272] Not all of the gifts of the Spirit are best used in the corporate setting, but some are designed to function best amongst groups of people.

God's heart is always to bless people with His Presence, and He will use the gathered church and the activity of the Holy Spirit amongst His people to call people to Himself. Sometimes, being a *"light to the nations"*[273] means that through the Church, the gifts of the Holy Spirit will spill over into the community around us to display concretely God's love and passion for the lost. There are times when gifts of deliverance, healing, faith and prophecy for example can be used among non-believers to show God's reality. If non-believers are not coming into the Church gathering, we must carry the reality of God's Presence with us out to where they are located.[274] Since the gathered community is now the temple of the living God, God's Presence is no-longer limited to a specific location in order for others to encounter Him.

Summary

Through the cross, God created the gathered Church to be a temple where His Presence can dwell. He intends it to be a blessing for the nations and to be a place where "foreigners" can encounter the tangible Presence of the Lord. The Gifts of the Spirit help to build up and cultivate

---

270 1 Corinthians 14:3, 6, 24-25.

271 1 Corinthians 14:3.

272 1 Corinthians 14:24-25.

273 Isaiah 60:1-3.

274 In 1 Corinthians 14:24-25 there is an unbeliever in the church gathering who is convicted by a word of prophesy. Often today, unbelievers do not come into the church gathering in order for a word of prophesy to have this kind of impact so we need to go out to where they are.

the Presence of God in the Church community. God's love flowing in and through the Church is key in making His Presence real to outsiders.

Key points in this chapter are:

1. Through the cross of Christ, God has formed for Himself a community of people who become a temple where He is worshipped and where His Presence dwells. This New Testament temple replaces the Old Testament temple of God. Through Jesus we are now a chosen people, a royal priesthood, a holy nation, a chosen possession of God set apart to declare His praises.
2. The Presence of God in the Church is a fulfillment of the blessing prophesied over the line and lineage of Jacob – that through Jacob all nations of the earth will be blessed. Now the Presence of God is more widely dispersed around the world to be a blessing to others.
3. The power of prayer is increased in the corporate setting when we realize that God Himself is with us and present to us. When we align ourselves with the will of God as we pray, we will see answers to prayer. God hears the prayers offered in this temple just like He did in the Old Testament temple of Solomon.
4. Our corporate life together influences how powerfully God can inhabit the gathered community. There needs to be the ability to repent and confess where we have sinned against others in the body of Christ. Holiness needs to be cultivated in the gathered community of believers.
5. The corporate life of the Church must cultivate and reflect the Presence of the Holy One of Israel. The gifts of the Holy Spirit are to be used in the corporate setting to build up the Church and cultivate the Presence of God.

Entering Into His Presence

Put on some worship music and spend time in the Presence of the Lord, inviting His Presence to come and fill you again. Repent, if need be, so that there are no barriers between you and God. Thank Him for forgiving you through Jesus.

Read again Solomon's Prayer of Dedication of His temple in 2 Chronicles 6:12-21 and God's response in 7:12-16. This time read it slowly and prayerfully imagining that **your church** is the temple that Solomon is praying over, that **your church** is the temple being dedicated. Imagine that **your church** is the long-planned-for temple that David and Solomon worked towards.

Pray for your church, that she would faithfully represent God in the world and be a place where His Presence is rich and strong. Forgive those in your church if needed. Repent if you have bad-mouthed the Church at all. Determine as much as possible to do those things that express love to others in your church and build them up in the Lord. Ask God to release spiritual gifts that build up His Presence in your church when believers gather.

Prayer

Lord, thank You for the Church. Help me to truly appreciate how it is Your gift to me so that I can grow in You. Make my church a place that is rich in Your Presence.

Lord, show me if I have sinned against Your Presence in the Church. May I love the Church as You love it. Help me to lay down my life for Your Church even as you did. I repent of the sins I have committed against others (be specific if necessary). Forgive me where I have maligned and bad-mouthed Your bride.

May Your Presence, Lord, fill my church so that You can be glorified through us. Make my church a blessing to the nations. Fill us with Your love for others. Help us to go out to where the "nations" are and not stay inside the safety of the Church walls.

Lord, release the power of prayer in my church. Align our wills with Yours so that we can see You act amongst us and through us. Increase our ability to be effective in prayer.

Anoint us with Your Holy Spirit. Release the gifts of the Spirit in us so that You can be glorified and people loved.

Bless us with Your Presence. We need You to be powerful and real amongst us. We need You.

In the precious name of Jesus, I pray,

Amen.

11

The Presence of God in the Individual Believer

God loves people. He created Adam and Eve so that He could dwell with mankind and enjoy relationship with them. He, even though He was the creator-God, came and spent time with them in "the cool of the day."[275] He enjoyed being present to them and them being present to Him. Adam and Eve's sin destroyed this intimacy, yet God initiated a plan that unfolds step by step in the Old Testament so that He could restore this lost intimacy. He does this through forming for Himself a community of people who will be characterized by His Presence. This is fulfilled through the cross and was talked about in the last chapter. He also, through the cross, destroyed every barrier to His Presence - including those that existed within the hearts of mankind - so that He could make the individual believer His dwelling place. This is the subject of this chapter.

THE TEMPLE OF THE INDIVIDUAL BELIEVER

The fifth dimension of the Presence of the LORD is the indwelling Presence of the LORD in the individual believer. God comes to us,

275 Genesis 3:8.

through the cross of Christ, to make each of us His dwelling place, His temple. This produces an intimate communion between the LORD and individual believers.

Many of the passages in the New Testament that refer to how the individual Christian is the dwelling place of the Lord use the plural 'you' form of the personal pronoun. However, the context suggests that, while Jesus and Paul are talking to a group of disciples, what they are saying applies to the individuals within that group. The reality seems to be that the Presence of God spills over and overlaps between the two. The line between the corporate and individual temples of God is fuzzier than most Westerners are comfortable with. Of course, the only reason we as both individuals and as a corporate gathering of believers can be a "temple" is through the sanctifying work of the cross of Christ in our lives.

One passage where we see the interplay of God being in both the individual and the gathered community of believers is found in John 14.

> *"And I will ask the Father and he will give you (pl.) another advocate to help you (pl.) and be with you (pl.) forever – the Spirit of Truth. The world cannot accept him, because it neither sees him or knows him. But you (pl.) know him, for he lives with you (pl.) and will be in you (pl.)."* (John 14:16-17)

In this passage Jesus talks about how after He leaves, He will send His disciples the Spirit of Truth who will lead them and guide them into truth. The corporate gathering of disciples through their acceptance and knowledge of the Holy Spirit prepares the environment for Him to lead and guide the community into truth. This "Spirit of Truth" does not live in the "world" (also a corporate identity) because He is not recognized and accepted by it. In other words, the work of the Holy Spirit is more easily recognized in the gathered community of believers because they are predisposed to accept His reality in their midst. However, part of the role of the Holy Spirit is also to bring the individual into truth. The community cannot live out the truth if the individuals in that community have not themselves accepted and submitted to truth. In this passage, while Jesus is focusing on how the Holy Spirit will lead and guide them as a group, it seems clear that the Holy Spirit will fulfill the same role within the individuals that make up that group. In order for the Holy Spirit to be "in" the community, He must also be "in" the individuals of the community.

The Presence of God in the individual believer is a little clearer in John 15:

> *"Remain in me, as I also remain in you (pl.). No branch (sing.) can bear fruit by itself; it must remain in the vine. Neither can you (pl.) bear fruit unless you (pl.) remain in me.*
>
> *I am the vine; you (pl.) are the branches. If you (sing.) remain in me and I in you (sing.),*[276] *you (sing.)*[277] *will bear much fruit; apart from me you (pl.) can do nothing. If you (sing.) do not remain in me, you (sing.) are like a branch that is thrown away and withers; such branches are picked up, thrown into the fire and burned. If you (pl.) remain in me and my words remain in you (pl.), ask whatever you (pl.) wish and it will be done for you (pl.). This is to my Father's glory, that you (pl.) bear much fruit, showing yourselves to be my disciples."* (John 15:4-8)

In this second passage, Jesus is using an extended analogy of a vine and branches to show that we, as disciples of Jesus, must live in Him if we are to bear fruit. We see the clear interplay of Jesus being "in" the disciples both as a group (verses 4, 7, 8) and as individuals (verses 5, 6). Although He uses the plural 'you' form in this passage talking to the disciples, He also uses the image of single branches being attached to the vine and emphasizes that each branch must be attached to the vine (remain in Him) if it is to bear fruit. Thus, the life of the vine (Jesus) passes to each individual branch as they all remain attached to Him. Both the individual and the gathered community of believers draws its life from Jesus to the

276 Literally this is – "the one who remains in me and I in him, he will bear much fruit . . ."

277 Similarly, this is literally – "if anyone does not remain in me, he is like a branch that withers . . . "

degree that they remain in Him and the Presence of the Lord fills all parts of the "vine" empowering them to bear fruit for the glory of the Father.

Both the gathered community of believers and the individual believer must create the environment that cultivates the life-giving Presence of the Lord in their midst. They do this by "remaining" in Jesus so that He can "remain" in them. They also do this by allowing the "words" of Jesus to bear fruit within their own lives[278] so they can bear fruit in the wider community. When the Gospel of Jesus is freely preached and its reality nurtured, God's Presence sustains and nurtures life, and, in this analogy, bears fruit that points to the reality of God and reveals His glory. Nothing in this world produces the kind of Presence that nurtures life like God's Presence does.

A passage that talks specifically about individual Christians being the temple or dwelling place of the Holy Spirit is 1 Corinthians 6:15-20:

> *Do you not know that your bodies are members of Christ himself? Shall I then take the members of Christ and unite them with a prostitute? Never! Do you not know that he who unites himself with a prostitute is one with her in body? For it is said, 'The two will become one flesh' But he who is united with the Lord is one with him in spirit. Flee from sexual immorality. All other sins a person commits are outside the body, but whoever sins sexually sins against their own body. Do you not know that your bodies are temples of the Holy Spirit, who is in you, whom you have received from God? You are not your own; you were bought at a price. Therefore honor God with your bodies.* (1 Cor. 6:15-20)

Here while Paul mostly uses the plural 'you' form, he is clearly talking to the gathered group of Christians as a gathering of individuals who are each one a temple of God. The emphasis is that since the holy God lives

278 In John 8 there is an extended dialogue between Jesus and those who are struggling to believe that he is the Messiah. In vs 37 Jesus says: "*. . . you are trying to kill me, because you have no room (in your heart) for my word.*" I prefer the French of this verse which indicates that they want to kill Jesus because they have not allowed his word to "penetrate" their hearts (". . . parce que ma parole ne pénètre pas en vous" (Louis Segond)) We need to allow the words of Jesus to penetrate our hearts.

in each one of us, having purchased us by the shed blood of His Son, each one of us is to live holy lives that honor His Presence in us. The previous verses to this passage talk about how we have been formed and made to be habitations of God[279] and were not created for sexual immorality (vs. 13). And, since Christ lives in us, we have the resurrection life of Jesus flowing in us (vs. 14). Therefore, since the cross of Christ and the work of the Spirit has united us with Christ Himself, to visit a prostitute[280] (vs. 15-16) and join ourselves sexually to her is to defile Christ in us (vs. 15). Sexual sin is different than other types of sin since when we join our bodies to another person sexually our spirits also join with theirs (we become "one flesh"[281] with them), and so our interior "being" gets impacted and touched by what we are doing. We need to recognise this, and flee any sexual immorality that might make our temples unclean and defile the Presence of God in us. It is clear here that since God dwells in the individual Christian, it has tremendous implications for how we are to live. The Presence of the Holy One in us requires His temple to be holy, consecrated and set apart for Him. If we are to cultivate and seek more of the Presence of God in us, there are certain things we must avoid.[282] This is true even if everyone around us does them. We are to live our lives as those who are designed by God to be HIS habitation and not fill our lives with other things that may defile us. We are to be God-full and idol free.

---

279 We were created in the image of God before sin entered the world and thus were made for Him and not for sin.

280 It is not just visiting a prostitute that is wrong, but any sexual sin where we become united with another person sexually in an improper way. We are the temple of the Lord and must keep that temple free of any type of uncleanness.

281 The "one flesh" is not just physically becoming "one" with the other. It is our whole being becoming united with the other. Sex involves a physical, psychological, emotional and spiritual union with the other person. It is not only a physical activity. This is why it is so powerful and affects us at multiple levels.

282 See Eph. 5:18: *"Do not get drunk on wine, which leads to debauchery. Instead be filed with the Spirit."* Also in Acts, the disciples and others spend ten days praying(and likely fasting) before they were filled with the Spirit. As they do this, they are avoiding the things that distract them from seeking the face of God. We need to be seeking more of the Holy Spirit and this often means separating ourselves from what keeps us from God (Acts 1:12-14; 2:1-4).

In addition, since our human nature has "fallen short" of the glory of God[283] and has been corrupted by sin, for the believer it is "normal" to fight *against* our human nature in order to live according to the pattern of holiness. While it is in vogue to hear people talking about how we must not put any limitations on our ability to express our "inner sense of self," we are called Biblically **not** to live according to our own nature, but according to God's. We are created in His image, and we find ourselves by coming back to that image. We are to be *"holy as He is holy"*[284] and the reason is so that His Presence in us can be strong, making us, as His temple, a holy and sanctified place. Relationship with the Holy One of Israel, and intimacy with Him, is more important than doing what is 'normal' according to our fallen human nature. Happiness and fulfillment are found in Him and not in ourselves or in the world. We were designed to thrive in the context of holiness. Unfortunately, sin has blinded our minds and spirits to who we really are, and we only re-discover ourselves when we come to God in repentance and live in holiness.

THE BLESSINGS OF THE PRESENCE OF THE HOLY SPIRIT RESIDING IN US

A passage that specifically mentions that the Holy Spirit resides in us is Romans 8. This chapter does not mention that the individual Christian is a "temple of God," but it does repeatedly mention the impact of the Holy Spirit residing in us and fleshes out for us the many blessings of His Presence. Structurally it is designed by Paul to be a literary "climax" where each point builds on the previous one until he comes to the culminating point that through Jesus Christ, because of the Presence of the Holy Spirit in us, we are more than conquerors and can never be separated from the deep love of the Father for us.

A section of this chapter that emphasizes in particular that the Holy Spirit lives in us is verses 9-11:

283 Romans 3:23.

284 Leviticus 19:2; 22:32; 1 Peter 1:15.

> *"You, however, are not in the realm of the flesh but are in the realm of the Spirit, if indeed* ***the Spirit of God lives in you****. And if anyone does not* ***have the Spirit of Christ****, they do not belong to Christ. But* ***if Christ is in you****, then even though your body is subject to death because of sin,* ***the Spirit gives life*** *because of righteousness. And if the Spirit of him who raised Jesus from the dead is* ***living in you****, he who raised Christ from the dead will also* ***give life to your mortal bodies because of his Spirit who lives in you****."* (Romans 8:9-11, emphasis added)

These verses indicate that the corporate gathering of believers is the gathering of those who "belong" to Christ[285] and have the Spirit of God living in them. As the Spirit of God lives in each member of the community, He releases them into life since He destroys the power of sin in them and brings them into righteousness.[286] In effect, He liberates them from bondage to sin which brings death,[287] so that they can experience the life righteousness brings.[288] The Holy Spirit who raised Christ from the dead also does something else: He brings that same resurrecting power of God and applies it to our mortal bodies, bringing physical vitality to our physical bodies. The "life" that comes from the Presence of God births health and life in us as He dwells in us individually.

From the rest of chapter 8, we see that the Holy Spirit in us also does the following:[289] He breaks the power of condemnation over us by applying the cross to our lives (vs. 1-4); He helps us keep our minds on the things of the Spirit rather than the things of the flesh (vs. 5-8); He helps us to live according to the Spirit and not the flesh (vs. 12-13); He adopts us into God's family and gives us an inner conviction that we are truly God's

285 They have been bought with a price 1 Corinthians 6:20.

286 Sin is death and righteousness is life. Romans 6:23.

287 Romans 6:23; Proverbs 10:16.

288 Part of what the Spirit is doing as He lives in us is applying the meaning of the cross of Christ to our lives and bringing us into the liberty purchased for us by the sacrifice of Jesus.

289 Most of these are only possible since the Holy Spirit lives in us individually.

children and now have intimacy with God as a Father (vs. 14-16); He gives us spiritual authority by making us heirs and co-heirs with Christ (vs. 17); He causes the liberty given by the Spirit of God to His children to spill over and impact all of creation (vs. 18-25); He helps us to pray even when we do not know how to pray (vs. 26-27); He causes all things to work together according to the love of God for us (vs. 28); He conforms us to the image of Christ and brings us into our destiny (vs. 29-30); He makes us conquerors and victors in Christ (vs. 31-33); Finally, He unites us with Christ so that nothing can separate us from His love (vs. 34-39). This is quite a list! All of these come from carrying the Presence of the Holy Spirit in our lives. The Holy Spirit catalyzes a transformation from sin and death to life and righteousness. The Holy Spirit helps us to grow from people who are struggling with condemnation to become people who are conquerors and victors who know we are truly and completely loved. Knowing God has chosen us and loves us and wants to make us His holy dwelling place showers dignity and honor upon us.

BUILDING UP THE PRESENCE OF GOD IN THE INDIVIDUAL CHRISTIAN

The gifts of the Spirit each have a context in which they function best. First Corinthians 14 suggests that prophecy or a word of knowledge or a word of instruction functions best in the corporate setting[290] and that speaking in tongues functions best privately.[291] The other gifts of the spirit seem to fall somewhere between these two.[292] All of the various gifts of the Spirit of God are intended to build up the Presence of God in our midst and equip us to express His love to the world. The gift of the Spirit that is particularly helpful to increase the Presence of God in the individual Christian is speaking in tongues. As is clear in 1 Corinthians 14, speaking

290 1 Corinthians 14:3-4, 6.

291 1 Corinthians 14:3-5 – unless God gives a message in tongues that is interpreted so that the church corporately can be edified (vs. 5).

292 For example, discernment is important in both the corporate and private setting.

in tongues involves our spirits speaking to God and praying without our minds being actively engaged (vs, 2, 14) and edifies us as individuals (vs. 4). Whereas gifts of the Spirit such as prophecy are more important in the corporate setting since they edify and build up the Church (see vss. 3, 4, 5, 6, 12, 19), we are still to pursue the gift of tongues as a means to help us as we pray and seek to increase our intimacy with God. In the corporate setting, Paul does not encourage speaking in tongues unless there is an interpretation so the Church can be edified by what God is saying (vs. 26-27). Yet in the private setting, Paul is happy that he speaks in tongues more than his audience does (vs 18). It is all a matter of context which gift should be emphasized where.

Part of the reason that tongues as a gift of the Spirit is more appropriate in the private setting is that it is easily misunderstood and appears foolish to others.[293] We normally do not know what we are praying since our minds are not engaged.[294] It occurs at a deeper level than the mind, spirit to Spirit as our spirits converse with God.[295] It is intended to build up humility in us and dependence on the Holy Spirit. It also does not produce unity within the corporate setting when practiced there.[296] Unfortunately what is intended by God to produce humility in us and unity in the church when used appropriately often produces the opposite when used inappropriately. I have seen the gift of tongues used in the corporate setting as a badge of pride as people try to show in front of others that they have been blessed by God. When used in this way, it shows the immaturity of the "practitioner" and shows that they still struggle with feeling like orphans in the family of God, insecure in the Father's love for them. This kind of usage does not invalidate the gift of tongues. It just needs to be practiced appropriately.

---

293 1 Corinthians 14:9-11.

294 1 Corinthians 14:14.

295 1 Corinthians 14:2.

296 Since what is said by people is not understood, we appear to one another as "foreigners" (1 Corinthians 14:11).

There are three reasons why praying in tongues in the private setting is helpful: it builds us up in the Lord; it helps us to align our spirits with the Spirit of God;[297] and it is helpful in spiritual warfare as we engage with spiritual forces we do not fully understand. We need to pursue and practice those gifts of the Spirit that build up the Presence of the Lord in us individually as His Temple.

THE PRESENCE OF GOD IN US MAKES US VESSELS OF HONOR

Holiness cultivates the Presence of God in us. We are to be holy as God is holy.[298] Holiness makes us useful to God, able to carry His Presence into a world that needs His love. 2 Timothy 2:20-21 indicates:

> *"In a large house there are articles not only of gold and silver, but also of wood and clay, some are for special purposes and some for common use. Those who cleanse themselves from the latter will be instruments for special purposes, made holy, useful to the Master and prepared to do any good work."*

Through the work of the Holy Spirit in our lives, we "cleanse ourselves" from the common things so that we become vessels of honor, useful to God our Master, set apart for "special purposes." When we do this, we prepare our lives to do "uncommon" things. Then God decides how to best use us as sanctified vessels. Now we can do great works for God without being defined or labeled by them. We are simply being used according to the purpose He has set us aside to accomplish.

We need to be ruthless with any personal sin that creeps into our lives as it always impacts far more than just us. It will touch our families, our jobs, our neighborhoods and much more. Sin brings death and disintegration. Holiness brings life and fruitfulness. Repentance, honesty and humility need to always be close to our hearts so that we can remain as

297 Thus it helps us with intercession.

298 1 Peter 1:15.

much as possible in the Presence of God so that our lives can be vessels of honor that lift up and bless the Lord.

THE PRESENCE OF GOD IN THE INDIVIDUAL TEMPLE OF GOD IS ROOTED IN HEAVEN

Second Corinthians 5 indicates that the house of God formed in us is rooted in Heaven:

> *. . . if the earthly tent we live in is destroyed, we have a building from God, an eternal house in heaven, not built with human hands. Meanwhile we groan, longing to be clothed instead with our heavenly dwelling. . .*
>
> *For while we are in this tent, we groan and are burdened . . . to be clothed instead with our heavenly dwelling, so that what is mortal may be swallowed up by life.* (2 Cor. 5:1-2, 4)

The Presence of God in us is a foretaste of what will one day occur in heaven. Our "tent" on earth is imperfect, subject to sickness and suffering so that we long one day to be clothed with the perfection of heaven. In this world we have challenges and difficulties.[299] It can be tough! We are at times confronted with our own feebleness. Yet the feebleness of our bodies is less important than what God is doing in us and where we are going. Our trials here give us a hunger for heaven where the reality of God's Presence will be more fully released to us. His Spirit has been given to us as a deposit on this future destiny.[300] Since He is in us, we have access to God's life and victory now. For many, this "deposit" of the Presence of God in them has been worth the pain and persecution they have experienced.

---

299 One of these challenges is that persecution is at its highest in 100s of years against Christians worldwide.

300 2 Corinthians 5:5.

BEING THE TEMPLE FOR THE SAKE OF OTHERS:

As I have said before, God has made us "Beth-El," the "house of God," so that we can be the "Gateway of Heaven" for others who do not know the LORD. We are the place where heaven is able to touch the earth because the cross of Christ bridges heaven and earth and makes heaven accessible through us. We have access to so much in Christ! Yet all around us are people who do not know our God, who do not know Jesus, who do not have access to the resources of heaven. Through the cross, the realities of heaven touch the earth when God's people allow God's Presence to flow through them and allow themselves to be God's temple on the earth. God saves us so others can be touched with His love.

Part of the reason that we are the dwelling of God on this earth is so that His "temple" can be where He meets the nations. The human tendency is to make the Church a place of exclusion, but this is not God's heart. Isaiah 56:6-7: "*. . . foreigners . . . I will bring to my holy mountain and give them joy in my house of prayer. . . for my house will be called a house of prayer for all nations.*" Jesus was offended at the religious leaders of His time for turning the temple of God into a place of corruption and greed. When He drove out the money changers from the temple, His explanation was: "*. . . Is it not written: 'My house will be called a house of prayer for all nations'? But you have made it a 'den of robbers'*" (Mark 11:17). The New Testament temple of God, formed by the blood and sacrifice of Jesus, is to be a "house of prayer for all nations." It is to be a place where the nations encounter the truth and reality of the Living God who loves them. One of the blessings of being individually the temple of God is that we can carry the vital Presence of God to where the nations are. In the Old Testament, there were some groups excluded from aspects of the temple worship – the blind and the lame (from the temple itself), Gentiles (from the outer court), women (from the inner court), men (from the Holy Place), priests (from the Holy of Holies). Only the High Priest could go anywhere in the temple, yet even he was afraid of going into the Holy of Holies and could die if he entered it with unconfessed sin. Now, however, through Jesus

Christ, all barriers have been destroyed.[301] Now anyone with a seeking heart – blind, lame, male, female, Jew, Gentile – anyone can come into His Presence if they come through Christ. It is Christ who sanctifies us and makes us able to freely enter His Presence. Our lives become the calling card of God towards those who do not know Him. May Zechariah 8:23 be fulfilled in us: *"This is what the LORD Almighty says: 'In those days ten people from all languages and nations will take firm hold of one Jew (or Christian) by the hem of his robe and say, 'Let us go with you, because we have heard that God is with you.'"*

We need to enlarge our expectation of what God can do through us. Remember, He is more active than we think. He is doing things right now in the people around us. As we allow God to fill us, we may even see a miracle.

Let me illustrate this with a story where you can see both temples at work. In January of 2014 I was leading an outreach to a large village in the country I work in. We were blitzing the area with many work projects, medical teams, a mural team (who painted murals on the walls of classrooms in a school), etc. One of the teams was a drama team that visited 13 villages doing skits and puppet shows. The area is strongly Muslim. The drama team visited one particularly strong Muslim village that allowed them to come since they wanted to see the puppets. As the team was packing up after the shows, the leader saw a young girl dragging herself through the dust. She was 11 years old and had never been able to walk. Compassion rose up in him (God's Spirit at work in him), and he asked the elders if the team could pray for the girl. They said "yes" since they did not expect anything to happen. The team gathered around the girl and prayed for her. The first time, nothing happened. They prayed a second time and strength came into her ankles. For the first time in her life she could support her weight on her ankles. God continued to work as they prayed (the Spirit at work through them). After praying five

301 Ephesians. 2:11-22; Galatians 3:26-29.

times she started to walk![302] The whole village was astonished! With one miracle, the village went from being strongly opposed to the Gospel to being wide open to it. As the drama team left, the villagers ran after them throwing gifts into the van. My son who was on the drama team said it was incredible! The elders later gave permission for the girl to choose to follow Jesus if she wanted to since Jesus had clearly chosen her. In the next year, four people from that village became Christians and every time the pastor (who was the translator for the drama team) visited the village, he was pulled into back rooms as people asked him to pray for various needs. There is now a Bible club that meets in the village. The entire village is in the process of being transformed by the power of the Gospel. This all happened because a group of believers allowed themselves to be the gateway to heaven for a crippled girl and her village. The Presence of God in them changed the village and gave it a different destiny. God fills us corporately and individually so that we can be His "Temple" for the sake of others.

There is another story that illustrates part of what I have been talking about. Surprise Sithole is a man who works with Heidi Baker in Mozambique. He has written a wonderful book called *A Voice in the Night*[303] where he tells the story of how God has led him through the years. At one point he tells how when he was living with his wife in South Africa, he was very poor and had no money. He was praying one day and felt God told him to walk with his wife and baby to a nearby village. When they got there, they sat down in front of a store, trying to figure out why God had led them there. As he prayed and was talking to God, suddenly a jeep stopped in front of him and two white men got out and came over to him. They handed him some money and said they could tell he

302 The girl still does not walk perfectly, but she does walk with the help of a staff. The change was so remarkable that the whole village recognized a miracle had occurred.

303 *Voice in the Night: The True Story of a Man and the Miracles that are Changing Africa,* Surprise Sithole, Chosen Books a Division of Baker Books, Grand Rapids. MI, 2012.

was a Christian by how he was sitting, and that God had told them to give money to a Christian in that place. Then they left. It was also significant that this was during the time of apartheid in South Africa. Surprise sat there trying to figure out how Christians sit! What I think happened was that the Presence of God within the two men caused them to recognize the Presence of the Lord in Surprise. When you cultivate the Presence of the Lord in your life, you never know where it will lead you!

When Jesus died for us on the cross, his intent was to reconcile mankind to God so that God could dwell with and in us. If we truly have the Spirit of the creator God in our lives, we should expect the miraculous to show up at times. There is a prophetic verse mentioned in Matthew 1:23 (from Isaiah 7:14) which indicates that Jesus is "Immanuel" which means "God is with us". If the Living God is truly with us, in our lives, this means that we are destined to do the impossible. Sometimes I think that the angels in heaven watch us, sitting on the edge of their seats, looking for what we will do with what God has given us through Jesus.[304] Sadly, many of us do not do much with it!

IMPLICATIONS FOR BOTH INDIVIDUAL AND CORPORATE LIFE:

The above has tremendous implications for both our personal life and our corporate life with others. Our personal walk with God influences how clean our temple is and how powerfully the Holy one of Israel can inhabit His temple. We need to repent and confess personal sin that defiles our relationship with God and impacts our relationship with others both inside and outside the Church. Personal and corporate purity and personal and corporate repentance are important for Christians. We need to do all that we can to keep ourselves in companionship with the Holy One of Israel, guarding His Presence in both ourselves and in the Church.

How we walk with God and other Christians influences how much we can impact the world. God's heart is that we are His temple so that

304 See 1 Peter 1:12 suggests that angels long to look into what the Gospel produces.

the nations come to Him. God loves family and intends that His family be composed of nations, tribes and languages from all over the world.[305]

Through the cross, we are sons and daughters of the living God, welcomed into His family. We are forgiven. We are clean. We have access to God. We have God's favor. We have access to God's love, peace, and joy, and to healing in all its dimensions. We have access to His Presence. And our position in His family gives us spiritual authority and dignity.

Through the cross, we are more than we think we are and have more than we think we have. We need to know who we are in the Presence of God. We are His dwelling place. The impossible is never far away when we have His Presence in us. Healing is as close to us as God is.

The Spirit of God in us gives life to our mortal bodies. This has powerful implications for healing. We can pray for healing, particularly for Christians, with confidence because the Spirit of God in them releases the resurrection power of God into their bodies as we pray.

God hears our prayers. In 2 Chronicles 7:15-16, God promises to hear every prayer prayed in the Old Testament temple. If God heard every prayer prayed in this inferior temple, how much more will He hear every prayer prayed in our hearts when we ARE the New Testament temple formed through the cross of Christ? Since our lives are the temple of God, His Presence is in us, and He hears even the quiet, whispered prayers no one else knows about. This truth produces confidence in prayer and the conviction of results. We have hope. We are heard. And our God is one who sees, hears and then comes down to deliver us in our need.

Even the highest Heaven and all the earth cannot contain and hold our God. Even these temples here on the earth[306] that He has formed through the blood of His Son cannot hold all of who God is. Yet His Presence is with us and calls us towards heaven where we will one day see all of who He is clearly.

---

305 Revelation 5:9; 7:9; 11:9; 13:7; 14:6.

306 2 Chronicles 6:18.

Summary

It is an incredible reality for us as individuals to be a temple for the Presence of the living God. This is only possible through the cross of Christ which has sanctified us and cleansed us from all of our sin so that we are now holy. Now the Holy One of Israel can come and live in us, writing His "laws" on our hearts. Now our inner person can be touched and shaped by the Presence of God. Now we as individuals become places of prayer for the nations. Now the real Presence of God can flow from us to bless others as we are obedient to God. The real Presence of God in us changes every aspect of our life for the better.

Key points from this chapter include:

1. Through the cross, God has destroyed every barrier between God and mankind, even those in the interior of mankind, so that He could make us as individuals His dwelling place.

2. God sends His Holy Spirit to lead us and guide us into Truth. He helps build our relationship with Jesus and our faithfulness to his teachings. As we remain "in" Jesus we are empowered to bear fruit as the life of God flows through us towards others.

3. Since we are the temple of God, we need to avoid sexual sin. Sexual sin more than any other type of sin, touches and impacts our spirits and can defile the Presence of God in us. As the temple of God each believer needs to cultivate holiness and faithfulness to God in their lives.

4. The Presence of the Holy Spirit in us blesses us in many ways. All of those who have the Holy Spirit living in them belong to Christ and have His life in them. The Holy Spirit adopts us into the family of God and brings each one of us the conviction that we are sons and daughters of God.

5. Our personal walk with God influences how clean our temple is and how powerfully the Holy one of Israel can inhabit His temple. We need to be ruthless with individual sin that cuts us off from the

Presence of God. Repentance, honesty and humility keep us close to God.

6. The reality that we are, as individuals, the temple of God is rooted in the reality of heaven. The Presence of God we experience now will be more fully experienced in heaven.
7. The gift of tongues is one of the gifts of the Spirit that is helpful in building us up individually in the Presence of the Lord. As we pray in tongues our prayers become more effective and powerful as God aligns us with His will.
8. We are made into the temple of God so that God can dwell in us and the nations can be blessed. God always has a heart for the outsiders and wants us to carry His Presence to bless the world around us. God wants to have a big family composed of members from every nation, tribe and language.

Entering Into His Presence

Put on some worship music and spend time in the Presence of God. As Francis de Sales indicated (chapter 6), sometimes it is helpful to look for the Presence of God in your own heart. Spend some time inviting God to increase His Presence in your life. Ask Him to show you anything in your heart that blocks Him or limits His Presence in you. Repent and ask forgiveness if necessary.

You are incredibly important and significant. God is in you. He has sought you out and called you by name into His family. Spend some time receiving God's love and favor. You are loved.

Prayer

God, I want to say again that there is no one like You in heaven or on earth. You sent Your son to die for me so that I could come into Your Presence, so that I could become Your dwelling place, Your temple. I am humbled and awed by this. Thank You for Your love for me. I am humbled that You see me as more valuable than the gold-lined temple of Solomon.

Lord, I want to be full of Your Presence. Search my heart and see if there is any wicked way in me. Show me where I need to repent so that I can have more of You.

Holy Spirit, come and lead me into Truth. Help me to understand the sacrifice of Jesus more and what He did to bring me into intimacy with the Father. Holy Spirit, bring me a deeper realization that I am truly a son (or daughter) of God. Show me that nothing can separate me from the love of the Father through Jesus.

Lord, fill me with a hunger for heaven. Fill me with a vision of what You are calling me towards. Do not let me get complacent here on earth and be satisfied with life here. I want more! I want You!

Jesus, send the Holy Spirit to anoint me and baptize me so that my intimacy with You is greater. Holy Spirit give me the gift of tongues so that I can be edified and built up in You. Help me to not get distracted by my pride so that I miss You. Holy Spirit do whatever is necessary in me so that I have more of You.

Father God, You love the nations. Make me a house of prayer for the nations. Help me to reach out – whether through prayer, giving financially or going – so that the nations can be blessed. Open up doors for the nations to come to You.

Make me so rich in Your Presence so that others see and sense Your Presence in me.

I love You.

In the precious name of Jesus I pray,

Amen.

12

The Presence of God in Worship

"Yet You are holy, O You who are enthroned on the praises of Israel." (Psalm 22:3, NASB)

"Let my people go, so that they may worship me."(Exodus 8:1)

"It is written: 'Worship the Lord your God, and serve him only.'"(Matt. 4:10, also Luke 4:8)

Every person is a worshipper, even those who claim that they do not believe in a "god", and what we worship produces fruit in our lives. Good or bad, what we worship[307] always influences our values, our priorities, and our lifestyles. It impacts our relationships with our neighbors and influences the destination of our lives. The question is always: who or what are we worshipping and is it worthy of our worship? The answer to this question impacts our entire life.

---

307 Worship is misunderstood in today's context. Instead of "worship" we could say what we orient our lives around or what we principally pursue or value as the supreme value in our lives.

WHEN WE WORSHIP GOD, WE ENLARGE HIS PLACE IN OUR LIVES.

We were created in the image of God. We were designed to find our fulfillment in relationship to Yahweh, the God of the Bible. We were designed to thrive in the context His Presence. True worship produces clarity in our spirits and mediates a revelation of the reality of the Lord to our hearts.

Psalm 22:3 indicates: *"Yet You are holy, O You who are enthroned on the praises of Israel" (NASB).* When we worship God in truth, His sovereignty over us and His Lordship in us expands. God is always Lord of Lords and King of Kings. He is Sovereign; we do not make Him so. Yet praise brings His sovereignty from the heavens into the personal domains of our lives and communities. Worship orients our lives rightly to Him and strengthens us in the Presence of God, establishing His authority in us. As has been mentioned before, life is primarily spiritual in nature. When we orient our lives around false spiritual values, around the wrong "spirits", it can destroy us. When we worship rightly, it liberates us.

Our ability to worship is linked to the level of freedom we experience. When our spirits, minds and hearts are bound, we cannot perceive God clearly and are not free to worship Him. Because it is so crucial, worship is a battleground. There are many forces at work, both spiritual and natural, to attract and entice us towards the worship of lesser "gods" that promise many rewards but do not satisfy. One of the greatest battles over correct worship seen in the Bible involves the Exodus events under Moses. God's heart is that we be free to worship Him.

EXODUS: A BATTLE OVER WORSHIP

It is hard to worship God when you are a slave. In fact, it becomes clear in the Exodus story that unless you are free, you cannot truly worship God. When there is an oppressive government system that is killing your children, it is even harder to worship the Lord. This is the start of the Exodus story: The Israelites had become subjugated to the Egyptians and were used as a slave labor force for building their cities and pyramids. The oppression became so intense that the Egyptians passed a law requiring every Israelite boy to be killed at birth. The Israelites, I would suspect particularly the mothers, cried out to God for Him to act. Since God is a God who sees, hears and comes down, He responded to their prayers by sending Moses to bring His deliverance to the people of God. Underneath the oppression and slavery were spiritual forces at work and false "gods" that caused the Egyptians to denigrate and abuse the Israelites.[308] Each of these "gods" were perceived to have some power and held sway over various aspects of Egyptian life. Yet whatever gods the Egyptians were worshipping did not result in them giving dignity, honor and value to the Israelites. In Exodus 7:16 Moses comes before Pharaoh and says: *"The LORD, the God of the Hebrews, has sent me to say to you: 'Let my people go, so that they may worship me*[309] *in the wilderness.'"* The Israelites were meant to be a people set apart to worship Yahweh only and to be His people. How can you worship God and be His people if you have no freedom to worship God in the way He wants? So, Moses says: *"Let my people go."* Pharaoh refuses and the battle is on!

Worship starts with knowing who or what you are worshipping. It starts with relationship. It seems that the Israelites barely remembered who Yahweh was. God tells Moses to tell the elders of Israel that "I am", the God of Abraham, Isaac and Jacob had sent him.[310] In Exodus 4:22-23, God calls the Israelites his "firstborn son" and tells Moses he is to tell Pharaoh to let God's "son go so he may worship me (God)." He also tells Moses that Pharaoh will not co-operate and will end up losing his own firstborn son in the process as God acts to liberate His "firstborn son." When Moses meets with the elders of Israel and tells them that the God of their fathers

308 You can say the same thing any time you see one group of people abusing and oppressing another, especially when the "abuse" is focused on the vulnerable. Anytime men, women or children are being killed, abused or oppressed, it is an attack on the image of God in them.

309 As Moses talks to Pharaoh it becomes more and more clear that the key issue is worship. In Exodus 5:1 Moses says let them go so they may hold a "festival" to God; in 5:3 it is "sacrifices"; in 7:16 it is "worship" as it is from then on in 8:1, 20; 9:13; 10:3, 7, 24; 12:31.

310 Exodus 3:13-16.

is *"concerned about them and has seen their misery, they bowed down and worshipped."*[311] This God who sent Moses in response to their pain is the same God who calls them His own and He has not forgotten them. Knowing that the God who covenanted with their forefathers was still committed to them and promised to free them stirs up worship.

Yet the Israelites had been in Egypt a long time.[312] They had acclimatised themselves to the Egyptian culture and gods. Even after they had physically left Egypt, they still had Egypt in their hearts and some level of attachment to the Egyptian gods. When Moses was on Mt. Sinai talking to God, they quickly fell back into idolatry.[313] God not only had to free the Israelites from their slavery in Egypt, He had to free them from their own idolatry so that they could worship Him. God told them in Exodus 6:6-7: *"I am the LORD, and I will bring you out from under the yoke of the Egyptians. I will free you . . . I will redeem you with an outstretched arm and with mighty acts of judgement. I will take you as my own people, and I will be your God. Then you will know that I am the LORD your God . . ."* These "mighty acts of judgement" were designed to convince both the Egyptians *and* the Israelites that Yahweh was the only true object of worship. God was crafting a nation known for having His Presence in their midst. To do this, He had to set them free with an "outstretched arm" so that they would truly "know" (tacit knowledge) that He is the LORD and be able to worship Him.

The plagues in Exodus 7-12 were aimed at the Egyptian gods.[314] The question was, which God had more power, which one was truly God? Which God

---

311 Exodus 4:29-31.

312 400 years according to Genesis 15:13; Exactly 430 years according to Exodus 12:40-41.

313 Exodus 32. Also see Deuteronomy 9:7-24.

314 Exodus 7:8-13 – snake God (staff of Moses); 7:14-24 – the Nile river turned to blood (god of Nile: Hapi); 7:25-8:15 – the frogs (goddess of fertility: Heket); 8:16-19 – earth is struck to produce gnats (god of earth: Geb); 8:20-32 – the flies (god of rebirth: Khepri); 9:1-7 – the livestock (goddess of protection: Hathor); 9:8-12 – boils on the people (goddess of medicine: Isis); 9:13-35 – hail (goddess of the sky: Nut); 10:1-20 – locusts (god of disorder and storms: Seth); 10:21-29 – darkness (the sun god: Ra); 11:1-9 – death of the first-born (the god Pharaoh). (from "Ten Egyptian Gods and Goddesses for ten Egyptian plagues" on Owlcation.com (updated Dec 14, 2018). See also Exodus 12:12: "...against all the gods of Egypt I will execute judgements – I am the LORD."

was truly worthy of worship? Little by little, it became clear that the God of Israel was far greater than every one of the Egyptian gods. Yahweh not only demonstrated control over the Nile, the frogs, the flies, etc., but by 8:19, the magicians of Egypt recognized that power, telling Pharaoh: "This is the finger of God." The magicians had some power. They were able to reproduce to some extent Moses' rod turning into a snake and the first two plagues (the Nile turned to blood, the control of frogs) but by the plague of gnats they admitted defeat. By the plague of boils, they could no longer come into the presence of Pharaoh, they were so undone by the plagues. Moreover, the territory where the Israelites lived was protected from each of the last five plagues. Clearly Yahweh was Lord over every god of Egypt,[315] and He protected His own.

God's intent was to teach both Israel and Egypt who was truly God. He needed Israel to learn to trust Him in the challenges they would face when He brought them into the Promised Land. God was also focused on the nations: He wanted all peoples to know that He was truly the Lord of all the Earth. Not only the plagues of Egypt but all He did to bring the nation of Israel into the Promised Land was to demonstrate to the surrounding nations that Yahweh was LORD, and that His Presence was with His people. Forty years later Rahab says to the Israelite spies who visited her in Jericho:

> *"I know that the LORD has given you this land and that a great fear of you has fallen on us, so that all who live in this country are melting in fear because of you. We have heard how the LORD dried up the Red Sea for you when you came out of Egypt . . . When we heard of it, our hearts melted in fear and everyone's courage failed because of you, for the LORD your God is God in heaven above and on the earth below."*[316]

Only the God of Israel is the great "I AM." When all the gods of this earth compete, He is the only one left standing. He is the one who created the world. He is the one who defines reality. He is the God who is defined

315 See Exodus 12:12 where God says He brings judgement on "all of the gods of Egypt."

316 Joshua 2:8-11.

by 'Presence'. There is no other god with His power, His sovereignty, and His love for those He has called into His family. As we see from Exodus 4:22-23 above, the spiritual battle is about God setting his "son" free so he can worship the Lord. There is no other God like this who is worthy of worship. Since we are all worshippers, we might as well worship the true God who alone can liberate us from all that enslaves us so that we can worship Him and come into fullness of life through that worship. True worship brings us into the Presence of the LORD of heaven and earth.

The Exodus events teach us several things. First, we need to be set free from all that enslaves us before we can truly worship the Lord. Second, Yahweh is sovereign. He is truly Lord. He is the only one with the power and love to set us free from our slavery and bondage. He is greater and more powerful than all that the world has to offer and is determined to bring us into "life." Third, we have lived in the world a long time and taken into our hearts the values and the "gods" of this world. We, therefore, become enslaved by worldviews and mindsets that do not honor God or the world He created. Fourth, we live as slaves when God wants us to live as His children. He has more for us. He is the only one who can bring us into the freedom of sonship/daughtership. He wants the free worship of sons and daughters, not the limited worship of slaves. He wants to take us on a journey into the "Promised Land" as we follow His Presence. He has a place of blessing for us. He is the only one with the power and might to take us there. Let's pursue and worship the great "I AM" and we will find that place of blessing.

THE CONNECTION BETWEEN "SONSHIP"[317] AND WORSHIP

In the Exodus events we see that slavery has robbed the Israelites of their ability to worship God freely as "sons." At the base level, the story

317 In this section, it is not only "sons" that are talked about but "daughters" as well. What applies to sons applies to daughters. To use "sonship/daughtership" gets clumsy but both are meant which is why I have "sons" or "sonship" in quotes.

is about the linkage between "sonship" to God and the worship of God. In the temptation narrative of Matthew 4:1-11,[318] we see the same two core issues. In Exodus, the children of Israel need to be freed from slavery so that they can freely worship God as "sons"[319] in intimacy with their Father-God. In Matthew 4, Jesus as the Son of God needs to keep himself in His identity as "Son" so that His intimacy with the Father is maintained. This is the foundation of His anointing as the Messiah. If Satan can successfully take Jesus out of a proper identity as "Son," He makes Him subservient to other "gods" and destroys His intimacy with the Father thus preventing Jesus from being effective in His calling from the Lord. In the temptation narrative the question is: Will Jesus deviate from being a trusting "Son" through obeying false "gods" that destroy His intimacy with His Father-God or not? Will Jesus act as a "Son" or as an "orphan/slave"?

An "orphan" is someone who has lost their parents and so does not have a parent who loves them. A "slave" is someone that has no position of status or significance in the family. In the sense I am using it here, an "orphan" or "slave," is someone that is not confident that they are truly loved. The result is that they constantly act to manipulate love from their "parent" or significant other so that they can feel that they have a position of significance and value in the "family." Many of us are like this. We have an inner sense of estrangement that makes us feel unloved. Some of this comes from our broken families of origin and this carries over into our relationship with God. Part of what the Gospel does is heal us so that we live our lives in confident relationship with our Father-God. It is about freeing us from what enslaves us so that we can worship Him as His children.

The story of Jesus' baptism and subsequent temptation is instructive. Just before the temptation narrative of Matthew 4, Jesus is baptised by John the Baptist. As He comes out of the water, the heavens are opened,

---

318 The temptation narrative is also recounted in Mark 1:12-13; Luke 4:1-13.

319 Exodus 4:22-23.

the Holy Spirit descends upon Jesus, and God the Father speaks in an audible voice. What He says is so significant: *"This is my Son, whom I love; with him I am well pleased."*[320] The Lord declares that Jesus is His Son, that Jesus is loved by the Father, and that Jesus pleases or has the favour of His Father on His life. This three-fold declaration of sonship by the Father is what is directly challenged by Satan in his three-fold temptation of Jesus a few verses later. If Satan can lure Jesus away from walking in his identity as the "Son" of God, he has won. It is no surprise that when Jesus successfully resists the temptations thrown at Him by Satan, He *"returned to Galilee in the power of the Spirit. . ."*[321] The basis of Jesus' anointing, that which allowed the Holy Spirit to remain on Him in power, was His confident identity[322] as the Son who had the love and favour of His Father on His life to accomplish the will of God on earth.

Each temptation Jesus goes through had two strands: first, is the temptation to act as an "orphan" rather than a "son;" second, is the temptation to listen to and obey false "gods" that will pull Jesus out of His identity as a "son" and away from intimacy and trust in His heavenly Father. God wants us to live with the anointing of the Holy Spirit on our lives that is based on a confident identity as His "sons" or "daughters." Satan will attack our identity through enticing us to listen to and follow other "gods" that rupture our intimacy with our heavenly Father, thus rendering us spiritually powerless. Giving in to temptation separates us from the Presence of God.

In the first temptation,[323] Satan attacked the first assertion of God that Jesus is God's Son. He said to Jesus: *"If you are the Son of God, tell these stones to become bread."*[324] We know that Jesus is indeed the Son of God

---

320 Matthew 3:17.

321 Luke 4:14.

322 Walking in his identity as the Son of God meant resisting temptations to sin and so kept Jesus in purity and holiness. If we understand "sonship" to God rightly it means staying "holy as He is holy."

323 Mathew. 4:1-4.

324 Matthew 4:3.

and we know that Satan knows this, so what is he trying to do? It was a temptation for Jesus to use His spiritual authority as God's Son in an illegitimate way to satisfy His own needs. God had anointed Jesus to release the Kingdom of God on earth. This anointing was real, and it was not given to Jesus to satisfy His own needs or for His own convenience. His anointing was to love people who were under the bondage of Satan and set them free. The anointing was God's love being poured out upon and through Jesus for the benefit of those who were hurting and estranged from God. Sonship is about using what God has given you in a way that is aligned with the will of the Father and His love for the world. It is not about doing something dramatic or selfish so that you can prove to yourself that you are truly a son or daughter of God. This is why Jesus as the Son of God committed himself to only do what the Father was doing.[325]

The Scriptural context of this temptation is important and shows us what "gods" are confronting Jesus. Jesus had just fasted for forty days and nights in the wilderness. He was starving. He was legitimately hungry. Satan is basically saying to Jesus: "Jesus, you are hungry. As the Son of God, you can make bread out of stones so just do it." The false "gods" are His physical appetites. You have physical needs – satisfy them! Yet if Jesus had let His own appetites "rule" Him rather than the will of God He would have sinned. He would not have demonstrated the trust and confidence in His Father that a true "son" has.

Jesus responded from Deuteronomy 8:3:[326] *"It is written: 'Man shall not live by bread alone, but on every word that comes from the mouth of God'"*[327] The original context of the verse he cites is instructive (verses 2-3). It says:

> *"Remember how the LORD your God led you all the way in the wilderness these forty years, to humble and test you in order to*

325 John 5:19.

326 Each response of Jesus referred to events from the Exodus of Israel from Egypt.

327 Matthew 4:4.

> *know what was in your heart, whether or not you would keep his commands. He humbled you, causing you to hunger and then feeding you with manna, . . . to teach you that* ***man does not live on bread alone but on every word that comes from the mouth of the LORD."*** (emphasis added)

In Deuteronomy, the Israelites were led by God into the wilderness. In Matthew 4:1, Jesus was led by the Holy Spirit into the wilderness. The Israelites were 40 years in the wilderness. Jesus was 40 days fasting in the wilderness. The Israelites were in the wilderness to be humbled and tested to see if they would keep the commandments of God. Likely Jesus saw a parallel with Himself, particularly in the context of the temptation of Satan. The Israelites were "humbled", caused to feel hunger, and then fed manna by God in the wilderness. They were dependent on the provision of God to survive. Likewise, Jesus, through His hunger becomes humbled and vulnerable in the face of His need for food.[328] The LORD gave the Israelites manna in the desert. If He wanted to, He could have given Jesus manna as well. For the Israelites, the manna came from God each day and nourished them. God used this experience to teach the Israelites that they must not live on food alone but on what comes from God Himself as their priority. Jesus in His hunger faced the same truth God was trying to teach the Israelites: hunger for God was more important than physical hunger, no matter how intense it was. Jesus needed to nourish Himself on what comes from God[329] before satisfying His own needs. This challenge came at the very beginning of the ministry of Jesus. In His ministry, Jesus needed to make it about God and not Himself and keep Himself in intimacy with His Father. The temptation was to not trust in the Father's love for Him as His Son and instead act to satisfy His own physical appetites.

328 This is one of the values of fasting: it humbles us and drives us to hunger after God rather than food. The human nature of Jesus means he was legitimately hungry.

329 There is a parallel here between Jesus nourishing himself on "every word that proceeds from the mouth of God" and John 6 where Jesus says he is the bread of life that has come down from heaven and people need to "eat" him in order to have life. Jesus practices what he preaches.

Jesus was determined to NOT fulfill Psalm 106:14 which applied to Israel in the wilderness: *"In the desert they gave into their craving; in the wilderness they put God to the test."*

After Jesus chose to focus on listening to the words that came from God more than to His own physical appetites, Satan now focuses on the second part of what God said to Jesus in Matthew 4: Are you really loved by God?[330] Satan took Jesus to the high point of the Temple and said: *"If you are the Son of God, throw yourself down (from the temple). For it is written: 'He will command his angels concerning you, and they will lift you up in their hands, so that you will not strike your foot against a stone'"*[331] The temptation was to not trust the love of the Father but instead have God *prove* His love for Jesus by sending His angels to save Him when He threw himself off the temple. Will Jesus trust that God loved Him as a "Son", or will He try to prove to Himself or to others that He was truly loved by God much like an "orphan" would? If Jesus threw Himself down, it would be a very public and dramatic action that would "prove" to doubters that He was truly loved by God. The false "god" we see here is the desire to be important and have the adulation of others. Another false "god" we see is doubt.[332] The sin is "testing" the love of God for Him in place of "trusting" that love.

Jesus responded: *"It is written: 'Do not put the Lord your God to the test.'"*[333] This is a citation from Deuteronomy 6:16. The original context is again helpful. Deuteronomy 6:13, 14 -16, 18 says:

> *"Fear the LORD your God, serve him only . . .*
>
> *Do not follow other gods, the gods of the people around you. For the LORD your God, who is among you, is a jealous God, and his anger will burn against you . . .*

330 Second temptation: Matthew 4:5-7.

331 Matthew 4:6.

332 In the Garden of Eden it was "Did God really say. . ."(Genesis 3:1). Here it is "Does God really love you?"

333 Matthew 4:7.

> ***Do not put the LORD your God to the test*** *as you did at Massah.*
>
> . . .
>
> *Do what is right and good in the LORD's sight, so that it may go well with you . . ..*" (emphasis added)

The context in Deuteronomy is the encouragement to fear and serve *only* the LORD. Massah was when the Israelites had no water in the wilderness and quarrelled with Moses, unsure if God was with them.[334] The question is: Will Jesus fix His eyes on following His Father or will He, like the Israelites, sin by challenging God and wondering if God truly loved Him and was with Him when He had need? Jesus indicated to Satan that He will not test or challenge the love of the Father for Him. He will choose to *trust* His love and believe that God is truly with Him. He will not listen to selfish ambition or doubt. Even if these "gods" are rampant in those around Him, He will not follow these gods.

The third temptation[335] challenged the truth that the favor of God rested on Jesus, that His Father was truly pleased with Him. Satan showed Jesus all the kingdoms of this world and their splendour[336] and then the clincher: *"All of this I will give you," he says, "if you will bow down and worship me."*[337] Jesus was in the wilderness alone. He did not have wealth or power, yet God proclaimed that He had the favour of the Lord on His life. Satan, however, challenged this truth: "How can you have the favour of God if all this wealth and power belongs to me? I will give you real favour. I will give you wealth, splendour and power. All you must do is worship me." The temptation for Jesus was not to trust that He truly pleased God and that He had the favour of God on His life and to evaluate that favour according to the world's values. The temptation was to seek status and significance in this world and not in the Kingdom of God. The false "gods" are power and wealth and splendour. We also see pride here, the desire to

---

334 Exodus 17:7.

335 Matthew 4:8-10.

336 Some translations say "wealth" in place of splendour.

337 Matthew 4:9.

be elevated above others.[338] Satan himself is another false "god". He tries to get the worship that only God Himself deserves. If Jesus submitted to Satan, He would be maligning the character of God[339] and choosing the things of this world as more important than the things of heaven. Every kingdom Satan showed Jesus was a temporary, finite kingdom on this earth which will be judged by God in the future. Only the King and His Kingdom endure for all eternity. Jesus would have been choosing to worship a lesser in place of the only true object of worship. He refuses to take favour that is not granted to Him by His Heavenly Father.

Jesus said to Satan: *"Away from me Satan! For it is written: 'Worship the Lord your God, and serve him only.'"*[340] His words were reminiscent of Deuteronomy 10:20. Again the context in Deuteronomy is helpful.

> *"And now, Israel, what does the LORD your God ask of you but* ***to fear the LORD your God, to walk in obedience to him, to love him, to serve the LORD your God with all your heart . . .***
>
> *For the LORD your God is God of gods and Lord of Lords, the great God, mighty and awesome, . . .*
>
> ***Fear the LORD your God and serve him.*** *Hold fast to him . . .*
>
> *He is the one you praise; he is your God . . ."* (Deut. 10:12, 17, 20, 21, emphasis added)

For Jesus, obedience to His Father was more important than the wealth and power Satan might give Him. The context refers to the Exodus events where God was marking out the Israelites as a people that would be characterized by His Presence as they followed, obeyed and loved Him. True worship leads us into the Presence of God. All the kingdoms of this world, like those shown to Jesus by Satan, were nothing in the light of the power and might of the Living God. He is the only true object of

338 Which is the sin of Satan himself. He desires to be greater than God and this is one reason that he tries to get Jesus to worship him.

339 Saying that what God gives is not true favour, in effect, calling God a liar.

340 Matthew 4:10.

worship. Jesus chose to serve the King of the Kingdom of heaven and not the "prince of this world."[341]

Through the substitutionary atonement of the cross, each Christ-follower is a "son" or "daughter" of God who is given the same favour and pleasure that God gave Jesus. Yet this will be challenged by Satan. If he can get us away from living as "sons" and "daughters" and instead striving to prove we are loved as "orphans" do, he has won. He will use the "gods" of our sensual appetites, our self-love, our pride, our desire for status and significance and even wealth and power to entice us away from trust and confidence in the love of our heavenly Father for us. Satan's strategy has not changed. He prefers that we are slaves and not "sons" who are free to worship in intimacy with the Living God. Yet we, like Jesus, must choose to serve and worship only the LORD. He is the one who loves us into life.

Both the Exodus events and the temptation narrative show us that it is false gods and our own bondage to them that will keep us out of the place of true worship and out of God's Presence. Yet the Presence of God in the lives of those set free to serve Him is a powerful proclamation of the reality of the truth of God's existence in the world.

TWO OTHER RIVAL "GODS" IN THE SCRIPTURES

Two other "gods" that we see in Scripture outside of the temptation narrative are money and sexual desire. The first connects to the "kingdoms of the world" Satan showed to Jesus and the second is related to giving in to our physical "appetites" mentioned above.

In Matthew 6:24 (also Luke 16:13) Jesus says: *"No one can serve two masters. Either you will hate the one and love the other, or you will be devoted to one and despise the other. You cannot serve both God and money."* Jesus here warns us that money is a rival god to Yahweh. You cannot serve God while at the same time serving money. One is exclusive of the other. Jesus had the favour of God on His life, but He was not rich: He trusted

341 John 12:31; 14:30; 16:11.

God for His needs. Sometimes people stay in slavery[342] because they cannot give up the financial resources they have access to as slaves. Following God is always about faith. Wealth is something you can see and pursue on this earth with your skills and abilities. It confers on you many blessings. It can be a challenge to rely on God, who you cannot see, rather than the riches of this world which are tangible. Yet it can also enslave us and rob us of His Presence. When you are obedient to the commands and will of God, many blessings result yet not all of these are financial. The blessings of the Lord are more profound than this. The underlying question is: Are we pursuing the things of this world or the Presence of God?

Another "god" is our sexual passions. In the Bible, we frequently see the enticement of sexual sin. Solomon had 700 wives and 300 concubines.[343] He may have been wise but he was also foolish. David had multiple wives.[344] His lust for Bathsheba led him to plan the murder of her husband.[345] In 1 Corinthians 6:15-16 a Christian man is defiling the temple of his body by having a sexual relationship with a prostitute. All these show that sexual passion when not reigned in, results in bondage, destruction and the rupture of our intimacy with God. Living as a "son" or "daughter" means keeping ourselves in sexual holiness and self-control, and not living as the slave of our passions. Yet this can be challenging because sexual activity promises sensual pleasure and gives the allure of intimacy with another. Whatever form it takes, when we listen to "gods" that entice us away from intimacy with our heavenly Father, we do not function as "sons" in our relationship with Him. God wants "sons" and

342 An example of this is the rich young ruler of Luke 18:18-25. He was invited to be a disciple of Jesus. He refused because he was wealthy. In the same way in the country I serve as a missionary, many people refuse to become Christians because of the financial cost of that decision in a Muslim milieu. When they become Christians they can be kicked out of their families and lose their jobs, homes, wives or husband and children.

343 1 Kings 11:3.

344 1 Samuel 30:5; 2 Samuel 3:2-5.

345 2 Samuel 11:1-21.

"daughters" who freely worship Him and who value intimacy with Him more than intimacy with anything or anyone else.

WORSHIP CHANGES US

None of us are where we need to be. We are on a journey, a pilgrimage towards God and the blessing of being in His Presence. To enter into the Presence of God we need to be changed. He is the Holy One of Israel and there is so much in us that is not "holy". Worship changes us. It is part of the process of sanctification as we invite the work of the Holy Spirit in our lives through the interaction of worship. It facilitates a revelation of God to our hearts. It enthrones God at the center of our life and empowers His Presence to transform us into the image of Christ.[346] We can never stay the same when we truly encounter God. Through worship, our "self" is confronted, and we are invited upward to something greater than ourselves. Through worship, something in our soul shifts and our lives become not about us but about Him and His beauty. Worship grows humility as we "meet" God in worship. As we "see" His glory we are transformed into glory.[347]

Isaiah 6 demonstrates the transformation that worship produced. Isaiah was in the temple worshipping when he encountered the LORD in His glory and majesty. He found himself in the Presence of the Living God, saw angels worshipping before His throne, and was shaken to the core of his being by what he saw and experienced. In the Presence of the Holy One of Israel, he realized his sin. Then as the Lord ministered to him, he became transformed into a man who was a powerful spokesperson for God. Isaiah was changed by his encounter with the LORD in worship. Honesty and humility permitted Isaiah's brush with God to transform him upward. Not every worship experience is an Isaiah 6 one. Yet, the potential is there any time we exalt the LORD through worship. True worship involves an encounter with God that changes us.

346 Romans 8:29.

347 2 Corinthians 3:18.

WORSHIP IS MANIFESTED THROUGH OBEDIENCE

Worship bears fruit in our lives. What we love reflects what we worship. The two Great Commandments of Matthew 22:34-40 are to love God with all our heart and our neighbour as yourself, but they are not possible without worship empowering us to love God. Then as we worship and love God with all we are, we can truly love our neighbour correctly. James 1:27 is a great verse that is often misunderstood. It literally says: *Worship*[348] *"that God our father accepts as pure and faultless is this: to look after orphans and widows in their distress and to keep oneself from being polluted by the world."* If you worship rightly, you love rightly. Love for God and for others is one of the primary fruits of worship: It shows we are rooted and attached to Him.[349] Obedience to the will of God is the evidence of true worship.

Jesus was able to resist the temptations of Satan for two reasons. First, He knew the Word of God and thus kept Himself in the truth. This empowered Him to recognize and resist the manipulations of Satan. Second, He deeply valued His intimacy with His Father and He was committed to having no other allegiances. He was committed to safeguarding His unity with the Father and refused to presume on God's anointing on His life. Instead, He chose in all circumstances to *"worship the Lord . . . and serve him only."*[350] Jesus' love for His Father and obedience to His will was something He never wanted to compromise.

HOW DO WE CULTIVATE HEARTS OF WORSHIP?

The above question is important. Ultimately, God needs to help us to have worshipful hearts so we begin by simply asking God to change us so that we can be people who truly worship Him alone. We ask Him to set

348 Most translations translate the word as "religion" but it is more correctly "worship".

349 John 15:5.

350 Matthew 4:10.

us free so that we can worship Him.[351] We need to be hungry for more of His Presence in our worship experiences as well as in our daily walk with Him. We need to fight against the false gods that compete for our allegiance. How do we do this? One key in the process of hungering for more of God is to fast regularly. Then as we feel physical hunger, we turn it into a spiritual hunger for God and ask Him to fill us with His Presence. We fast because we hunger for God and not the things of this world. Fasting also cultivates humility as we see our weakness and see how easily we can be led by physical appetites. The strength of our physical hunger forces us to be honest and can turn us towards the higher values of heaven.

Another important question is: What do we really want? Do we want to be "set free" so that we can worship God? For me, worship involves a constant battle as I seek to make my life about Him and His Presence. Since Jesus defeated Satan's attacks through His knowledge of the Word of God and His awareness of the character of His Father, I spend time daily in the Scriptures so that I can be rooted in the truth of who God is and grow in my experience of His love for me. It is Truth that will set me free to worship God.[352] Knowing the truth and trusting in the goodness of God, I evaluate every temptation and every "good thing" I am tempted with by the Word of God.

I want my life to be centered on God, so I ask Him to change my desires so that my life is not focused on myself. I say "yes" as often as I can to the Lord to maintain a heart of obedience. I seek to cultivate holiness and repentance so that I can stay in the Presence of God as much as possible, living at the foot of the cross.

All the above is part of cultivating a heart of worship. I know that as I walk in my identity as a loved child of God who has His favor and love, determined to pursue a deeper unity with my heavenly Father through

351 Echoing what Moses said to pharaoh in Exodus 8:1.

352 John 8:32.

worship, He will anoint me to love people as He did Jesus,[353] and He will be glorified. It is all about Him.

Summary

Worship is one of the most powerful and consistent ways we can come into the experienced Presence of God. One of the reasons for this is that it enthrones God as Lord in our hearts. Worship helps us to come into a right relationship with God as Father and clarifies what it means to be His child. God, through worship, liberates us and changes us in positive, God honoring ways. False worship however enslaves us. Let us pursue His Presence through worship.

Key points in this chapter include:

1. Everyone is a worshipper. We need to make sure that who or what we worship is worthy of our worship.
2. Sometimes we need to be set free from what enslaves us before we can truly worship the Lord. God is committed to bring us out of our slavery into the liberty of being His loved children. The question becomes: what "gods" keep you from worship of the living God?
3. God wants us to be free to worship Him because this alone will bring us the life and fulfillment we need. We were created in His image and thrive in His Presence when we worship Him.
4. Some of the false "gods" we may need to be freed from are: the tyranny of our fleshly appetites; self-love; pride and the desire for greatness; money; and sexual love. Pursuit of all of these "gods" produces bondage and not freedom.
5. Worship changes us. Through our encounter with God in worship He can transform us and change us into the people the world needs.

353 Luke 4:14

6. Worship is seen in what we love and what we obey. Jesus is our model of one who was committed to keeping His unity with His heavenly Father at all costs.
7. We press into the Lord so that we can be a person who are characterized by intimacy with God and love for people. Let's cultivate humility, honesty, holiness and love in your daily life. Let's live close to the cross.

Entering Into His Presence

Put on some worship music and just spend time in the Presence of the Lord. Read the declaration of sonship God gave to Jesus in Matt. 3:17 and hear Him say it to you (put your name in the declaration and change "son" to "daughter" if necessary). Repeat the phrase over and over again until it resonates in your heart. You are loved and you have God's favour on your life through Jesus.

Thank the Lord for His love and receive it. Ask for a deeper revelation of His love for you.

Ask the Lord to examine your heart and reveal any areas where you may be worshipping other "gods." Spend some time asking the Lord if you are using your time, energy or money in the right way as how you use these three things will show you the false "gods" you are worshipping.

Do you spend daily time in the Word of God? Spend some time working on a schedule that will allow you to regularly spend time in the Scriptures.

Is worship a regular part of your life? Ask God to show you how you can incorporate worship more regularly.

Prayer

Lord, set me free so that I can worship You. Show me where there are any "false" gods in me so that I can renounce and forsake them. Set me free from any false "gods" that come from the culture I live in so that I am 100% Yours. Lord, please, take "Egypt" out of my heart even as You set me free from my place of bondage so that I can live in the promised land of Your Presence. I want to worship You with all my heart. Change me so that I can fully worship You.

Increase Your Presence in my life as I worship You. Unite my will with Yours. Make me Your instrument, Your hands and feet in this world.

Help me to love You more and empower me to see and love my neighbour. Help me to love them as You love them. Show me any "widows" or "orphans" around me that need to be loved by You through me.

I declare that You are the LORD of lords and King of kings. You alone have all power. You are the great "I am" that created the world, and Your reality is the only reality that counts. Enlarge my view of who You are.

I receive Your affirmation of me: that I am Your son/daughter; that I am loved deeply by You; and, that I bring You pleasure. I thank You for choosing me before the foundation of the world. I thank You for sending Your Son so that I could be Your child. Teach me all that this means. Show me what it truly means to be Your son/daughter and to have Your love.

I enthrone You in my heart.

I worship only You.

I love You.

In the precious name of Jesus I pray,

Amen.

13

The Presence Of God In Love

"Dear friends, let us love one another, for love comes from God. Everyone who loves has been born of God and knows God. Whoever does not love does not know God, because God is love. . ." (1 John 4:7-8)

EVERY TIME WE LOVE OTHERS WE REFLECT THE GOD WHO IS LOVE

Since humans were created in the image of God, part of the glory of humanity is our ability to love. The creator God IS love.[354] Everything about Him manifests what love is. When we doubt this, it means we misunderstand both love and who God is. Since we were created in God's image and God is love, His love then calls us into our identity. To the degree that we express God's pure, holy love, to that degree we call others into their true identity as well. Wounds keep us from our identity. Love that heals, opens up our hearts to walk in who we were created to be by God. This is one of the reasons that a good marriage is so powerful. Love in the family, based on God's love for us, nurtures and calls every member

354 1 John 4:8, 16.

of the family into their identity and releases them into fruitfulness. When the love expressed in families is broken or abusive, it destroys what it is meant to build.

First John 4:7-8 says: "*Dear friends, let us love one another, for love comes from God. Everyone who loves has been born of God and knows God. Whoever does not love does not know God, because God is love.*" These verses show that love has its source in God. We love others because that is how God expresses Himself in the world. Second, those who love show that they "know"[355] God and have been "born of God." They demonstrate that they are not of this world but instead have their origins in God. One of the indicators that people are children of God is that they can love others as God does.

In verses 11-12 and 16, John adds the following: "*Dear friends, since God so loved us, we also ought to love one another. No one has ever seen God; but if we love one another, God lives in us and his love is made complete in us. . . . God is love. Whoever lives in love lives in God, and God in them.*" Here John emphasizes again that we are to love one another because we have been loved by God. When we know God, our love reflects the love we have received from Him. Our love also makes the invisible God visible. Since God is love, our actions of love reveal what God is like. Loving others keeps us in the Presence of God. When we love, we live in God and He in us.

These verses show that God's love, when expressed, is evangelistic. It demonstrates that God is real and makes Him visible to the world. It has its source in God and is modeled after the love we have seen and experienced from God. It attracts people towards God.

In our own setting in an Islamic country, my wife and I are always looking for practical ways to show our Muslim friends that God loves them. We have done micro-enterprise projects and did a feeding program for children (mostly boys) who were living with a Muslim religious

355 Here we have the tacit dimension of knowledge. They "know" God and his love because they have experienced it.

leader being taught the Qu'ran, but did not have enough food to eat. Once a week, we provided these children with a nutritious meal with yogurt and rice. A Christian lady in the community prepared the food and fed the boys. One day she went to a local store to buy supplies. The Muslim shop owner asked why she was buying so much. She explained that there were some missionaries who had heard that the boys with this religious leader were not getting enough to eat so they were sponsoring a nutritious meal for them. He was surprised and asked more questions. She said that we believed that God loves Muslims and so when we saw the need, we responded to it. The shop keeper asked if we were Christians. The lady said "yes." Then the shop keeper said: "Huh! I have never heard of Christians loving Muslims like this before!" When she told me this story, I was shocked since Christians should be leading the way when it comes to loving others.[356] We love because God who is love lives in us. We know the Father better than anyone else and so we can show the world what love is like more clearly than anyone else can.

THE GOSPEL IS ABOUT THE LOVE OF GOD FOR THE WORLD

Jesus came to die and give his life as a ransom[357] for the people of this world who were under bondage to sin and the domination of Satan so that we could be cleansed from our sin, forgiven and restored into relationship[358] with the Father. Jesus came to crush the head of the serpent[359] and destroy the works of the devil.[360] He came so that we could live our lives in the Presence of God and so God could live in us. He came so that

356 See John 13:35: "*. . . everyone will know that you are my disciples, if you love one another.*"

357 Matt. 20:28; Mark 10:45; 1 Cor. 6:20.

358 Heb. 10:14-18.

359 Gen 3:15.

360 1 John 3:8.

we could become a holy place consecrated to the worship of God and become His temple.

The central message of the ministry and preaching of Jesus was the coming of the Kingdom of God[361] to the earth. He taught and proclaimed the kingdom of God with power and the Presence of God in His life was manifested in miracles of healing and deliverance.[362] These miracles were evidence of the love of God for the sick and oppressed. When Jesus sent out His disciples, He told them to preach the Kingdom of God and heal the sick.[363] When He sent out the 72, He told them the same thing.[364] Jesus was motivated and moved by compassion[365] to preach the kingdom of God and love people who needed to be healed and set free.

After His death and resurrection, Jesus told His disciples to stay in Jerusalem until they were equipped with power from on high so that they too could bring the Kingdom of God from heaven to earth. After being empowered by the Holy Spirit, Peter preached with power and 3000 people were saved. The power of the love of God was also on display with signs and wonders.[366] God's love for people is displayed when people are healed and delivered. When we do not press into God, do not seek His empowering so that people can be healed and set free, we sin against the love of God for the world. The kingdom of God has come to the earth. It is "Good News." God loves the people of this world. He sent His Son to set us free and usher us into the freedom that only the love of the Father can bring us. He sent His Spirit to anoint us and empower us to love on people, to heal them and set them free. His love is to be manifest in and through the Church. What difference does any "god" make on earth if He never actually enters into the pain of people to help them? How attrac-

361 Matt. 4:17, 23-24; 5:20; 6:10; 10:7; Luke 4:43; 9:2, 27, 60; Mark 1:15; 4:11, 26, 30; 9:1, 47; 10:14, 15, 17, 24, 25; 12:34; 15:25; 15:43; John 3:3, 5.

362 Matt. 4:23-24; 9:35.

363 Matt. 10:1, 7-8; Luke 9:1-2.

364 Luke 10:1, 9.

365 Matt. 14:14; 9:35-36.

366 Acts 2:43.

tive is any "god" who is helpless to heal and deliver, or if he is not "real" in the experience of the hurting? The Good News of the Gospel is that through Jesus Christ the Kingdom of God has come to the earth to love and change people, to break oppression and bondage. Now as the Church pursues intimacy with God the Father, and seeks the empowering of the Holy Spirit, the powerful love of God and the Presence of God can be manifested in their midst for the hurting.

This kind of love changes and transforms people. It is the kind of love the world needs and longs for.

THE TWO GREAT COMMANDMENTS

At one point a man came to Jesus and asked him what the greatest commandment of the law was. Jesus replied in Matthew 22:37-39: *'Love the Lord your God with all your heart and with all your soul and with all your mind'. This is the first and greatest commandment. And the second is like it: 'Love your neighbor as yourself.'"* The greatest thing we are to do in obedience to the will of God is to love God with everything we are and to love our neighbor as well. Since God is love, obedience to the will of God involves love. Jesus adds in verse 40: *"All of the Law and the Prophets hang on these two commandments."* If we truly learn to love God and others, everything else falls into place. In the Law, the requirements were laid out for how people were to come into the Presence of God. In the Prophets, people were constantly called back into obedience to the Law. What Jesus is saying is that if we truly love God with all our heart, mind and soul, we will be staying away from sin. We will be fulfilling the requirements of the Law. If we love, we won't need the prophets to call us back to God. And our ability to love our neighbor is empowered since the love of God in us and in our communities expresses and teaches us how to love others. Love not only keeps us in the Presence of God but results in obedience to the will of God and produces holiness in character. The first sign that we genuinely love God is that we love our neighbor.[367] We can only love our neighbor rightly if we love God wholly.

Another aspect of the first of these commandments is that as we pour ourselves out on the task of loving God, we become "known" by God[368] and become people who are conformed to His will. There is a communion of Spirit, heart to Heart and an obedience that comes out of our love for God. We may be known as people who cast out demons and do all manner of "miracles" in the name of Jesus; we may think we are doing the will of God, but if we do not love God, we are not known by Him and are even called "evildoers."[369] It is not those who do miracles who are known by Him, but rather those who love, trust and obey him. It is those who act in conformance to the will of the 'bridegroom' because they love Him and his bride who show they are truly in relationship with the bridegroom and are thus 'known' by Him.[370] Once again this is the tacit dimension of knowledge, as we love God, we know Him and He knows us.

IN ORDER TO LOVE OTHERS, WE NEED TO LOVE OURSELVES

Matthew 22:39 indicates that we are meant to love others as we love ourselves. One of the greatest barriers to us loving others is the brokenness of our own souls. All of us have grown up in homes with parents who were to one degree or another dysfunctional, unable to love us with the unconditional, complete love that is found in the heart of God. The result of this is a faulty self-identity and a warped ability to love ourselves. What the second commandment suggests is that any inability to love ourselves impacts our ability to love others. This is why chapter one

367 1 John 4:20.

368 See 1 Cor. 8:3: ". . . *whoever loves God is known by Him.*"

369 Matt. 7:21-23.

370 As in the parable of the 10 virgins – the 5 foolish virgins shame the bride and groom by their foolish actions and are cut off from entering the marriage banquet because the groom says: "I don't know you." Their actions show they do not truly love him and so he does not "know" them (Matt. 25:12).

is so foundational – the basis of our self-knowledge must come from God Himself who formed us and created us "in His image."[371] As we make God the context of our lives, His love forms and shapes us into who we are meant to be in Him. His deeply affirming love for us heals us and calls us into who we really are and empowers us to both know and love ourselves. Then out of the confidence and internal 'rest' that this brings to our hearts and spirits, His love for us overflows to others.

So, if we do not love themselves in the truest way (with humility, gratitude, and the enjoyment of who God made us to be), we can never truly love others. It is God's love for us in our deepest hearts that allows His Presence to flow through us to bless and love the world. We cannot see the second commandment fulfilled without starting with the first commandment to love God with all our being so that we can know and experience His love for us. Loving God and knowing His love for us empowers us to love others.

Another aspect of this is that since God is holy and His holiness cannot be separated from His love, His love for us will encounter our unholiness and call us to repent so that we can be freed to be more like Him. Sin entangles[372] and corrupts our self-image and distorts our ability to see both God and ourselves clearly. Without embracing holiness, we cannot grow in our ability to know and love ourselves and so cannot grow in our ability to love others. A corrupted self-love produces a corrupted ability to love others. What the world longs to experience is a love that is pure and undefiled by sin. This means that we, as bearers of God's love, are to be holy as God is holy[373] so that we can love as He loves.

---

371 Genesis 1:27.

372 See Hebrews 12:1-2: "*. . . let us throw off everything that hinders us and the sin that so easily entangles. And let us run with perseverance the race marked out for us, fixing our eyes on Jesus . . . .*"

373 1 Peter 1:15-16.

LOVE MAKES GOD INTELLIGIBLE TO THE WORLD

The great chapter of the Bible on love is 1 Corinthians 13:

> *"If I speak in the tongues of men or of angels, but do not have love, I am only a resounding gong or a clanging cymbal. If I have the gift of prophecy and can fathom all mysteries and all knowledge, and if I have a faith that can move mountains, but do not have love, I am nothing. If I give all I possess to the poor and give over my body to hardship that I may boast, but do not have love, I gain nothing.*
>
> *Love is patient, love is kind. It does not envy, it does not boast, it is not proud. It does not dishonor others, it is not self-seeking, it is not easily angered, it keeps no record of wrongs. Love does not delight in evil but rejoices with the truth. It always protects, always trusts, always hopes, always perseveres.*
>
> *Love never fails. . . . And now these three remain: faith, hope and love. But the greatest of these is love."* (1 Corinthians 13:1-8, 13)

The love talked about in this chapter is not the love we normally see. It is not fleshly love. It is not sexual love. It is patient, kind, and not envious. It is forgiving and forgetful of wrongs committed. It protects, trusts and perseveres. It is "agape" love, the kind of love we see in God and that flows from God. This kind of love when manifested in the lives of people makes God understandable to the world. It shows people what God is truly like. You only get this kind of love by pressing into God and spending time in His Presence.

This kind of love also makes the Gifts of the Spirit intelligible. The Gifts of the Spirit are meant to be used to build up the Church and they do this when practiced in the right way. They are meant to draw us closer to God, but they will only do this when used in the context of love. Love, not the Gifts of the Spirit, makes us into the kind of people God wants us to be. Love makes the Gifts of the Spirit into part of a song of God's love for the world. Without love the Gifts of the Spirit are only noise. Any experience of love can affirm who you are to some degree, yet this "God" kind of love calls and affirms who you truly are without any deception or bias.

GOD TEACHES US HOW TO LOVE

"Now about your love for one another we do not need to write to you, for you yourselves have been taught by God to love each other." (1 Thess. 4:9)

God teaches us how to love one another. It is the Holy Spirit as He leads us and guides us into all truth[374] who helps us to live out God's love. It is His Presence in us that helps us to love according to His nature and character. The quality of love indicates whether we are willing to be taught by God. The humble grow in love, the proud and stubborn do not.

When we press into God and experience His love, He teaches us what true love really is and empowers us to show it to others. Pressing into God means that we purposefully create time and space for God in our lives and pursue those activities that empower us to encounter His Presence. So, we seek God – and wait for Him to speak. We worship and listen to the voice of God speaking to us as we engage our hearts with His. We go through our day acting as if we truly are in the Presence of the living God and include Him in our thinking and activities. We seek to live as if the living God is always near. It is never God that drifts from us, unless we engage in purposeful sin, but it is us who drift from God. We fast and tell God we hunger and thirst for more of Him – and wait for God's Presence to respond to our hunger like manna descending from heaven. We remind ourselves that God is the foundation of all reality and invite Him to be our reality and our foundation. Then, God's Presence and love will gradually come to characterize us. His reality, love and glory will begin to be manifested in our relationships and peo-

374 John 16:13.

ple will be drawn to the light of the Gospel. Everyone needs to be loved. As we cultivate God's Presence in love, we start to change the world through the love of God flowing through us. For the sake of the world, we need to cultivate our intimacy with our Father-God.

Summary

Love makes God visible and understandable to the world. We all need love and were designed by God to thrive in a context of love. Since the Bible says that *"God is love,"* this means that every time we experience love we are experiencing an element of the nature of God, and every time we love others, we show them an aspect of God's nature as well. Loving God and experiencing His love for us enables us to love others as they need to be loved. Yet God's love cannot be separated from His holiness, so we need to show others love that is pure and undefiled. It is this kind of love that transforms and liberates. This love is only found through a relationship with God Himself and living in His loving Presence.

Key points in this chapter include:

1. Since we are created in the image of God, part of the glory of humanity is that we can love others. God is love. His Presence in us empowers us to love others as they need to be loved.
2. True love is evangelistic, calling people into a relationship with their heavenly Father. When we love people, we show them God.
3. Jesus came to the Earth to bring the kingdom rule of God. He died as our sin-sacrifice so that we could be re-united with our heavenly Father. Part of the kingdom rule of God on earth is bringing healing and deliverance to people. We sin against the love of God for people when we do not release healing and deliverance to the hurting and oppressed.
4. The two Great Commandments show us that when we love God rightly, His love can be released to our neighbor.

5. When God's "agape" love is shown to the world it makes God understandable. When the Gifts of the Spirit are expressed in the context of love, they point to the One who is love and make Him understandable as well.
6. God is committed to teach us how to love if we are willing to be taught.

Entering Into His Presence

Put on some worship music and spend time with God. If there are areas in your life where you have not felt loved, give these over to God and invite Him into these areas.

Give God your wounds, those areas where you have not been loved rightly by others. Invite God into those deep, love-starved parts of your heart. Ask God to reveal the full depth of His love for you. Yield to God those places where you have been hurt by life and ask God to heal them by His love.

Tell God that you need Him to teach you what love is really like. Wait in His Presence. Receive His love for you.

Prayer

Lord, I need to know Your love for me. Sometimes I feel like I cannot love others because I do not love myself. Help me to forgive and love myself as You do.

Lord, I give You my wounds. I forgive those that have hurt me (be specific if you can). I turn to You right now and invite Your love into my heart. Heal my heart I pray. Make it whole so that I can love others as You want me to do.

Lord, show me Your love for me. Teach my heart about Your love. I want to be taught by You so that I can love others with Your love. I long for the whole world to know Your love – how wonderful You are.

Come, Holy Spirit. Anoint me and empower me to be a healing balm to the wounded and to bring freedom to those You love. Help me to be a carrier of the Good News of the Gospel. Bring Your kingdom down to the earth with power to love people into wholeness. God, do more than I know to ask. Be Lord! Release Your love I pray.

Overwhelm me with Your love. Help me to carry it to others.

In the precious name of Jesus I pray,

Amen.

14

Experiencing the Presence of The Glory of the Lord

"The god of this age has blinded the minds of unbelievers, so that they cannot see the light of the gospel that displays the glory of God. . . .

For God, who said. 'Let light shine out of darkness,' made his light shine in our hearts to give us the light of the knowledge of God's glory displayed in the face of Christ." (2 Cor. 4:4, 6)

GOD'S GLORY IS NOT ALWAYS EASY TO SEE

Three people can be looking at the same beautiful sunset. The first is moved to tears by its beauty; the second, thinks the sunset is pretty, but no big deal; the third, wonders what the fuss is about and would rather be watching TV. Not everyone has the ability or willingness to see the glory of a beautiful sunset. Similarly, not everyone is able or willing to see the glory of the Lord. It's paradoxical. The glory of the Lord can be overwhelming, powerful and deeply confrontive, yet not everyone can perceive it. And, sometimes seeing it, want to run from it. It challenges our presuppositions about life, about who we are, and about who God is. Encountering the Glory of the Lord can be one of the most powerful manifestations of God we will ever experience. It can shake the very foundations of our lives. Just look at what happened with Isaiah: he "saw" the Glory of the Lord and was so overwhelmed by the experience that he thought he would be killed by that glory. Resistance to truly "seeing" the Glory of the Lord can be deeper than it is for experiencing any of the other dimensions of God's Presence. God's glory, His beauty and His wonder, is present everywhere God is, yet, why do we have trouble entering in? Let's look at several possible reasons for this.

The first reason is simply that the god of this world has blinded people to the glory of the Lord, especially as it is seen in the face of Christ. Second Corinthians 4:4 says: *"The god of this age has blinded the minds of unbelievers, so that they cannot see the light of the gospel that displays the glory of God."* There is a spiritual dimension at work here. Satan does not want us to see God clearly, particularly in the face of Christ, and works to blind us to His glory.[375] As we come into the light of the Gospel and turn our hearts to Christ, the "blindness" in our hearts is taken away[376] and we become empowered to see the glory of the Lord in the face of Jesus.[377] This is a transforming work of the Spirit in our lives which occurs as our minds and hearts are renewed.[378] If we cannot see the glory of the Lord in the face of Christ,[379] it may be difficult to see it anywhere else. Since the Son is the image of the invisible God, Jesus makes God visible to us, in Christ we see all that God is. This includes His love, His beauty, and His glory. Satan resists us coming to Christ and being freed by the Holy Spirit to see and contemplate the glory of the Lord.

A second reason we have a hard time experiencing the glory of the Lord is that we can be afraid of His glory. It can be terrifying! God is so

---

375 2 Cor. 4:6.

376 2 Cor. 3:16.

377 The Transfiguration event is one moment when the Glory of God in Jesus is revealed (Mark 9:2-8).

378 Romans 12:1.

379 Col. 1:15,19: *"The Son is the image of the invisible God . . . For God was pleased to have all of his fullness dwell in him."*

"other" than us, so pure and so holy that we want to run and hide when He draws near in His power and Presence.[380] It takes courage to embrace the transformation necessary to truly "see" the Lord with unveiled faces. There is an Old Testament story where Moses is transformed as he spends time in the Presence of God so that his face glows, and the Israelites are afraid to look at him.[381] Moses ends up accommodating their fear by covering his face with a veil but takes it off when he returns to the Presence of the Lord.[382] Referring to this story, Paul explains[383] how even today, this "veil" caused by fear separates us from God. Yet, as we turn to Christ, this "veil" is taken away so that we can truly see the Lord and be changed by His glory into people who more fully resemble Christ.[384] In 2 Corinthians 3:18 Paul implies that it is precisely this contemplation of God's glory with "unveiled faces" that changes us into God's image. We need to let go of our fear of the power of God's glory and turn to the Lord. As we come to Him, if we are willing to be changed, God will shine His light on our hearts, and we will be *"transformed into his image with ever-increasing glory"* (2 Cor. 3:18). It is about intimacy, face-to-face time with the LORD. It is about receiving His love and allowing it to drive out our fear.[385] As we are transformed, we become increasingly able to display the glory of the Lord in our own lives. Moses became known as a man who spoke to God "face-to-face, as one speaks to a friend"[386] and ended up unknowingly displaying God's glory to others.[387] In other words, as we are courageous

---

380 See as an example, the response of Adam and Eve to the Presence of the Lord in the Garden of Eden – they run and hide (Gen. 3:8-10).

381 Exodus 34:29-35.

382 This shows also that Moses was not afraid of entering into and encountering the glory of the Lord, but the Israelites were.

383 2 Cor. 3:7-18.

384 2 Cor. 3:18 and Rom. 8:29 – contemplating God's glory changes us into His image.

385 1 John 4:18.

386 Exodus 33:11.

387 Exodus 34:29: *"When Moses came down from the Mountain . . . he was not aware that his face was radiant because he had spoken with the LORD."*

enough to enter the Presence of the LORD "face-to-face," we are changed so that the Lord becomes more visible to others through us.

Third, there is also a mystery to being able to see or hear the Lord. It seems people may have different sensitivities to God's voice or Presence. There is a passage from John 12:28-29 that illustrates this. As Jesus is talking to his disciples about his upcoming death, He suddenly cries out: *"Father, glorify your name!"* God responds with an audible voice, but the people around do not hear it the same way. After Jesus cries out, John reports: *"Then a voice came from Heaven. 'I have glorified it and will glorify it again.' The crowd that was there and heard it said it had thundered; others said an angel had spoken to him."* Some of those present heard a voice speak (John apparently was able to distinguish the words). Others said it was thunder. Some said it was an angel speaking. Different people heard the voice of God differently. You see a similar thing in Paul's Damascus Road experience. Paul was confronted by God and heard a voice asking him: *"Saul, Saul, why do you persecute me?"* (Acts 9:4) It says in verse 7: *"The men traveling with Saul stood there speechless; they heard the sound but did not see anyone."* In Acts 22:8 recounting the same story, Paul says: *"My companions saw the light, but did not understand the voice of him who was speaking to me."* Paul heard God speaking clearly, yet some of the others were not able to distinguish the words except that it sounded like someone speaking. Not everyone sees or hears God the same. Some of the reasons for this could be attributed to the other factors mentioned below,[388] but one reason could simply be that not everyone is equally sensitive to the Lord's Presence.

A fourth reason is that not every person, whether Christian or non-Christian, has the same openness to seeing or hearing the Lord. We need to have eyes and hearts that are open to see Him in order to see the glory of the Lord and be receptive to His voice. In the ministry of Jesus

388 Particularly the issue of unbelief which is emphasized in John 11. This is one of the most common reasons people cannot "see" or "hear" God. Part of this is because unbelief hardens our hearts and makes us unable to perceive the actions or voice of the God who speaks softly.

we see clearly that not everyone was willing to see or hear what God was saying. In Mark 4:9 and other passages[389] Jesus finishes parables with a refrain similar to "Whoever has ears to hear, let him hear."[390] After the parable of the Sower, Jesus declares this phrase,[391] and then the disciples come to Jesus and ask him why He speaks in parables to the crowds. [392]Jesus responds by saying that basically not everyone is willing or truly open to "hearing" His words. Yet, speaking to the disciples, Jesus says to them (Matt. 13:16): *"But blessed are your eyes because they see and your ears because they hear."* Jesus explains the parables more fully to the disciples because they are willing to "see" and "hear" what God is doing and saying. In Revelation, speaking to the Seven Churches (and therefore speaking to "believers") Jesus says the same refrain at the end of each of His messages to the Churches.[393] So, even among Christians there can be an unwillingness to perceive correctly who God is and what He is doing in our midst.

A fifth reason relates to why people are unwilling to truly "hear" or "see" the Lord. In Matthew 13, Jesus says that the crowd around them are unwilling to "see" or to "hear" God because of the hardness of their hearts. Therefore, one of the main reasons[394] people do not listen to God or are unable to "see" Him is because their hearts have become hard, seemingly due to conscious choices they have made.[395] Why do people develop hard hearts? Hebrews three and four give us some insight as the author comments on a pivotal event in the history of the nation of Israel.

389 See Mark 4:23; 8:18; Luke 8:8; 14:35; Matt. 13:9, etc..

390 Not all of them are identical in wording.

391 Matt. 13:9.

392 Matt. 13:10-17.

393 See Rev. 2:7, 11, 17, 29; 3:6, 13, 22.

394 Since contemplating the Glory of God changes us (see 2 Cor. 3:18), I think that some of the time people do not "hear" or "see" God because they are unwilling to change. Of course, the question becomes: why are they unwilling to change? Is hardness of heart the foundational reason? Perhaps this is what Jesus is saying in Matt. 13:10-17.

395 In Matt 13:15, the language Jesus uses to describe these people suggests they have purposefully chosen to close their eyes and ears to the Lord.

The entire nation gathered at the edge of the Promised Land, ready to go in, but ended up refusing to do so. The result was a 40-year exclusion from the Promised Land until the death of every one of the adult Israelites who refused to go in except for Joshua and Caleb. Why did they refuse to enter the Promised Land? The root was unbelief and a lack of trust in the goodness of God that caused them to turn away from Him and disobey His voice. Hebrews 3:12, 15-16, 19 says:

> *"See to it, brothers and sisters, that none of you has a sinful and unbelieving heart that turns away from the living God. . .*
>
> *As has been said, 'Today if you hear his voice do not harden your hearts as you did in the rebellion.' Who were they who heard and rebelled? . . .*
>
> *(19) So we see that they were not able to enter (the Promised Land) because of their unbelief."*

This passage indicates that a sinful, unbelieving heart turns away from the Presence of the Lord and refuses to follow Him. "Hearing" the voice of God involves a choice: trust or unbelief? Refusing to listen to God's voice hardens our hearts and can result in our hearts becoming hard enough that we no longer hear His voice. The result of this unbelief then becomes rebellion, disobedience, and exclusion from the blessing of the Lord. This means that since the people of God chose to walk in unbelief, their exclusion from the Promised Land resulted in an inability to see the Glory of the Lord. In other words, their unbelief resulted in them being excluded from the place where God had chosen to display His glory and power as He led His people into their destiny. Some people are unable to see the Glory of the Lord because they are so filled with unbelief that their hard hearts have placed them outside of God's Presence.

We see similar things in the ministry of Jesus. For example, in John 11 when Lazarus was raised from the dead, some people saw an incredible miracle and believed in Jesus (John 11:45; 12:11). Others, observers at the same event, did not see anything other than an inconvenience and a source of disturbance (John 11:46, 48; 12:10). Lazarus was raised from the dead, yet they could not see the glory of God this event displayed. Their unbelief led them down a path of disobedience and rebellion that resulted in their exclusion from the glory of the LORD. Ignoring the voice of God is not the way to enter His Presence! It takes faith to "see" the glory of the Lord. It takes faith and trust in the Lord to keep your heart soft and receptive to His voice.

A sixth reason people may not see the Glory of the Lord is a lack of worship that is linked to a belief in God's goodness. God responds to the praises of His people, especially when they are joined with consecration to Him and a declaration of His goodness. 2 Chronicles 5:13-14 says:

> *". . . the singers raised their voices in praise to the LORD and sang: 'He is good; his love endures forever.' Then the temple of the LORD was filled with the cloud, and the priests could not perform their services because of the cloud, for the glory of the LORD filled the temple of God."*

In chapter 6, Solomon praises the LORD and acknowledges His greatness and goodness (vs. 4-11). Then he consecrates the temple to the LORD in a powerful prayer of dedication (vs. 14-42). As he finishes this prayer, fire falls from heaven on the burnt offerings and consumes them and:

> *". . . the glory of the LORD filled the temple. The priests could not enter the temple of the LORD because the glory of the LORD filled it. When all of the Israelites saw the fire coming down and the glory of the LORD above the temple, they knelt down on the pavement with their faces to the ground, and they worshipped and gave thanks to the LORD saying, 'He is good; his love endures forever.'"* (2 Chron. 7:1-3)

Twice in chapters 5-7 we see worship and a *declaration of God's goodness* linked to a powerful manifestation of His glory. If we want to see God's glory, we worship the Lord, declare and trust in His goodness and love, consecrate ourselves to His service, and we may see God responding with an outpouring of His glory!

A last key to being able to see the glory of the LORD is to embrace holiness. It is the pure in heart who will 'see' God.[396] This is one reason that unbelieving, hardened hearts do not see the glory of the LORD. If they did see it, it would destroy them. Holiness is always deeply confronting to who we are. It challenges and transforms us. It breaks our pride and arrogance producing humility and grace. It is better to fall on the cornerstone so that we are broken and renewed rather than be crushed by it when it falls on us.[397] Isaiah discovered this as he saw his own sin in the Presence of the glory of the LORD. It shattered him, yet, as he listened to the LORD, he was able to enter his calling as a powerful prophet. Being in the Presence of the glory of the LORD changes us. Are we willing to "see" the glory of the LORD? Do we really want it? If we do, then let's pursue holiness so that there are fewer barriers to His Presence in our lives.

It is worth asking yourself, what is your capacity to see the glory of the LORD? Do any of the above points resonate with you? Then do what you can to be able to truly "see" the LORD and "hear" His voice. Gaze at the face of Jesus and see the glory of the LORD there since Jesus cannot be separated from His glory.

THE GLORY OF THE LORD IN THE NEW COVENANT

> *"Now if the ministry that brought death, which was engraved in letters of stone, came with glory, so that the Israelites could not look steadily at the face of Moses because of its glory... will not the ministry of the Spirit be even more glorious? If the ministry that brought condemnation was glorious, how much more glorious is the ministry that brings righteousness! For what was glorious has no glory now in comparison with the surpassing glory. And if what was transitory came with glory, how much greater is the glory of that which lasts!"* (2 Cor. 3:7-11)

---

396 Matthew 5:8.

397 Matt. 21:44.

The glory of the Old Testament Covenant was tremendous, but still does not compare to the glory of the New Testament Covenant. The Old Covenant was superficial and exterior, the New Covenant goes deeper and transforms the interior man. The Old Covenant brought death (since the law kills) and was written on stone tablets,[398] yet it came with power and might at Mt Sinai.[399] The New Covenant brings life and is written on human hearts[400] and came with the hidden glory of the cross by a work of the Spirit of God.[401] The first brought condemnation through the law, the second brings righteousness through the cross.[402] What God does in human hearts is much more glorious than what He did on stone tablets at Mt. Sinai. Jesus as the mediator of a better covenant mediates the glory of the Lord to us. We need to have eyes to see the wonder and the glory of the cross.

It is intriguing to compare Mt Sinai and Pentecost. At Mt Sinai, God came down upon the mountain with fire and smoke and tremendous power.[403] Moses was given the Old Testament Law for the Israelites, but while he was spending time with God on the mountain, in the glory of God, the people were sinning down below. They made an idol of gold and worshipped it. Moses descended, angry at the people, and 3000 people were killed as the Levites went through the camp with swords bringing the judgement of God to the people. In the New Testament, at Pentecost, a feast celebrating the giving of the Law of God at Mt. Sinai, the fire of God fell on the disciples in the upper room. In the Old Testament, the fire of God fell to consume the consecrated sacrifice or to destroy the

398 2 Cor. 3:7.

399 Exodus 19:16, 18:*"On the morning of the third day there was thunder and lightning, with a thick cloud over the mountain, and a very loud trumpet blast. . . Mount Sinai was covered with smoke, because the LORD descended on it in fire."*

400 Heb. 8:9-10. See also Romans 2:15 and Ezekiel 11:9 and 36:26.

401 2 Cor. 3:8.

402 2 Cor. 3:9.

403 Told in Exodus 19-20, 32.

sinner.[404] In Acts chapter two, it fell to make living sacrifices out of consecrated lives to take His Gospel to the nations. The result is 3000 people saved who received eternal life. At Mt. Sinai, 3000 sinners go from life to death. At Pentecost, 3000 sinners go from spiritual death to spiritual life. Which has the greater glory? The answer is clear: The New Covenant of grace which brings life rather than death through the Gospel of Christ.

THE GLORY OF GOD IS SEEN IN THE INTERPLAY OF CLAY AND THE POWER OF GOD

"We have this treasure in jars of clay to show that this all-surpassing power is from God and not from us." (2 Cor. 4:7)

As we are formed into the image of Christ,[405] we become increasingly able to display the glory of God. There is something incredible about seeing the glory of God in the interplay of "clay" or fragility and the power of God. The troubles and suffering of this world craft God's glory in us, the jars of clay.[406] The "ordinary" becomes extra-ordinary because we have made our lives about the eternal and brought Him into the ordinary. Our humanity becomes touched with a power and a glory greater than ourselves and this makes God more visible precisely because we are human and frail.

Another aspect of this relates to the fragility of our humanity. Life can be hard. We are not guaranteed comfort or even a lack of pain. God's glory is often seen in the cracked and broken vessels that hold on to the goodness of God. This brings hope. It brings life during the struggle and pain. Jesus bore the cross, He was not granted immunity from it. Yet through embracing the pain and the shame of the cross, Jesus brought

404 See Lev. 9:24; 1 Chron. 21:26; 2 Chron. 7:1; 1 Kings 18:38; Lev. 10:2; 2 Kings 1:12; Numb. 16:35.

405 Rom. 8:29; 1 Cor. 4:6.

406 2 Cor. 4:17; 1 Peter 4:13-14.

God's redemptive plan to fruition. God enters into suffering to walk with us through it. This is part of His glory.

THE GLORY OF GOD IS SEEN IN THE "FIRE" AND THE "CLOUD"

Humans are oriented towards the physical world, to what they can see, hear and touch with their senses. This is why believing in the unseen spiritual world with an unseen God who actually helps them with the challenges of life can be difficult. This is the challenge of faith. Many choose not to fight this battle and prefer to fall back on to what they "know" (or can see) to be real, not understanding or accepting that the foundation of this world is the spiritual world.[407] There were times in the Old Testament when the Living God wanted to make a particular impact on those He was in the process of setting apart to be His people; those who would be used by Him to bring freedom and deliverance to the world. It was important that a distinguishing feature of their national identity became that they were a people marked by His Presence.[408] To this end, God chose moments to physically manifest His powerful Presence to His people so that they could see and hear His reality. The more powerful these moments, the more the national identity would be marked by them. Yet, He did not want idolatry to result from these moments[409] so the form He chose to use was commonly either "fire" or a "cloud." Neither "form" could easily become a physical idol. These powerful manifestations of

---

407 Part of this is due to sin: unredeemed mankind has spirits that are "dead" and not able to perceive the spiritual world clearly. Faith that sees God clearly is a work of grace.

408 See Exod. 33: 15-16: *"Then Moses said to him, "If your Presence does not go with us, do not send us up from here. How will anyone know that you are pleased with me and with your people unless you go with us? What else will distinguish me and your people from all the other people on the face of the earth?"* Deut. 4:7: *"What other nation is so great as to have their gods near them in the way that the LORD our God is near us whenever we pray?"* Deut. 4:37: *"Because he loved your ancestors and chose their descendants after them, he brought you out of Egypt by his Presence and his great strength."*

409 Deut. 4:15-20.

God's Presence were so intimidating and overwhelming they were often called revelations of His glory. Sometimes God comes in such power that no matter what resistance you may have in your heart to "seeing" Him, you become overwhelmed with the reality of His glory and might.

There are three series of events in the Old Testament marked out by this kind of powerful physical manifestation of the glory of the Lord. These are the Exodus events, the inauguration of the Tabernacle and the Aaronic priesthood, and the consecration of Solomon's temple.[410] In the New Testament the glory of God is seen in events in the life of Jesus (particularly his birth,[411] transfiguration[412] and death[413]), and in individual Christians as they make God visible[414] in their lives. Revelation also reveals that the fullness of the glory of God will be seen in heaven which is our destination.[415]

The Exodus events are about God calling and forming a nation into people who truly worship the LORD and are characterized by His Presence. In the initial events of Exodus,[416] God shows His glory by liberating the nation of Israel from their slavery and showing them and the Egyptians that He is greater and more powerful than all the Egyptian gods.[417] Repeatedly God acts powerfully and miraculously among the Israelites to demonstrate His power and sovereignty and reveal His glory. He parts the waters of the Red Sea so the nation can escape from the army

---

410 Although there were many other times when God revealed His glory such as with Isaiah (Isaiah 6) and with Elijah and the prophets of Baal (1 Kings 18).

411 Luke 2:9-13 (esp. vs 9, 13).

412 Mark 9:2, 3, 7.

413 Matt. 27:54; 28 :2-4; Mark 15 :38-39 ; Luke 23 :47; 24 :4-5.

414 Acts 4:33. God's glory is seen when He acts in power through believers.

415 See for example Rev. 15:8.

416 Exodus 1-14.

417 As mentioned in chapter 12, the ten plagues and the liberation of the Israelites was a battle over worship. See Exod. 14:17, 18: (17) "*. . . I will gain glory through Pharoah and all his army. . . (18) The Egyptians will know that I am the LORD when I gain glory through Pharoah, his chariots and his horsemen.*" See also Exodus 12:12 – God brings judgement on all the gods of Egypt.

of Pharaoh (Exod. 14: 21-22); He goes before them in a pillar of cloud by day and leads them by a pillar of fire by night (Exod. 13:21-22); He provides manna for them to eat daily for 40 years in the desert (Exod. 16:1-32; Josh. 5:12) and even quail to eat at times (Exod. 16:13);[418] He provides water miraculously when the nation needs it (Exod. 17:1-7; 20:1-13); He gives them miraculous victory in battle (Exod. 17:8-15); He parts the waters of the Jordan River and leads them into the Promised Land (Josh. 3:1-17); and He dramatically and powerfully destroys the mighty walls of Jericho and leads His people to victory there (Josh. 6:1-21). All of these show His glory, yet it is the events at Mt Sinai that powerfully marked the identity of the nation.

Mt Sinai was where God descended to teach the Israelites about His holiness and how they could only enter His Presence through sacrifice. It was at Mt Sinai that the Levitical sacrificial system was inaugurated, and the Aaronic priesthood started. It was extremely important because it prepared the nation for the future coming of the Messiah and gave an understanding of the significance, necessity and meaning of the death of Jesus on the cross. It needed to be such a powerful event because the whole future of the nation would be impacted by it. At Mt Sinai, the glory of the LORD descended on the mountain in an unusual way, shaking and covering the mountain with fire and smoke.[419] The Presence of God was powerful, majestic, glorious, and holy. The people of God, particularly the leaders, were invited to draw near to the Presence of God on the mountain but could not do so without consecrating themselves.[420] They were afraid, and rightly so, as they ran the risk of being killed if they came into His glory lightly. They pleaded with Moses to be their spokesperson and to enter in alone, leaving them at the foot of the mountain, promising

418 The quail and particularly the Manna are linked to a display of the glory of the LORD "in the cloud" (Exod. 16:7, 10).

419 Exodus 19:16-19; 20:18; 24:15-18 - the mountain shook for 6 days before the LORD calls Moses up to meet him.

420 Exodus 19:10-15. Aaron is invited up in Exod. 19 :24 ; Aaron, Nadab, Abihu and 70 elders in Exod. 24:1, 9-11; Joshua in Exod. 24:13.

that they would do what God told them to do through Moses.[421] They heard the voice of God speak to them out of the fire and smoke.[422] They saw His glory and majesty and they were terrified to get too close to it.

What happened in the lives of Moses and the others is instructive. Moses chose to enter the glory of the LORD and stayed there for 40 days straight. As he went to the top of the mountain, he was transformed and changed by his encounter with God. He conversed with God and became a man who hungered and thirsted for a deeper knowledge of God. After he came down from the mountain Moses set up a "tent of meeting" where he could meet with God[423] and, while immersed in the cloud of the glory of God that had descended on the tent, cried out: *"Now show me your glory!"*[424] God responded: *"I will cause all my goodness to pass in front of you and I will proclaim my name, the LORD, in your presence."*[425] Moses became a leader who talked to God face-to-face as one talks with a friend.[426] He became an intimate with the Living God. He became a man who knew and loved God's Presence. He became one of the most powerful prophets of God, speaking and teaching the people of God the things revealed to him in the context of his relationship with God. He was transformed into a godly leader through time spent in the Presence of God.[427] Meanwhile, those who were too afraid to draw near to the glory of God, were left unchanged. Outside of the Presence of the glory of God, their true character came to the fore. When Moses was on the mountain, in the glory, they pressured Aaron to make them an idol to worship,[428] in-

421 Exodus 20:19.

422 Deut. 4:11-12, 33-36; 5:23-24.

423 Exodus 33:7-11.

424 Exodus 33:18.

425 Exodus 33:19.

426 Exodus 33:11.

427 It is instructive that Joshua was the only other person it seems that went with Moses up the mountain (Exod. 24:13; 32:17) and who stayed in the Presence of God in the tent of meeting (Exod. 33:11). It was Joshua who became the next leader of the nation after Moses.

428 Exod. 32:1-10.

sisting Moses must be dead since he had stayed so long on the mountain. Refusing to draw near the Presence of God on the mountain, they drifted into idolatry. Aaron and the other leaders were called by God to lead the people of God towards the things of God, instead they lead them into sin. Fearing that they would be killed by the holiness of God on the mountain, many of them were killed by God in judgement for their idolatry.[429]

When we deal with any blockages, whether fear or sin or unbelief, and dare to enter courageously into the Presence of God, we will in the same way be transformed into people who can fulfill His calling on our lives. When we don't, we lose out. As we say "yes" to God we start to enter the path of our destiny.

THE GLORY OF GOD IN THE TEMPLE OF GOD

Twice in the Old Testament God descends and "settles" on the temple of God with such power that the priests and other worshippers cannot stand.[430] The first is when both the Tabernacle is consecrated and the Levitical priesthood inaugurated with the consecration of Aaron as High Priest. In Exodus 40 we have a description of the completion and consecration of the Tabernacle. In Leviticus 9 we have the inauguration of the priesthood of Aaron.

> *"Then the cloud covered the tent of meeting, and the glory of the LORD filled the tabernacle. Moses could not enter the tent of meeting because the cloud had settled on it, and the glory of the LORD filled the tabernacle. . . .*
>
> *So the cloud of the LORD was over the tabernacle by day, and fire was in the cloud by night, in the sight of all the Israelites during all their travels."* (Exod. 40:34-35, 38)

---

429 Exodus 32:18 – 3000 people were killed by the Levites for their idolatry and more died later in a plague due to their sin (Exodus 32:35).

430 This heavy, thick Presence of the glory of God is often called the "shekinah" glory of the Lord. In both events, God's Presence appears like a thick, heavy cloud and fire comes out of the Presence of God to consume the sacrifice of the people.

> From Leviticus 9: "*. . . the entire assembly came near and stood before the LORD. Then Moses said, 'This is what the LORD has commanded you to do, so that the glory of the LORD may appear to you. . . .*
>
> *Moses and Aaron then went into the tent of meeting. When they came out, they blessed the people; and the glory of the LORD appeared to all the people. Fire came out from the presence of the Lord and consumed the burnt offering and the fat portions on the altar. And when all the people saw it, they shouted for joy and fell facedown.*" (Lev. 9:5-6, 23-24)

In the first passage, as soon as Moses finished setting up the tabernacle (vs. 33), God came down powerfully and "settled" on it. His Presence was so powerful that even Moses could neither stand nor enter the Presence of God. God was visibly there with the people. It says that the Presence of God was seen as a cloud during the day and at night there was fire visible[431] inside the cloud (vs. 38). During "all their travels" in the wilderness, the visible Presence of God was with them, settling on the tabernacle and leading the way when it was time to move. You can see how the reality of the Presence of the glory of God leading His people became imbedded in the identity of the nation of Israel.

In the Leviticus passage, we see that God responded to the actions of the people of God. They, in obedience to God, set up the priesthood of Aaron and carried out the sacrifices according to the laws given by Moses. Then Moses says they will see the glory of the LORD. As Aaron and Moses came out of the tent of meeting after completing the sacrifices (correctly), the glory of the LORD appeared, fire came out of the Presence of the LORD[432] and consumed the sacrifices they had laid out. The people fell on their faces in worship and joy. As the people of God

431 God is often called a "consuming fire" in the Bible (Exod. 24:17; Deut. 4:24; Isa. 30:27 (tongue is a consuming fire), 30:30 (arm is a consuming fire); 33:14; Heb. 12:29).

432 Fire often comes out from the Presence of God.

were faithful and obedient, God honored their faithfulness and showed them His glory.

The second time this powerful "Glory cloud" settled on the temple of God was at the consecration of Solomon's temple.[433] In 2 Chronicles 5:13-14; 6:1-2 it says:

> "*. . . the singers raised their voices in praise to the LORD and sang: 'He is good; his love endures forever.' Then the temple of the LORD was filled with the cloud, and the priests could not perform their service because of the cloud, for the glory of the LORD filled the temple of God.*
>
> *Then Solomon said, 'The LORD has said that he would dwell in a dark cloud; I have built a magnificent temple for you, a place for you to dwell forever'*"
>
> From chapter 7: "*When Solomon finished praying, fire came down from heaven and consumed the burnt offering and the sacrifices, and the glory of the LORD filled the temple. The priests could not enter the temple of the LORD because the glory of the LORD filled it. When all of the Israelites saw the fire coming down and the glory of the LORD above the temple, they knelt on the pavement with their faces to the ground, and they worshipped and gave thanks to the LORD saying, 'He is good; his love endures forever'*" (2 Chron. 7:1-3)

In chapter 5, it almost seems that God descends upon the temple, revealing His glory as a response to His people declaring His goodness. Solomon had spent years building a magnificent temple for the LORD. Finally, it was ready for God to dwell there. God descended powerfully at its consecration, His glory filled the temple, and the priests could not stand in the Presence of the glory of God. They worshipped the LORD affirming His goodness and love. Again, as with the consecration of the priesthood, fire came out from the Presence of God and consumed the

433 This event is also in 1 Kings 8:10-11.

priestly sacrifice. In chapter 7, we see that a revelation of the glory of God was again linked to a declaration of His goodness by His people.

God has a heart to bless and fill His temples as people consecrate them to Him and worship there. In fact, the temples of God became marked by His Presence and glory. May each one of us as temples of the LORD consecrate ourselves to Him, worship Him and be filled with His glory and fire![434]

On the mountain of Sinai, God's powerful glory descends with His holiness. With the tabernacle, the inauguration of the Aaronic priesthood and with Solomon's temple, it is after the consecration of these items and people that the glory of God descends in power. Yet in Leviticus 10 we have the tragic story of two of the sons of Aaron, on the *day after* they were consecrated as priests, being consumed by the fire of God when they wrongly and sinfully did not follow the laws set out by God for the priesthood (Lev. 10:1-2). Holiness is the only way that someone can enter the Presence of God's glory and live. Isaiah in 33:14 asks the question: "*Who of us can dwell with the consuming fire? Who of us can dwell with everlasting burning?*" Yet in the next verse he answers: "*Those who act righteously and speak what is right . . .*". Only the righteous can live with the consuming fire![435] The consecration of our lives made possible by Christ's sin-sacrifice is the only entry point into the Presence of the glory of God. God gives us the impossible standard to be holy as God is holy (Lev. 11:44, 45; 19:2; 20:26; 21:8; 1 Pet. 1:6). Through Jesus this becomes possible as we apply His sacrifice to our lives. Obedience to the will of God releases the possibility of encountering His glory.

---

434 As happened at Pentecost in Acts 2.

435 This is instructive for our ideas of hell. When Satan and others are thrown into the lake of "fire" (Rev. 20:14-15), it is only the sinful that are burned by the consuming fire of God. The righteous are not burned by the fire since they are pure through the blood of Jesus. It is people's sin that makes hell a torment. If they were righteous, the fire of hell would have nothing to burn in them.

One of the things we see in those moments when the Glory of God descends on the temple is that people have a physical response to the glory of God. When God's glory descended on the tabernacle, Moses could not enter it (Deut. 40:34-35). When the fire came out of the Presence of God and consumed the sacrifice at the consecration of Aaron and his sons, the people fell on their faces in joy (Lev. 9:24). When the glory of God descended on Solomon's temple, the priests could not enter the temple and when the fire consumed the sacrifice, the people knelt on the ground praising God with their faces to the ground (2 Chron. 7:1-3). It is almost like their physical bodies were so overwhelmed by the powerful Presence of God that they short-circuit. There are other points in the Scriptures where men fell as if they were dead in the Presence of God or angels.[436] They lost control of their bodies and, perhaps, this is why the Presence of the glory of God can be so scary.

Another aspect of this is that through Jesus we, as believers, are now a kingdom of priests,[437] called to minister to the Lord and mediate between God and those that do not have access to His throne room. It is a high and holy calling. Yet when the glory of God falls as it does in 1 Kings 8:10-11 and other passages, the priests cannot do their priestly service. This shows that everything we might do and are called to do for the Lord is to be laid down in the presence of the glory of God. His presence, His glory, supersedes everything else. We need to find those moments where we put aside our service to the Lord and for His people to fall down before His glory.[438] His glory is far more important than anything we might do for Him. This is especially important when we realize that through Jesus, we become the temples His glory fills. May His glory shine in and through each one of us as we lay down our service to Him in the light of His Presence.

436 Matt. 28:2-4; Rev. 1:17; Dan. 10:7-11; Ezek. 1.28.

437 1 Peter 2:9.

438 See Ezekiel 44:4

THE GOODNESS OF GOD AND THE GLORY OF THE LORD

The goodness of God is closely linked to His glory. Earlier we saw that the people of God sang and proclaimed the goodness and love of God when the glory fell on the temple.[439] In Exodus 33:18 we see the same when Moses asked God to reveal His glory to him. God responded that He would reveal His goodness to Moses and proclaim His "name" to him.[440] God then proclaimed His goodness and faithfulness. God's goodness IS His glory – and holiness is part of His glory as well. Holiness is always good, goodness is always holy. They are always together. At the waters of Meribah, for example, God was gracious to the Israelites and provided water for them in the desert, an act of love, yet it says that through this event God was "proved holy among them" (Nb. 20:13). The essence of the glory of God is His goodness, and this is not separated from His holiness.

JESUS AND THE GLORY OF GOD

Jesus is the visible representation of the invisible God. Thus, it is no surprise that His whole life was tinged and flavoured by the glory of God. From His birth[441] to His death[442] the glory of God and the miracle power of God abounded in His life and ministry. Over 40 specific miracles are recorded in the Gospels, but He did many more than those recorded.[443] These were all demonstrations of the love and power of God to break the bondage of Satan in the lives of people. Each one of these reveal the

439 2 Chron. 5:13; 7:3.

440 Exod. 33:19. In other words, reveal to Moses God's inner nature. The next chapter in Exod. 34:5-6 God again proclaims His "name" to Moses, proclaiming His goodness and faithfulness.

441 Luke 2:9, 14.

442 Matt. 27:51-54.

443 There are 66 specific miracle stories but many of these are duplicates. We Know that He did many other miracles from such passages as Matt. 4:23-24, 8:16 and 14:35-36 where He healed all who came to him, Luke 7:21 where many were healed and even raised from the dead and John 20:30 where Jesus "*performed many other signs in the presence of his disciples, which are not recorded in this book.*"

glory of the LORD to those whose hearts are open to see it. Another key event where we see the glory of God in Jesus is the Transfiguration of Jesus recorded in Matt. 17:1-8; Mark 9:2-8; and Luke 9:28-36. Peter as an eyewitness also refers to it in 1 Peter 2:16-18.

Philippians 2:6-8 talking of Jesus says that He:

> *"Who, being in very nature God, did not consider equality with-God something to be used to his own advantage; rather, he made himself nothing by taking the very nature of a servant, being made in human likeness. And being found in appearance as a man, he humbled himself by becoming obedient to death – even death on a cross!"*

Jesus emptied Himself of His Godly prerogatives, taking on human limitations out of obedience to the plan of God to redeem the world. He became the "Messiah", the "anointed one" of God at His baptism[444] when the Holy Spirit not only came upon Him but remained on Him.[445] Jesus did all of His miracles because God was with Him, as one anointed by the Holy Spirit to destroy the works of Satan.[446] We see the glory of God through what Jesus did because the Presence and anointing of God was on His life. Yet, despite limiting the expression of His divinity, Jesus remained God. One of the moments we see this is in the transfiguration event where it is as if Jesus peals back His "hiddenness" and shows Peter, James and John something of the glory He had with God since the beginning. His face shone "like the sun,"[447] His garments became white "as the light," then a bright cloud covered them and a voice spoke out of the cloud affirming the Sonship of Jesus (*This is my Son, whom I love. Listen to Him!"*)[448]. The disciples were overwhelmed by this moment and fell

---

444 John 1:33.

445 Here we see a distinction between Jesus and us. The Holy Spirit remained with Jesus because Jesus guarded his purity before God and did not sin.

446 Acts 10:38; 1 John 3:8.

447 Matt. 17:2; Mark 9:2-3; Luke 9:29.

448 Matt. 17:5; Mark 9:7; Luke 9:34-35.

on their faces.[449] They were overcome by fear and could not stand in the Presence of this "cloud" overshadowing Jesus. It is reminiscent of Moses in the tent of meeting where God powerfully met Moses and showed him His goodness and the face of Moses shone due to the Presence of God on him. When Jesus descended from the mountain, the remaining disciples with others saw Jesus and were "overwhelmed with wonder and ran to greet him."[450] Unlike Moses, Jesus did not cover His face.

In this event in the life of Jesus, prayer precipitated an encounter with the glory of God. The Presence of the glory of God "shone" through Jesus and God descended in a cloud that overshadowed the top of the mountain. Then God spoke – and it is not what you would expect: He affirms the Sonship of Jesus and how much He is loved by His heavenly Father.[451] He also affirmed that Jesus was someone who must be listened to by the disciples.

Peter later refers to this moment as a moment when the majesty, honor and glory of Jesus were revealed[452] and warns us prophetically to pay attention to the words spoken to Jesus *"as to a light shining in a dark place, until the day dawns and the morning star rises"* in our hearts (2 Peter 1:19). This revelation of sonship (or "daughtership") which was at the core of Jesus' encounter with the glory of God on the mountain is something that we need to take in and make our own. Now as children of God purchased through the blood of Jesus and adopted into the family of God, God speaks the same words of affirmation to us. One of the revelations embedded in any encounter with the glory of God is the revelation that we are loved and accepted by our heavenly Father through Christ. This revelation needs to grow in us until it "shines" like the morning star, filling our hearts with the light of the God's love. Part of the wonder and glory of God is that He calls us His children. If we want to know the

449 Matt. 17:6.

450 Mark 9:15.

451 Echoing God's declaration over Jesus at His baptism in Matthew 3:17.

452 1 Peter 1:16-18.

glory of God, let's press into the Father and grow in our understanding of what it means to be His child. Then the glory of God will be seen in and through us when we come into our identity as a son or daughter of the Living God. And don't forget to declare His goodness!

THE GLORY OF GOD IS SEEN IN EVERY DIMENSION OF THE PRESENCE OF GOD

We can catch a glimpse of the glory of the Lord at each of the dimensions of the Presence of God outlined so far. God cannot be separated from His glory no matter the manifestation of His Presence. When love is on display, for example, we can see the beauty of the glory of the Lord. When someone is healed, the glory of the Lord is on display. When we worship, we can at times feel and sense the glory of the Lord. We can see Him in others and in our Churches. However we access His Presence, it is always glorious if we have the eyes to see. One way to cultivate the ability to "see" the glory of the Lord is to cultivate His Presence in each of the dimensions discussed in this book. Let's look for His activity in our lives. Acknowledge His sustaining Presence. Look for Him in His Word. Seek for Him in Worship. We can consecrate ourselves to be His temple and welcome His Presence in our lives and the life of our Church. We can value the Presence of the Lord when we meet with other Christians. Let's love Him and love others, seeking to display His Presence in our relationships. We add Presence to Presence. As we do these things, our hearts will become predisposed to "see" His glory when it is there. Remember also that God is not a "safe" God. He is an amazingly powerful and loving one that will transform everything about our lives as we pursue His Presence.

Every time we see an eruption of the power of God, we see part of the glory of the LORD. Powerful healings, lives transformed by love, all of these are demonstrations of the glory of God.

How do we become conformed to the image of Christ? We worship God; we love the goodness of the LORD; we embrace holiness; we gaze at the glory of the LORD in the face of Jesus. We become what we love.

As we pour out our lives on loving Jesus, God by His Spirit will work to transform our lives into the image of His Son.

Summary

There are many blockages that can prevent people from seeing the glory of the Lord. If we want to truly see and encounter the glory of God, we need to get rid of any barriers in our life to God's Presence and seek more of Him. Living in appreciation of His goodness and His enduring love will often result in seeing a greater manifestation of the glory of God. Embracing holiness and living lives consecrated to Him are also important. God's glory is truly magnificent and any encounter with it can be life-changing!

Important points from this chapter include:

1. It is not always easy to see the glory of the Lord. There are several reasons for this which include: Spiritual opposition, particularly to us seeing God's glory in the face of Christ; the fearsome nature of His glory; our willingness or unwillingness to see it; the softness or hardness of our hearts; and the level of our personal worship and holiness.

2. The glory of the Lord in the New Covenant is greater than that revealed in the Old Covenant. Now God can be more intimate with His creation and draws closer to those who love Him.

3. The glory of God is seen in the uncomfortable interplay of "jars of clay" and the power of God. Our feebleness makes God's glory more obvious since His strength is made perfect in our weakness.

4. God revealed His glory in the Exodus events as He showed His reality to His people and marked them out as being a people who carried His Presence. His Presence and glory are what gave them victory and what led them into the Promised Land.

5. The glory of God descended on Mt Sinai and powerfully impacted the people. Majesty, holiness and power are all part of the glory of God.

6. The glory of God dwells in His temple, those places consecrated and set apart for His Presence. He blesses and fills the temples dedicated to Him.
7. Goodness and holiness are part of the glory of God. You cannot have the glory of God without His goodness and holiness.
8. The glory of God is seen clearly when His power is displayed, confronting and destroying darkness and bringing His life to people. When the works of Satan are destroyed, God is glorified.
9. The glory of God is seen in each dimension of the Presence of God. The way to see more of the glory of God is to add Presence to Presence – worship God, honor His Word, cultivate His Presence in our individual and corporate lives, and love others – these together invite the Presence of the glory of God.

Entering Into His Presence

Put on some worship music and invite the Presence of the Lord. Give God your love. Worship Him. Tell Him that you want more of Him. Invite Him to show you His glory.

If there are any of the "blockages" to seeing the Lord mentioned in this chapter that resonate with you, bring them to the Lord and ask Him to help you. Repent where necessary. Tell Him you want His love to overpower your fear of His glory.

Ask the Lord to show you His goodness. Spend time just receiving His love for you.

Prayer

Oh Lord, I want to see Your glory. Show me if there is anything in me that blocks me from seeing Your glory. Please, Lord, open my eyes to see the glory of God in the face of Jesus. Take any fear from me – help me to rest in Your great love for me. I give You my heart – circumcise it, cutting off disobedience, unbelief, or resistance to seeing You from my heart. Give me a heart of flesh so that I can see You clearly.

Lord, I want to tell You today that I am willing to see Your glory. I say "yes" to You.

Make Your Presence so strong in me that Your works shine through me. At times I feel so fragile, show Yourself in my weakness.

Lord, Jesus has formed me into a temple for Your Presence. I consecrate my life right now to You. Make me holy as You are holy. Fill Your temple with Your glory right now. Make my life shine with Your Presence.

Lord, show Your power through me. Touch others through me. Let Your glory be displayed through me as I am obedient.

Show me Your glory.

In the precious name of Jesus I pray,

Amen.

Part III:

What Now?

The real Presence of the Living God is transformational. Yahweh is the giver of life. He is its source. It is the responsibility of each of us to make the beauty and glory of God and of His bride, the Church, visible in the world. If others do not see the truth of the nature and character of God in and through us, will they ever see and discover the truth about God? To do this we must be changed, be transformed into the image of Christ so that the world can *"see your good deeds and glorify your father in heaven."*[453] This happens only through living in and embracing the real Presence of God and allowing His Spirit to form and shape us.

This section describes how we need to let the light of God shine in the darkness of this world so that the beauty of the Presence of God in His Church is seen clearly. We will also look at how to keep ourselves in the Presence of God. God is available to those who seek His face, and He has given us the cross so that we can enter and stay in His Presence. Only as we "live in Christ" will the world see clearly our Lord in us. In addition, healing is something that flows from God's very nature. When He is

453 Matt. 5:16; 1 Peter 2:12.

present, healing erupts because He IS life. We can expect that since this is true, when we nurture the real Presence of God in all its dimensions, we will see people healed through the living Presence of the Lord as we experience it. We need to nurture the ongoing Presence of God in our lives so that we can be the world changers God is calling us to be.

15

Displaying The Glory Of The Lord

"At that time the kingdom of heaven will be like ten virgins who took their lamps and went out to meet the bridegroom. Five of them were foolish and five of them were wise. The foolish ones took their lamps but did not take any oil with them. The wise ones, however, took oil in jars along with their lamps. The bridegroom was a long time in coming, and they all became drowsy and fell asleep.

"At midnight the cry rang out: 'Here's the bridegroom! Come out to meet him!'

"Then all the virgins woke up and trimmed their lamps. The foolish ones said to the wise, 'Give us some of your oil; our lamps are going out.'

"'No,' they replied, 'there may not be enough for both us and you. Instead, go to those who sell oil and buy some for yourselves.'

"'But while they were on their way to buy the oil, the bridegroom arrived. The virgins who were ready went in with him to the wedding banquet. And the door was shut.

"Later the others also came. 'Lord, Lord,' they said, 'open the door for us!'

"But he replied, 'Truly I tell you, I don't know you.'

> *"Therefore keep watch, because you do not know the day or the hour." (Matthew 25:1-13)*

The above passage, the Parable of the Ten Virgins from Matthew 25:1-13, is an important one that calls us to display the beauty and glory of the bride of Christ amidst the darkness of this world. In its immediate context, though, it has an eschatological application which is usually all people see in this passage. The key verse is verse 13 where Jesus says that since we do not know the exact hour when He will come, we are to keep watch and be prepared for his imminent return. This parable clearly has an eschatological application and gives us an entirely pertinent warning and counsel. However, there is something else in this passage that touches on how we are to relate to the darkness around us.

The more obvious "end of times" application was for the masses who followed Jesus around; to the disciples, however, Jesus added a more subtle thread of meaning and challenge. This becomes clearer when we consider the connection this passage makes to the great themes of Matthew.

THE BATTLE BETWEEN THE LIGHT AND THE DARKNESS

One of the themes in Matthew that surfaces in this passage is that of light breaking into darkness. Here is Matthew 4:12-13, 14-17:

> *"When Jesus heard that John had been put in prison, he withdrew to Galilee. Leaving Nazareth, he went and lived in Capernaum . . .*
>
> *. . . to fulfill what was said through the prophet Isaiah:*
>
> *'Land of Zebulun and land of Naphtali, the Way of the Sea, beyond the Jordan, Galilee of the Gentiles – the people living in darkness have seen a great light; on those living in the land of the shadow of death a light has dawned. . . "*

From this we see that in the life and ministry of Jesus there is a direct fulfillment of a prophetic passage from Isaiah 9:1-2 talking about light coming into the darkness of this world. Through Jesus: *"those living in darkness have seen a great light; on those living in the land of the shadow of death a light has dawned*" (Matt. 4:16; Isaiah 9:2). Jesus then chooses the 12 and immediately starts to preach and proclaim the good news of the Kingdom of God and heal the sick[454] implying that the new community He is developing is actively pushing back the darkness through doing what He did: preaching about the coming of the kingdom and healing the sick.[455]

Then in Matthew 5:14-16, Jesus more explicitly teaches His disciples that they themselves are light in a dark world. In verse 14, He tells the disciples, "*You are the light of the world... (vs. 16) in the same way, let your light shine before others, that they may see your good deeds and praise your Father in Heaven.*" A key battle in this world is between light and darkness. The "good deeds" that the disciples do would be how they shed light amidst the darkness of this world. You see this in missions, but you see it everywhere. We are the light of the world!

My parents were missionaries in Africa for 49 years and over the years risked their lives many times. The following is a story that illustrates the battle between light and the darkness that is occurring all around us. One day my father was holding some evangelistic meetings in a village in Uganda. By the third day, he was stirring up some opposition among the local witchdoctors and started to notice that the Africans were looking at him in a funny way. In the meeting that afternoon, he noticed two men sitting on the front row glaring at him through the whole service. It was obvious they did not want him there. He also started to feel sick as the afternoon wore on. At one point he asked the interpreter why the locals were looking at him strangely. The man reluctantly told my father that the locals were waiting for him to die. My father was startled and asked why they were doing this. The interpreter explained that the two men who had

454 Matt. 4:18-23.

455 See Acts 10:38 where Jesus goes about *"doing good and healing all who were under the power of the enemy."* And 1 John 3:8 where it says that the reason the Son of God appeared was to destroy the devil's work. Clearly what Jesus did was part of pushing back darkness.

glared at him during the service were local witchdoctors who had placed a curse on him and told people he would die by the next morning. He went on to say that these men were very powerful and had placed a curse on a young girl who dropped dead when she went to get water at the river. My father went into his tent and read the Word of God, worshipped for a bit and then fell asleep. In the middle of the night, he suddenly woke up and felt a heavy evil Presence in his tent. He tried to rebuke it in the name of Jesus, but it felt like something grabbed his throat and he could not talk. He kept battling and eventually was able say the name of Jesus, rebuke the spirit in the name of Jesus and it left. He fell asleep again. When he woke up in the morning, he felt fine. The next morning the Africans were shocked to see him alive and flocked to the meetings. Obviously, my father's God was more powerful than the witchdoctors'! One of the first people to accept Jesus that day was one of the two witchdoctors. Light always triumphs over darkness!

We are the light of the whole world! This means that if you were not around, the darkness in our world would be greater! You do not know your influence in the world. Yet if we more fully understood who we are, our impact would be greater. We are the light of the world because the Presence of the Lord shines through us.[456]

The same battle between light and darkness is seen in this Parable of the Ten Virgins.

MARRIAGE CEREMONIES IN FIRST CENTURY PALESTINE

In order to understand the depth of this parable, we need to understand the marriage practices of first century Palestine. Normally both the bride and groom would dress up, and this would take time. When the groom was ready, usually by the afternoon, he would travel with members of the wedding party to the home of the bride. In the afternoon, the rabbi would arrive and once all were gathered, he would initiate the

456 See John 8:12, 9:5 where Jesus calls himself the "light of the world."

ceremony. Sometimes they would have to wait for everyone to assemble at the bride's house before they could start. If the bride and groom belonged to two different synagogues, there would be two ceremonies with each Rabbi presiding over their own ceremony. Once this was over, there would be a procession from the home of the bride to the home of the groom where there would be a large feast for all the guests and the whole wedding party. Often this procession would be at night, although, even if it was not, lamps would be used to symbolize the Presence of God and the desire of the guests that the bride and groom receive the blessing of God. So, we see light symbolizing the Presence of God; and oil symbolizing the Presence of the Holy Spirit or the anointing of God.

Since our culture is so different to that of first century Palestine, there are a number of items in the parable that need clarification: who were these "virgins" and why were they important? What was their task? Why did they need the lamps? What was so bad about what the "foolish" virgins did?

First, who were the "virgins" in the parable? The "virgins" are the bridesmaids. In the culture of that time, bridesmaids would be chosen by the bride to fulfill this role. They would normally be unmarried women who looked forward eagerly to their own marriage and so could celebrate with the bride on her wedding day. Single girls it was assumed would be virgins.

Why were the "virgins" important? What was their task? These bridesmaids had two tasks: to help the bride prepare for her wedding, and to help with the processional. The latter task is the one we see here. During the processional, they again had two jobs: to light the path in the darkness so that the bride and groom could find their way; and, to raise up their lamps in the darkness so that the beauty of their friend, the bride, could be seen on this special day. They celebrated with the bride and groom, and they wanted everybody in the village to celebrate with them, even those who were not part of the wedding party. This is why there were ten of them, one or two could light the way, but more were needed to make sure there was enough light to see the beauty and glory of the bride!

The lamps were needed because often the processional occurred at night, and without the lamps they could not make sure that the beauty and the glory of the bride were visible, and they could not light the path for the wedding couple in the darkness. These were not small lamps, but normally oil-soaked rags on top of a pole which burned brightly but needed more oil every 15-20 minutes. Without the lamps the bridesmaids could not do their job and failed the bride, who had thought they were her friends.

It seems extreme that the foolish virgins are condemned so harshly. Why was it so terrible when the "foolish" virgins did not have oil? The basic reason is because they could not do their job. Their laziness and lack of preparation let their friend down on her big day. They could even have ruined the wedding processional itself. In addition, their actions reflected negatively on the groom. It was the groom's responsibility to provide the funds for the bridesmaids to buy the lamps and the oil. The "foolish" bridesmaids had all the funds they needed to buy all the oil they needed but, shockingly, had not bothered to do so. If the bridesmaids did not have enough oil or if there were not enough bridesmaids, it implied the groom scrimped on what was provided. The result was that both the groom and bride as well as their families would be dishonoured in the sight of the entire village.

So, how did the presence of the bridesmaids relate to the coming of the groom? Although part of their job had been completed as they helped the bride prepare for her wedding, the more important role was during the processional which they could not do before the groom arrived. Once he came, they could do their job but only if they had prepared for it. This was a huge celebration with a jubilant processional involving singing and dancing.

Imagine it with me. The bride and groom are finally married. It is late, but the main event has occurred. Now the newly married bride and groom leave the bride's home to journey through the darkness to the home of the bridegroom for the grand feast. As they leave the bride's home, the voice rings out: "The bridegroom is here!" The bridesmaids scramble to trim their lamps and re-fill them with oil so that they can burn brightly. The lamps only last 20 minutes before they need more oil, so it is clear they need to get them ready. Five of the bridesmaids have their oil and quickly get their lamps ready; five of them do not have enough oil and after trying to beg some from the others, run off to try to get more. Yet, they should have planned ahead. That was their responsibility. They knew they would need oil, and they had all the funds needed to purchase the oil they needed. Their laziness now costs the bride and reflects on the groom. The other bridesmaids cannot give the foolish ones any oil since if they ran out, none of the bridesmaids could do their job and it would be a disaster!

Meanwhile, the people in the village hear the music and songs approaching. Finally, the wedding procession itself draws near. As they look out into the darkness to catch a glimpse of the bride in all her glory, they are shocked to see only five bridesmaids. Did the groom not want everyone to see the beauty of his bride? Was he too cheap to pay the costs for the ten bridesmaids normally used? Did he not love his bride? Did the bride not have enough friends to find ten people to help her celebrate her special day? It was so hard to see the beauty of the bride in the darkness! What a shameful thing to only have five bridesmaids!

As the procession arrives at the home of the groom, both the bride and groom have been shamed in the eyes of the village and may never live it down. In particular, the groom has been shamed as the costs of the bridesmaid's supplies were his responsibility. It is no surprise that the groom disowns the bridesmaids. They have shamed him and dishonoured his new bride. They have proven that they do not have any real love for her. She had thought they were her friends; they have revealed how little they truly loved her.

THE APPLICATION OF THIS PARABLE TODAY

Now, let us apply this parable to ourselves. In this parable, the bride represents the Church who is the "Bride of Christ."[457] The groom represents

457 Eph. 5:22-33; Rev. 19:7-9; 21:9.

Jesus.[458] But what about the bridesmaids? They represent Christians – all those who love the bride and the groom. What is the task of these "bridesmaids'? Their task is to shine their light in the darkness in such a way that the glory and the beauty of Jesus and His bride, the Church, are clearly seen! Matthew 5:16: "*. . . let your light shine before others, that they may see your good deeds and glorify your Father in Heaven.*" Now THIS is the essence of missions and of the Christian life: to let the light of God so shine before men that they see the beauty of the bride and His Presence with us and that the Father is glorified.

What is the oil? It represents the anointing and empowering of the Holy Spirit. We need the "oil" of the Holy Spirit so that we can shine brightly in such a way that people "see your good deeds and praise your Father in Heaven." The "foolish" here are those who have not done the necessary preparations to do their assignment. They have not pursued the Presence of the Lord in such a way that God's Presence, His light, characterizes them. By not having enough of God in their life, or not giving God enough of themselves, they cannot ensure that the beauty and glory of Jesus and of His Church are clearly seen in the darkness of this world. Because of this, they let their friend, Jesus, down, bring shame to His name and dishonor His bride.

How do we get this "oil" in our life? We do this by cultivating the pathways to His presence mentioned in this book. We need to have a well of "oil" in our lives if we are to "shine" in the darkness effectively. We cannot count on what others have in the Lord. We need to pursue His Presence ourselves. We must press into God, pray, seek His face, worship Him and as we do so, the "light" will spill out around us. If we do not do this, we risk shaming the Lord since the people in the darkness, those who need the love of the Lord, will not be able to see the true beauty of His Bride, the Church. We must keep trimming our "lamps" so that they shine brightly in the darkness. Will we display the beauty of His bride, the

458 The "Lamb" in Rev. 19:7-9.

Church, or not? Will we be able to do those "good deeds" by the power of the Holy Spirit to push back the darkness?

We would never try to do a painting project with no paint, no brushes, no rollers, no plastic covers, so why would we think we can shine and make the love and beauty of Jesus evident in the world without the "oil" of his Presence flowing in our lives?

Just as the bridesmaids were chosen specifically to shine in the darkness so the beauty of the bride was seen. We are here on this world because God believes in us. He thinks that we can make a difference. He believes we can bring light to the darkness by how we live. Today Jesus continues to do His work through believers like you and me. Just like with Jesus, through us God wants those "living in the land of the shadow of death" to have His light shine on them.

"Foolish" Christians are those that do not pursue the Presence of the Holy Spirit in their own lives so that they have enough of God to "push back" the darkness of this world. Jesus as the groom has given us all we need to shine brightly. Let's go out and get more of the "oil" of the Holy Spirit so that we can do this!

Let's be people who can bring glory and honour to Jesus and His Church.

> *"But you are a chosen people, a royal priesthood, a holy nation, God's special possession, that you may declare the praises of him who called you out of the darkness into his wonderful light. Once you were not a people, but now you are the people of God; once you had not received mercy, but now you have received mercy. . .*
>
> *Live such good lives among the pagans that, though they accuse you of doing wrong, they may see your good deeds and glorify God on the day he visits us."* (I Peter 2:9-10,12)

Summary

We are here on the earth is to illuminate the beauty and glory of Jesus and His Bride amidst the darkness of the world. We are the light of the world, and the world needs us to shine with the power of the Spirit of God so that it can see the wonder of God's love for it. We honor God as we shine with His love and show His reality.

Key points in this chapter include:

1. We are in a constant battle between light and darkness. Jesus in His ministry brought the light of God to those living in the "land of the shadow of death." We continue this ministry today.
2. We are the light of the world. Without our lives expressing the Gospel, the world would be a darker place.
3. Our role as Christians is to shine in such a way that the beauty and glory of the Bride of Christ and of Jesus, the Bridegroom, are clearly seen.
4. We need to be pursuing the Presence of the LORD in our lives so that we have enough of the Presence of God to shine brightly in the darkness.
5. God is glorified when Christians make His love and glory evident.
6. "Foolish" Christians are those who ignore the responsibility to be full of the Holy Spirit so that the darkness of this world can be pushed back.

Entering Into His Presence

Put on some worship music and spend time in the Presence of the Lord. If you are married, pull out your wedding photo and spend time looking at it, remembering that special day. If you are single, think back to the wedding of one of your friends. Wasn't the bride beautiful? Think of the beauty of the bride and apply it to your own life. God wants his bride's beauty to be seen by the world!

Ask God to show you how He sees the Church. Ask Him to help you show that beauty to others. Ask God to help you and your church to live such good lives before the people around you that they will see your good deeds and give glory to your God. Ask the Lord to show you how your church corporately can shine more with the light and the love of God in the darkness of the world.

Luke 11:13 indicates that your Heavenly Father will give the Holy Spirit to those who ask Him, so spend some time asking the Lord for more of His Holy Spirit. Ask God to reveal to you what you need to do to receive more of Him. Do you need to fast and pray more specifically for the Holy Spirit as the disciples did in Acts one and two? What about your church? Ask the Lord to show you how your church can cultivate an attitude of wanting and seeking more of the "oil" of the Holy Spirit?

Prayer

Jesus, thank You that You love Your bride. Help me to love her like You do.

Lord, fill me with Your light so that I can be used by You to push back the darkness. Help me to continue Your ministry of releasing light to those that are living in the "land of the shadow of death." Teach me what it means to be the "light of the world."

Lord, help me to live in such a way that the beauty and glory of the Church and of Jesus are clearly seen. Unify my church so that corporately we glow with the light of Your love for the world. May you be increasingly glorified and visible within us as we act in obedience to Your love.

Holy Spirit, I need more of You so that I can be prepared to do the good works You give me to do. Fill me with Your Presence. Make me hungry for You so that I press into You. Give me a fire and a passion for Your glory to be displayed.

Be glorified in me and in Your Church.

In the precious name of Jesus I pray,

Amen.

16

Living in The Power of His Presence

"Worship the LORD in the splendour of his holiness;
tremble before him, all the earth." (Psalm 96:9)

"I am the vine and you are the branches.
If you remain in me and I in you, you will bear much fruit;
apart from me you can do nothing." (John 15:5)

"Consecrate yourselves, for tomorrow the LORD
will do amazing things among you." (Joshua 3:5)

The Presence of the Lord is able to transform us into the kind of people we need to be for the sake of the world. We need to allow His Presence to change how we live and relate to others so that we can be midwives for the Presence of God. The Lord is calling to the world.[459] Our responsibility is to reduce the barriers to hearing His call so that people can come into the embrace of His Presence – and be changed into His likeness. For

459 As happened in Isaiah 6 with Isaiah.

others to discover the power of the Presence of the Lord, we must rest in that Presence ourselves as much as we can.

A PATHWAY INTO THE POWER OF THE PRESENCE OF THE LORD

Before entering the Promised Land, Joshua told the people of God: *"Consecrate yourselves, for tomorrow the LORD will do amazing things among you."* (Joshua 3:5). This instruction was to prepare the people for the powerful Presence of the Lord to be with them and go before them into the Promised Land. Without the consecration, it is doubtful they would have seen the "wonders" God would do on their behalf. The next day, the Levites carried the Ark of the Covenant (the Presence of the LORD) and went ahead of the people. When they got to the Jordan River, they were to cross over to the middle and stand there with the Ark. As soon as the first priest's foot touched the river, the waters divided and separated. It was not some powerful leader, it was not the staff of Moses, it was not Joshua that parted the waters: it was those unnamed priests who carried the Presence of the Lord. This was to demonstrate to the people of Israel that the wonder working Presence of the LORD was with them.[460] The Presence of the Lord is powerful for the effecting of miracles. His Presence was all the Israelites needed to deal with the giants and fortresses in the Land God was taking them into. If we want to see the same powerful, wonder-working Presence of the Lord in our own lives we also must "consecrate ourselves" to the Lord and follow His Presence into the place to which He is leading us.

Later, we see that it was obedience to the voice of the Lord that gave victory to the Israelites at Jericho. The battle plan to take the fortress of Jericho was bizarre. Yet when the people of God were obedient and marched around the city walls as God said, the fortress fell.[461] It was almost too easy!

---

460 Joshua 3:7, 10.

461 Joshua 6:1-25.

Next came the city of Ai and it did not go so well. One person among the Israelites coveted gold and disobeyed God after the battle of Jericho by stealing some and so God withdrew the blessing of His Presence from the people. They attacked Ai thinking they had the Presence of God and were defeated with 36 of them dying.[462] The Presence of the Lord brings victory, not military might. Sin and disobedience drove away the powerful blessing of the Presence of God. At Ai one person sinned, and, tragically, 36 people died because of it. Our sin always impacts those around us. We may think our sin is private and that it only affects us, but this is not true. With the city of Ai, Achan's sin put the entire nation outside of the protecting Presence of God and brought them defeat. Moreover, we see that the sin of Achan also caused the death of his entire family.[463] It might seem harsh, but sin always sows death into our relationships and communities.[464] Sin seriously weakens the people of God. The way back into the Presence of God was consecration[465] and excising from the nation the sin that had driven out the blessing of the Presence of the Lord. The Lord told Joshua: " . . .*you cannot stand against your enemies until you remove them* (the sin and the things Achan had stolen)."[466] If we want to stay in the Presence of the Lord we need to embrace consecration and obedience to the Lord as well as individual and corporate holiness.

Later, Paul in First Corinthians 10:1-13 recounts how the Israelites were blessed with the cloud of the Presence of the Lord leading them: they walked through the Red Sea on dry land, they experienced the provision in the desert of both manna and water, yet they drifted into idolatry and sexual immorality. They did not live in their consecration to the Lord. In effect, they sinned against the Presence of the Lord in their midst. The

462 Joshua 7:5.

463 Joshua 7:24-25.

464 Rom. 6:23: "The wages of sin is death."; also Prov. 10:16: ". . . the earnings of the wicked are sin and death."

465 Joshua 7:13.

466 Joshua 7:13.

result was that the judgement of God fell on them.[467] When God is acting powerfully in our midst, we must be careful not to take it for granted and drift into sin. The severity of God's judgement is always greater when God is more powerfully acting amongst His people. If we want more of God, we need to know what we are asking for. God's powerful Presence acts against sin just as it releases blessing on the righteous. The Presence of God makes the ordinary extraordinary, but it is never safe.

THE PRESENCE OF GOD IS INTERTWINED WITH HIS GOODNESS

In the consecration of both the tabernacle[468] and the temple of Solomon,[469] God's Presence was so powerful that Moses as well as the priests could not enter the tabernacle/temple. Sometimes the Presence of the Lord is so overwhelming that it overloads us. These moments when God and His glory descended in such a powerful way were preceded by consecration, worship, sacrifice and the affirmation of His goodness and love.[470] God loves it when we honor His goodness and declare it to ourselves and to our communities. It is as if it encourages God to increase an outpouring of His good Presence upon His people.

We see a similar theme of acknowledging the love of the Lord in a powerful victory God gave to King Jehoshaphat in 2 Chronicles 20. In verses 21-22 it says:

> *After consulting with the people, Jehoshaphat appointed men to sing to the LORD and to praise him for the splendour of his holiness as they went out at the head of the army, saying: 'Give thanks to the LORD, for his love endures forever.' As they began to sing and*

467 Paul mentions 23,000 dying due to sexual immorality in vs. 8, others killed by a plague of snakes in vs. 9 and still others killed by an angel of the Lord due to their grumbling against the Lord and Moses in vs. 10.

468 Deut. 40:34-35; Lev. 9:24.

469 2 Chron. 5:14; 7:2.

470 2 Chron. 5:13; 7:3: *"He is good, and His love endures forever"*

praise, the LORD set ambushes against the men of Ammon and Mount Seir who were invading Judah, and they were defeated.

Again, we see consecration: praising God for the splendour of his holiness implies they have consecrated themselves to that holiness. Jehoshaphat put worshippers at the head of the army and as they marched, they sang, thanking the LORD for his enduring love. Knowing that the Presence of the LORD brings victory, not the force of arms, Jehoshaphat put worshippers at the forefront of the battle. As they praised God and thanked Him for His love, the approaching army was ambushed and killed. It says in 2 Chronicles 20:24: "*When the men of Judah came to the place that overlooks the desert and looked toward the vast army, they saw only dead bodies lying on the ground; no one had escaped.*" Consecration with worship and praise that acknowledged the enduring love of God released the powerful Presence of God to protect His people and brought them victory. God linked the power of His Presence to the actions of His people. What we do impacts whether the power of the Presence of God is released to accomplish the will of God. It seems, in particular, that praising God for His love and goodness causes God to respond with the power of His Presence.

There is an assumption in the Biblical accounts mentioned above that God is a God who speaks. He personally interacts with His people who seek His will. When they do what He says, He blesses them with the power of His Presence. This shows that we need to cultivate the lifestyle of a "listener." Like Samuel, we need to say to the LORD: "*Speak, for your servant is listening.*"[471] As the people of God obeyed the voice of God, God acted. If we want to experience more of the power of the Presence of the Lord, we need to value and pursue the intimate Presence of God. God wants to have a dynamic, living, vibrant relationship with each one of us. He wants us to "consecrate ourselves" so that tomorrow we will see God do "mighty acts" among us.

---

471 1 Sam. 3:10.

GOD'S PRESENCE HEALS

I made the comment earlier that healing is not something that God does, it is something He IS; that when we encounter the real Presence of God, we do not just encounter part of who He is, but ALL of who He is. In God there is a complete unity between His works and His being. He heals because of who He is. I have found that when we create an environment where there can be a "God encounter," we will more likely see a manifestation of healing in the lives of those present. This is why many healing conferences include powerful worship which prepares and invites the deeper Presence of God in the gathered community of God.

God's Presence heals and this can be seen in many of the "dimensions" of the Presence of God mentioned in this book. First, His sustaining Presence in the world means that God acts in the lives of both Christians and non-Christians to sustain and nurture their lives. He loves everyone and is active in bringing them health. This is one of the reasons we have medicine is in the world. God has created within humanity the ability to find out and determine the cycles and patterns of life and God uses this to nurture life through medicine in various forms. Medicine is one of the tools in God's toolbox of healing.

God's Word also heals. Psalm 107:20 indicates that God "sent out his word and healed them." Since God's Presence heals and God is a healing God, any time the Word of God is clearly declared,[472] the Presence of God in the Word can release faith and healing to those who receive what is preached. There are many stories of this kind of thing in the histories of revival. Just a quick story of this from our own ministry. I was preaching in a small church in Canada and had been praying beforehand for a word of knowledge that indicated what God wanted to do. As I was praying, I felt a strong tingling in my left thumb but no specific pain. At the end of the message as I invited people to come forward for prayer, I gave the word of knowledge about a problem in a left thumb but said that I was

---

472 Whether the spoken Word (preaching, testimony, etc.), the written Word or Jesus as the Word of God made flesh.

not sure what the injury or exact problem might be. It turned out that there were three people who each had a different problem with their left thumb (probably why it was not specific). The first person was healed as she listened to the message. She came into the service with the problem, but realized at the end of the message, that she was healed. The second was healed as she came forward for prayer and the third was healed as we prayed for him. After the service the first lady came to me and thanked me for our ministry. She was a young mom who was left-handed and had fallen and badly sprained her left thumb and had found, since she was left-handed, that she could not do many things with her young child. Even carrying her child had been painful. She had been asking God to heal her. While she was talking to me, she had her child on her left arm and told me that she could not hold her child like that before the service. No-one had prayed for her. God came to her during the preaching and healed her.

The Presence of God in the Church heals. A man told me the following story. He had struggled for a while with pain in his hips and back. He knew we would be at his church on Sunday and was somewhat familiar with us since we had been there before. That Sunday, he got out of the car in the church parking lot and as he walked towards the church building, he felt his pain level decreasing. This stirred up faith and he believed he was going to be healed. Then as he was in the service, the pain continued to decrease until by the end of the service he had no pain at all. At the end of the service, he walked around and found he was healed. This could be God's Presence in the church linked with the Presence of God in the preached Word of God, but his healing started as he entered the place where the church met.

Love heals. I have seen several cases where people start to feel better emotionally as we pray and often it is because they sense the love of God for them. Often with the experience of love comes a reduction in their pain level. As well, physical and spiritual bondage can be linked to heart wounds and as these are healed, physical healing and deliverance can result.

Worship heals. One person told me this story. She had a frozen shoulder that meant she could not lift her right hand above her shoulder. She was in a service where there was wonderful worship, and she got caught up in it. Suddenly she realized that both her hands were in the air above her head as she worshipped. She thought: "Wait a minute, I can't lift my right hand that high!" As she lifted her arm up and down and tested the situation, she realized that she had been healed as she worshipped the Lord.

The power of the Presence of the Lord heals. An African friend of ours and his wife were the only people in their family who were Christians. I had visited the family and prayed for his elderly father who was close to 100 years old. As I prayed, he seemed to be healed of TB. This had a large impact on my friend who decided to share the story of Christmas with his extended family who were mostly Muslims. His aunt was a hunchback and, as long as he had known her, she had a sizeable hump on her upper back. After Christmas that year, the family gathered for the New Year's celebration, and he took the opportunity to tell the family about the story of Christmas. Then he invited the Holy Spirit to come. It fell with power on several of them, in particular on the aunt who fell to the ground under the power of the Spirit. When she got up from the ground, her back was normal. I asked my friend about this and how it happened. He said, "I'm not sure. All I know is that when she fell to the ground, she had the hump on her back, but when she got up, it was gone." I was introduced to the aunt whose back looked totally normal. It was as the power of God fell on her that she was healed. I suspect it was more a deliverance than a healing[473].

The Presence of God in us and in the Church means that He hears our prayers and His character means that He responds.

473 See Luke 13:10-16 where a woman is healed of something to do with her back that was caused by an 18 year demonic bondage.

There is always a mystery with healing. We are not in control. God is. Yet getting involved in praying for the sick gives you an opportunity to see God's love in action and get a glimpse of His glory.

We are to be midwives of the Healing Presence of the Lord to others, bringing the love and life of God to those who do not know Him.

THE IMPORTANCE OF KEEPING YOUR HEART SOFT

When the nation of Israel came to the border of the Promised Land under Moses, they did not enter because of their unbelief. They disobeyed God because they doubted that the Presence of God[474] with them was enough to deal with any giants or fortresses in the land. Instead, they listened to their fear. Hebrews compares the Promised Land to entering the "rest" of God. God has a place of "rest" and "peace" for each of us, but it must be entered through faith and trust. We can do great things in the "Promised Land" but it is through rest not work. God does everything by His Presence with us.[475]

The key to entering the "rest" of God is to have a heart that is soft and responsive to the voice of God.[476] Doubt and unbelief hardens our hearts and produces rebellion and disobedience. Instead of trusting and obeying God's voice, we listen to and believe in the deceitfulness of sin and turn away from the living God.[477] We doubt His goodness. Saying "no" to God always produces less than the promise of His Presence and the blessing that flows from it. There will always be giants, fortresses and obstacles that stand against us entering the Presence of God and that place of rest in Him.

We humans are choosers by nature. Sin entices us to choose the swamp that looks firm rather than the rock that is in the shadows. What

474 Heb. 4:2.

475 See also Exodus 14:14: "The Lord will fight for you; you need only to be still."

476 Heb. 3:7-11, 12, 15; 4:7.

477 Heb. 3:12.

we choose is often influenced by what voice we choose to listen to. Heb. 3:15: "*. . . Today if you hear his voice, do not harden your hearts as you did in the rebellion.*" Choose to listen to the still small voice of the Lord, obey it and enter into the rest of God. Do not let sin, doubt, and unbelief creep into your heart and lead you away from the vital Presence of the Lord.

PATHWAYS TO HIS PRESENCE: FOUNDATIONAL PIECES

Previously we have talked about entering the Presence of God or getting more of God, but how do we **KEEP** ourselves in the Presence of the LORD? We will start with some foundational pieces for staying in the Presence of God if we are to grow in our experience of His Presence.

1. We need to take the holiness of the LORD *seriously*. He is the Holy One of Israel, and we cannot enter His Presence or stay there without embracing holiness. In ourselves we are not holy. None of us are: we have all "*fallen short of the glory of God.*"[478] Yet God has paid the price so that we could be made holy by the blood of Jesus. He has invited us into His Holy Presence. We stay in the Presence of God when we live close to the cross. When we sin, we repent, go to the cross, get forgiven and then we continue. We need to understand that holiness is not a burden of "do's" and "don'ts," but it is a prescription for living life well. Holiness keeps us close to the author of life and helps His life flow in us. So, we cultivate those actions and attitudes that keep our lives holy so that we can rest in His Presence. We embrace the need to change, adding consistent practices of repentance, humility, honesty, obedience and worship to our lives.
2. We also value our relationship with God, nurturing intimacy with Him through His Word and through worship. We seek to live our life as if we really believe that Jesus is the "bread of life"[479] and that

478 Rom. 3:23.

479 John 6:35, 48, 51.

"man does not live on bread alone but by every word that proceeds from the mouth of God."[480] So, it is good to start each day with quality time with God. Then, let the Presence of God go with you into the rest of the day.

3. Treat the Lord as a person, knowing that we can quench or grieve the Holy Spirit.[481] Realize that some of the activities we engage in do not encourage the Holy Spirit to stay with us. We must be aware of what the Holy Spirit might think of what we do and so we invite His Presence with us everywhere we go.
4. Seeking to increase our obedience to the Lord, we make "yes" the stance of our hearts towards Him. He will honor our desire to be obedient and will draw near to us as we do this. Obedience keeps us in the Presence of God.[482] We live our lives with Him as our friend and partner.
5. We hunger for more of God and so ask Him for more. We fast and turn our physical hunger into a hunger for God, pursuing His Presence. We never want to settle down in our relationship with God. When we do settle down, we lose our way. We are always on a pilgrimage towards the deeper Presence of the Lord. Honor the Lord's Presence and He will honor you with His Presence. Understand that the Presence of God is the key to fruitfulness.[483]
6. It is good to remind ourselves of the testimonies of what God has done in the past and in the present, honoring the activity of God in the lives of those He loves and asking Him to do again what He has done elsewhere. We need to build up our faith in the actions and love of God so that our view of God is enlarged.

480 Matt. 4:4; Deut. 8:3.

481 Eph. 4:30.

482 John 15:20.

483 John 15:4,5-6.

7. Each one of us has been bought with a price[484] when Jesus laid down his life for us. So, we honor our debt to God, living our lives as if we are not our own but belong to Him.
8. Access to the deeper Presence of God is through Jesus. Only through Jesus are all barriers between us and God destroyed so that we can come into clear communion with God the Father. He is the *only* "way" into the Presence of the Father.[485]

PATHWAYS TO HIS PRESENCE: THE EIGHT DIMENSIONS.

It might be easy as you go through this section to feel overwhelmed as it seems like there are a lot of things to do. I would suggest over the next week or ten days, taking one or two points or "dimensions" mentioned below each day and apply them to your life, especially those points that resonate with you. Take as much time as you need. Remember that the goal is to grow in your experience of the Presence of God as you apply what is mentioned. You could also go through the "**Entering Into His Presence**" sections at the end of each chapter. Each of us might find a different pathway to His Presence that we find more useful.

The General Presence of God:

1. Cultivate an awareness of God with you through Jesus Christ. God is everywhere present but He is only close through Jesus. Turn your heart as often as you can towards an awareness of Him.
2. Follow the advice of Francis de Sales from chapter 6:
    (a) Since God is universally present, look for signs of His Presence in your own life and determine to meet that Presence wherever you are;

484 1 Cor. 6:20.

485 John 14:6.

(b) Remind yourself that God is not only in the place where you are, but most particularly present in your heart and mind which He lights up with His Presence;

(c) Fix your mind on the thought that Jesus in His ascended humanity looks down from heaven on those who seek Him. He watches over us from heaven even when we are not aware of it;

(d) Imagine that Jesus in his humanity is with you now as a friend. Talk to him as a friend as you go through your day.

To summarize: Be conscious of God's Presence with you. Keep your focus on Him in your heart. Act as if he is a good friend always with you. Look for His Presence and honor it. Thank the Lord when you notice His Presence.

The Sustaining Presence of God:

Be thankful for every gift He brings you, for every sign of the favor of the Lord on your life. Thank the Lord for His Sustaining Presence with you and your loved ones. Notice and be thankful for signs of health and provision. Be grateful for all He does do for you. Thankfulness is a doorway into His Presence.[486] Tell Him when you need His Sustaining Presence and invite it in your life.

The Presence of God in His Word:

1. Honor the Word of God. Read it in order to encounter God. Make the source of your life "every word that proceeds from the Mouth of God"[487] and expect that God will speak to you through His Scriptures. Ask the Lord to show you something daily to apply to your life.

2. Ask God to breathe on His Word by the Holy Spirit so it brings life to your heart, soul and mind. Ask forgiveness for when you have

486 Psalm 100:4.

487 Matt. 4:4.

seen the Scriptures as only "dry bones" and ask God to make it living for you in your experience. Honor the Presence of the Holy Spirit in His Word.

3. Determine to be a person whose words line up with the will of God so that His Presence can bless others as you teach, preach, pray and share with those around you.

4. Nurture your faith through reading and listening to testimonies of what God has done in the lives of others. Invite God to do the same in your own life.

The Presence of God in the Church:

Honor and value the Presence of God in the corporate gathering of the Church. Refuse to bad-mouth or speak negatively of the Bride of Christ. Repent where you have done this. Speak blessing on the Church when you think of it. Treat the Church in the same way you would want to be treated as a bride (or as you would want your bride to be treated). Ask God to give you His love for the Church. Honor and value the place of the Church in God's plan to redeem the world.

The Presence of God in the Individual Christian:

1. Consecrate each part of your life to God. Honor His Presence in you and with you. Commit yourself to the pursuit of holiness for His sake as well as your own. Recognize that each domain of your life is sacred.

2. Invite the Presence of the Holy Spirit to fill His temple. Ask God to cleanse and purify every 'room' in your temple and chase out any idols or unclean presences.

The Presence of God in Worship:

1. Embrace where God is in your life. Don't get bogged down with where He is not. Be a worshipper and love His Presence. Seek it in your life and you will find it.

2. Enthrone Jesus at the center of your life. Do this through worship. Invite the kingdom of God to come to the earth and make your life

the "Bethel" where Heaven meets earth. Set up worship as a regular activity you do in "your temple".

The Presence of God in Love:

1. Decide to love the Lord your God with all your heart, mind and soul and your neighbor as yourself. Love people and ask the Lord to increase your ability to love others. You will find the Presence of the Lord when you choose to love people. Pursue the anointing and empowering of the Holy Spirit so that you can love others more.
2. Recognize that the "LORD is good and His love endures forever."[488] It was this declaration at the dedication of the temple of Solomon that released and invited the powerful Presence of the Lord. The recognition of the Lord's goodness and love for us honors His Presence with us and invites Him to come more powerfully into our lives. See His goodness in your life and you will be able to let His goodness flow to others. Knowing you are loved empowers you to love others.

The Presence of the Glory of the Lord:

1. Consecrate your life to God and recognize His goodness and love for you. This invites the outpouring of the Glory of the Lord on your life.
2. Ask God to remove from your heart any barriers to seeing His glory. Embrace a heart that is soft and obedient before the Lord. Deal with any sin so that coming into a deeper experience of the "glory" of the Lord will not destroy you. Be honest in your relationship with God and pursue more of His Presence.

Pathways to His Presence: Final Words

1. Nurture in your life any of those things that nurture the Presence of God. Live your life as if every part of it is sacred.

488 Psalms 106:1; 107:1; 2 Chron. 5:13; 7:3.

2. As much as you can, add Presence to Presence. Stir up each one of the dimensions of the Presence of God we have talked about. Read and honor the Word of God, worship the Lord, recognize His Presence with you every time you think of it, and bless God for how He is sustaining your life. Give more of yourself to God and you will find more of Him in your life.

Summary

The Church is victorious when the Presence of God is cultivated and honored. She becomes feeble when sin is present in the lives of people in the Christian community. Living lives that are consecrated to and passionate for the Lord empowers us together to be overcomers. Humility and trust in God are key for us to keep our hearts in the right place before God. Pursuing the Presence of God and cultivating lives that are oriented to remaining in His Presence is what the world needs from us. For their sake, we love God and pursue His Presence.

Entering Into His Presence

Put on some worship music and spend time saying "yes" to the Lord. Declare to Him that He is good and that His love endures forever. Ask Him to increase His Presence in your life. Give Him your heart and ask Him to help you keep it soft.

Go through the above suggestions for keeping yourself in the Presence of God. Focus on one of them and spend the day going back to it again and again. Take another one tomorrow and keep doing this until you start to feel more of the powerful Presence of the Lord in your life.

Prayer

Lord, today I want to listen to Your voice and say "yes." Help me to always keep my heart soft before You and obey You.

Lord, I consecrate myself to You again right now. Take my life and make it a temple for You, a place consecrated to worshipping You. Fill

Your temple with Your Presence. Wash me and make me clean. Cleanse Your temple of any darkness.

Lord, I declare that You are good and that Your love endures forever. Thank You for Your goodness towards me. Thank You for the love You have poured out upon me. I bless You for all You have done for me.

Examine my heart and show me if there is any wicked way in me. Change me so that I am more like Your Son. Help me to embrace repentance and honesty. Be strong in me for the sake of Your Church and for the wider world.

Lord purify Your bride. Make Your Church clean and pure so Your Presence can be strong in her. Bless Your Church with Your Presence. Increase the power of Your Presence in Your Church.

I honor You. I honor Your Presence in me. I honor Your goodness and love in my life.

Thank You for Your powerful Presence with me.

In the precious name of Jesus I pray,

Amen.

17

Some Concluding Thoughts

"And he called the place Massah [testing] and Meribah [quarreling] because the Israelites quarrelled and because they tested the LORD saying, "Is the LORD among us or not?" (Exodus 17:7, brackets added*).*

"As the deer pants for streams of water, so my soul pants for you, my God. My soul thirsts for God, for the living God. Where can I go and meet with God?" (Psalm 42:1-2)

IS THE LORD AMONG US OR NOT?

God is calling us to be a people who are characterized by His Presence. This 'call' is a theme of the Scriptures as Yahweh repeatedly expresses His desire that His people be His possession,[489] a nation that is distinctly

489 A common phrase is: "I will be their God and they will be my people." See Joshua 24:18; Jeremiah 7:23; 10:16; 11:4; 12:6-14; 13:11; 24:7; 30:22; 31:1, 33, 38; Gen 17:7, 8; (35:11); Deuteronomy 29:13; Exodus 6:7; Leviticus 26:12; Genesis 17:7, 8; 35:11; Ezekiel 36:28; 37:23; Joel 2:27; 1 Samuel 12:22; 1 Kings 6:13; 8:51, 53; 2 Kings 11:17; Psalm 95:7; 1 Chronicles 22:10; Hosea 1:8-10; 2:23; Zechariah 3:10-11; 8:8, 23; 13:9; Titus 2:14; Revelation 21:3-4, 7.

different from any other nation on Earth. In the Exodus events, God led the Israelites powerfully, dramatically and visibly because He wanted to craft among them the conviction that they were a people set apart by the Presence of the living God. Yet, what does it mean to have the Presence of the living God with us? If we understand this rightly, it changes everything because when God is among us, everything He is accompanies His Presence. Every single one of us will have challenges and problems in this life. How does the Presence of God among us empower us to overcome these problems?

In Exodus, God led the people of Israel through the desert with a column of smoke by day and a pillar of fire by night. Every moment of every day the people of God saw clear evidence that God was powerfully with them. You would think as they followed Him, that, surely, they would not encounter any problems! Yet in chapter 17, God led the people of God to a place called Rephidim where there was no water for either them or their herds to drink.[490] Why would He lead them to a place without water? He knew the people needed water, yet, after all they had experienced of His Presence, would His people trust Him to bring them through this next challenge? Evidently not, as the people quickly became upset and even wanted to stone Moses for bringing them to Rephidim.[491] The real issue was not the leadership of Moses but the significance of the Presence of God with them. Was God truly among them or not?[492] And knowing God was with them, would they trust His Presence? Moses cried out to God and then obeyed God, and the result was that abundant water was provided for the people -- more than enough for everyone. At Rephidim the people "tested" God and this testing[493] was a lack of belief or trust in

---

490 Numbers 1:46 and 2:32 indicate that there were 603,550 men so this probably meant at least three times this number of people in total adding in women and children. It was a large crowd of people with their herds requiring a huge amount of water!

491 Exodus 17:2-4.

492 Exodus 17:7.

493 The Hebrew word for "testing" is Massah and after this event, this place was called "Massah". It became a symbol of testing God by not trusting in His love.

God's love for them. They saw His Presence, but they did not trust that His Presence meant His love and provision were also there.

When God comes and lives in us as His temple, all of Him comes to dwell with us. A challenge for us becomes: "Is the LORD among us or not?" And will we trust His Presence? If Yahweh is truly with us, then we must become a people who trust the Presence of God who is among us and show this by how we live.

In Matthew 4:5-7, during the second temptation event, Satan challenges Jesus to throw Himself down from the temple to 'prove' God's love for Him. Jesus quotes from Deuteronomy 6:16 which refers to not putting the LORD to the test as the Israelites did at Massah. At Massah, as shown in Exodus 17, the Israelites doubted that God's Presence with them meant His love was also with them. Jesus, as the Son, refused to test God's love as the Israelites had. So: Is God among us or not? If He is, we can trust that Presence like Jesus did. We can trust that His love, provision and that all He IS, comes with His Presence. No matter the problems we may face, with God's Presence, we have everything we need.

I challenge you, the reader, as we finish this book to hold onto the Presence of God in your life. He is with you! And when He is with you, you have everything you need.

IT IS HIS GOOD PLEASURE TO GIVE YOU THE KINGDOM

In Luke 12:29-34, Jesus describes characteristics that are meant to characterize His disciples. In the first part, verses 29-31, He contrasts His followers and pagans. The disciples of Jesus are not to set their hearts on what they can eat or drink and are not to be anxious (i.e. they are meant to trust God's love). In contrast, the pagans chase after the things they think they need, thinking that they have to provide these things for themselves. The children of God are different, trusting that God is with them and that He knows exactly what they need – and knowing this, will provide it. The people of God, instead of seeking after the things of this world, are to seek after the Kingdom of God, fixing their attention on the higher things of heaven. They can do this because God is with them, and they can trust His Presence.

Then Jesus goes on in verse 32 with these beautiful words: *"Do not be afraid little flock, for your Father has been pleased to give you the kingdom."* Seeking the kingdom of God is about submitting to the rule and the reign of God, about submitting to the claims of His Presence with us. It focuses us on heaven and releases us to enjoy the fruit of His Presence. There is no anxiety there because we trust His love. When we seek the kingdom of God, we will find it because it is God's good pleasure to give it to us. Then Jesus goes on to tell the disciples to sell their possessions and give to the poor (verse 33) and build up for themselves a treasure in heaven that can never be taken from them. They can do this because trust in the love of God empowers them to be counter-cultural in how they relate to possessions. They are to loosen the ties that bind them to this world and pursue heaven. How can we do this amidst the pressures and needs we face in life? By trusting the Presence of God with us. When He is with us, we have everything we need. Our heavenly Father gives us the kingdom we seek as we trust His Presence and His love for us. Love, power, glory, peace, all of these come with His Presence. His Presence is all we need.

Trust His Presence! Is He not among us? Trust His Presence!

AS A DEER PANTS FOR STREAMS OF WATER . . .

I hunger, I thirst for more of God. I thirst for the living God, a God that makes a difference, a God that is alive and real. Where can I find this God? Where is He that I can get to know Him and bring His reality into my life? In a sense this book has been an attempt to answer these questions. As we learn about and walk on the various pathways to God's Presence mentioned in this book, our lives will be transformed by the reality of God and by His deep love for us. We were designed for God. We need Him to find ourselves. What is more, the world needs us to come into our true identity in God so that it can discover that He is the answer it needs.

There are huge problems all around us: personal, social, and global. How can we solve them? Only in Christ. Only by finding the solutions through the creativity and power of the living God. Only through truly knowing and encountering the living God and drawing our life from His.

In Philippians 3:7-10, 12-14 Paul says:

> *But whatever were gains to me I now consider loss for the sake of Christ. What is more, I consider everything a loss because of the surpassing worth of knowing Christ Jesus my Lord, for whose sake I have lost all things. I consider them garbage, that I may gain Christ and be found in him . . .*
>
> *I want to know Christ – yes, to know the power of his resurrection and participation in his sufferings, becoming like him in his death . . .*
>
> *Not that I have already obtained all this . . . But one thing I do . . . I press on toward the goal to win the prize for which God has called me heavenward in Christ Jesus."*

Nothing is of more value than knowing Christ Jesus. We see in Paul a hunger, a thirst, to know Christ more. He has given up everything just to draw closer to Christ, to be found in Him. So, he focuses his life on pursuing Christ. He wants to be changed by knowing Christ into becoming like Christ. We need to do the same.

I pray for each reader that a hunger for God will rise up within you. May Paul's heart and passion be yours. May you thirst and hunger for more of God. May you walk down each pathway into His Presence, pursue each dimension of the Presence of God to discover His beauty and come to know His glory. May you find the Lord and grow in Him so that you become all He wants you to be. May He be your center. As you do this may you become the world changer God wants you to be.

Seek and embrace the Presence of the LORD. His love for you is deep and passionate.

Partial Bibliography:

Augustine. *Confessions*, translated by Rex Warner. 1963. Mentor Books. New York.

Bernard of Clairvaux. *The Love of God and Spiritual Friendship*. James Houston (editor). 1983. Multnomah Press. Portland Oregon.

Bowler, Arnold. *I Sat Where They Sat*. 2011. Castle Quay Books. Pickering, Ontario, Canada.

Brother Lawrence, *The Practice of the Presence of God*, reprinted 2005. Shambhala Publications. Boston, Massachusetts.

Clark, Randy. *There is More! The Secret to Experiencing God's Power to Change Your Life*. 2013. Chosen, A Division of Baker Publishing Group. Minneapolis, Minnesota.

Clark, Randy & Miller, Craig. *Finding Victory When Healing Doesn't Happen: Breaking Through With Healing Prayer.* 2015. Global Awakening. Mechanicsburg, PA.

De Sales, Francis. *An Introduction to the Devout Life.* Reprinted 2013. TAN books. Charlotte, North Carolina.

Johnson, Bill. *Hosting the Presence: Unveiling Heaven's Agenda.* 2012. Destiny Image Publishers. Shippensburg, PA.

Mezirow, Jack, Robert Kegan, Mary Field Belenky, Ann V. Stanton, Laurent A. Parks Daloz, Stephen D. Brookfield, Kathleen Taylor, Patricia Cranton, Judith Beth Cohen, Deborah Piper, Elizabeth Kasl, Dean Elias, Lyle Yorks, Victoria

J. Marsick, Edward W. Taylor, Colleen Aalsburg Weissner. 2000. *Learning as transformation: Critical perspectives on a theory in progress.* San Francisco, CA: Jossey-Bass.

Polanyi, Michael Polanyi. *Personal Knowledge: Towards a Post-Critical Philosophy*. 1958. University of Chicago Press, Chicago.

Satyavrata, Ivan. *The Holy Spirit: Lord and Life Giver.* 2009. IVP Academic. Downers Grove, Illinois.

Sithole, Surprise. *Voice in the Night: The True Story of a Man and the Miracles that are Changing Africa.* 2012. Chosen Books a Division of Baker Books, Grand Rapids, MI.